BrightRED Study Guide

CfE HIGHER

BUSINESS MANAGEMENT

William Reynolds and Nadene Morin

BrightRED
PUBLISHING

First published in 2014 by:
Bright Red Publishing Ltd
1 Torphichen Street
Edinburgh
EH3 8HX

Reprinted with corrections 2015, 2017, 2019

A CIP record for this book is available from the British Library.

ISBN 978-1-906736-58-3

With thanks to:
PDQ Digital Media Solutions Ltd, Bungay (layout) and Sue Moody, Bright Writing (copy-edit).

Cover design and series book design by Caleb Rutherford – e i d e t i c.

Acknowledgements
Every effort has been made to seek all copyright-holders. If any have been overlooked, then Bright Red Publishing will be delighted to make the necessary arrangements.

Permission has been sought from all relevant copyright holders and Bright Red Publishing are grateful for the use of the following:

Images licensed by Ingram Images (pp30, 100, 101 & 107); Roger Alexander (CC BY 2.0)[1] (p 6); supergenijalac/iStock.com (p 6); Kevin Dooley (CC BY 2.0)[1] (p 6); David Wright/Creative Commons (CC BY-SA 20)[2] (p6); Logo © Innocent Drinks (p 8); whitemay/iStock.com (p 9); kontrast-fotodesign/iStock.com (p 10); tupungato/iStock.com (p 12); SoopySue/iStock.com (p 14); Logo © The City of Edinburgh Council (p 14); The BBC name and logo are trade marks of the British Broadcasting Corporation and are used under licence (p 15); Logo © The Scout Association (p 16); whitemay/iStock.com (p 16); Image © The Big Issue (p 17); monkeybusinessimages/iStock.com (p 18); ragsac/iStock.com (p 20); Extracts adapted from http://www.bbc.co.uk/news/business-27413189 and http://wecyclers.com/ © The British Broadcasting Corporation & Wecyclers (p 21); DagDurrichPhotography/iStock.com (p 24); The passage 'Tougher times on the high street' taken from Business Review Volume 17 Number 3 February 2011. Reprinted by permission of Philip Allan (for Hodder Education) (p 24); CREATISTA/Shutterstock.com (p 26); webking/iStock.com (p 28); 4774344sean/iStock.com (p 28); BrianAJackson/iStock.com (p 29); kirstypargeter/iStock.com (p 29); 71gazza/iStock.com (p 36); jfmdesign/iStock.com (p 37); Andreyuu/iStock.com (p 40); violetkaipa/iStock.com (p 44); AndrewSoundarajan/iStock.com (p 44); versevend/iStock.com (p 44); Niloo138/iStock.com (p 44); Samohin/iStock.com (p 46); manaemedia/iStock.com (p 46); illusob/iStock.com (p 46); stuartmiles99/iStock.com (p 47); TonyBaggett/iStock.com (p 48); A diagram © Tesco Plc (p 48); stockyimages/iStock.com (p 50); duckycards/iStock.com (p 50); SirikulT/iStock.com (p 51); lucato/iStock.com (p 53); scyther5/iStock.com (p 53); ryanmatthewsmith/iStock.com (p 54); Logo © Long Tall Sally (p 56); gvictoria/iStock.com (p 57); Two extracts taken from http://www.educationscotland.gov.uk/Images/BusinessDecisionAreas1v3_tcm4-303474.doc © Crown copyright 2012. Contains public sector information licensed under the Open Government Licence v1.0. (pp 58–59); Craig Sanders Photography © Steven Morin (p 59); ginosphotos/iStock.com (p 60); JackF/iStock.com (p 60); vitanovski/iStock.com (p 61); pressureUA/iStock.com (p 62); fieldwork/iStock.com (p 66); robtek/iStock.com (p 66); rypson/iStock.com (p 67); wellphoto/iStock.com (p 70); Advert © Innocent Ltd (p 71); lenscap67/iStock.com (p 73); Vichly44/iStock.com (p 74); Rawpixel/iStock.com (p 75); Jag_cz/iStock.com (p 81); egal/iStock.com (p 83); The passage 'New car giant' taken from Business Review Volume 17 Number 3 February 2011. Reprinted by permission of Philip Allan (for Hodder Education) (p 90); KITEMARK and the BSI Kitemark device are reproduced with kind permission of The British Standards Institution. They are registered trademarks in the United Kingdom and in certain other countries. Diagram sourced from www.Kitemark.com - Copyright © 2014 BS (p 92); BS5750/ISO 9000 Copyright © 2014 BSI. All rights reserved (p 92); CE Mark © European Union, 1995-2014 (p 92); Royal Warrant image © Tagishsimon (CC BY-SA 3.0)[3] (p 92); The British Lion Quality mark © British Egg Industry Council (p 92); Logo © Investors in People (p 92); BSI case study taken from http://businesscasestudies.co.uk/bsi/quality-through-standards/introduction.html. Copyright © 1995-2014 Business Case Studies LLP (p 92); Logo © Ethical Trading Initiative (p 96); Logo © The Fairtrade Foundation (p 97); hroe/iStock.com (p 98); ms_seal/iStock.com (p 98); simonkr/iStock.com (p 100); Kevin.B (CC BY-SA 3.0)[3] (p 101); Kgbo (CC BY-SA 3.0)[3] (p 102); The passage 'Self-service checkouts: Love them or hate them' taken from Business Review Volume 17 Number 2 November 2010. Reprinted by permission of Philip Allan (for Hodder Education) (pp 102–103); piovesempre/iStock.com (p 104); Tesco case study taken from http://businesscasestudies.co.uk/tesco/recruitment-and-selection/workforce-planning.html. Copyright © 1995-2014 Business Case Studies LLP (p 105); BernardaSv/iStock.com (p 105); RyanKing999/iStock.com (p 108); AVAVA/iStock.com (p 109); AndreyPopov/iStock.com (p 109); monkeybusinessimages/iStock.com (p 110); Sergey Nivens/iStock.com (p 111); Case study of KFC QLD Restaurants © Collins Restaurants Queensland Pty Ltd (p 113); Wolterk/iStock.com (p 113); Ljupco/iStock.com (p 115); kschulze/iStock.com (p 116); Viktor_Gladkov/iStock.com (p 116); monkeybusinessimages/iStock.com (p 117); FireAtDusk/iStock.com (p 122); michaeljung/iStock.com (p 126); pressdigital/iStock.com (p 126); shironosov/iStock.com (p 127); psphotograph/iStock.com (p 128); dibrova/iStock.com (p 129); kzenon/iStock.com (p 130); alphaspirit/iStock.com (p 131); joxxxxjo/iStock.com (p 132); fotek/iStock.com (p 133); funky-data/iStock.com (p 134); Antonprado/iStock.com (p 136); Fantasista/iStock.com (p 138).

(CC BY 2.0)[1] http://creativecommons.org/licenses/by/2.0/
(CC BY-SA 2.0)[2] http://creativecommons.org/licenses/by-sa/2.0
(CC BY-SA 3.0)[3] http://creativecommons.org/licenses/by-sa/3.0

Printed and bound in the UK.

CONTENTS

INTRODUCTION

INTRODUCING CfE HIGHER BUSINESS MANAGEMENT

Business organisations come in many different structures and sizes, ranging from the local sole trader to the global multinational organisation. All of these organisations are important to both the local and the international economy, because they create employment, income and wealth for society. All organisations, irrespective of their size, require skilled and talented entrepreneurs to lead them through the cyclical nature of the global economy.

As consumers and employees, we interact with businesses every day and depend on business organisations to produce goods and services to satisfy our needs and wants. The study of Higher Business Management will help you to understand the role of business in society and the key functional areas of business organisations. It will also help you to develop and apply skills for learning, skills for life and skills for work.

DON'T FORGET

Marketing is one of the most important functional areas of a large organisation. It is important that consumers are made aware of an organisation's products and services, or sales and profits are unlikely.

DON'T FORGET

Employees are one of the most important resources to any organisation.

DON'T FORGET

Financial management is vitally important if organisations are to generate profit and maintain liquidity.

DON'T FORGET

Reference will be made to the impact of technology on business management throughout all three units.

HIGHER COURSE CONTENT

The Higher Grade course comprises three main units of study:

UNDERSTANDING BUSINESS (HIGHER)

This unit focuses primarily on the range of different types of organisations in our economy, with emphasis on large-scale organisations such as public limited companies.

In this unit you will study the structure and objectives of business organisations, how they achieve growth and the internal and external factors that can impact on their success. You will gain an understanding of the conflict of interests between different groups of stakeholders and how the actions of one stakeholder can impact on another.

MANAGEMENT OF MARKETING AND OPERATIONS (HIGHER)

In this unit you will study how the marketing function is used to influence consumer behaviour and the importance of using market research to give business organisations a competitive edge. There will be a particular focus on the marketing mix.

The study of operations examines the processes and procedures used by organisations to produce their goods or services in an efficient and ethical manner including inventory management, production methods and quality assurance.

MANAGEMENT OF PEOPLE AND FINANCE (HIGHER)

In this unit you will gain an understanding of how organisations recruit and maintain an effective workforce, including training and motivating employees. Organisations must also ensure that they adhere to all forms of employment legislation and maintain harmonious working relationships with employees.

You will also examine the sources of finance available to different organisations and how managers can budget to ensure good cash flow. You will gain an understanding of the importance of financial statements and how organisations use ratio analysis to interpret these accounts to help them make key business decisions.

COURSE ASSESSMENT – EXTERNAL

QUESTION PAPER

The question paper is worth 90 marks (75% of the total). It consists of two sections:

1 – A case study with short answer questions from any areas in the course. 30 marks.

2 – Four topic-based questions drawn from any areas in the course. 60 marks.

ASSIGNMENT

This assignment gives you an opportunity to apply your knowledge and understanding of business and business concepts. It will require you to make decisions, solve problems, draw conclusions and present and communicate your findings. You will be required to collect information, analyse and evaluate business data and produce a business report.

 ONLINE

Check out two specimen assignments at www.brightredbooks.net

EXAM HINTS

Before you start answering questions in the external exam paper, you should identify the key 'command word' used in each question. This will ensure that you tailor your response to the demands of the question being asked.

Command Word	Meaning
State	Listing or bullet points would be acceptable here.
Suggest	More than just naming or stating. Put forward a recommendation or advise on a possible course of action.
Outline	Identify key features and provide a brief description where appropriate.
Describe	Give a description and use examples where possible as part of the description.
Explain	Give a definition and an example as to how something may or may not be affected.
Discuss	Give advantages and disadvantages where possible. Use examples to expand your answer and, if possible, give a conclusion to your answer.
Compare	You must be able to compare the similarities or differences between the items, again giving a conclusion if necessary. A key word that you can use in this type of question is 'whereas'.
Justify	You must be able to give reasons why a certain course of action is being taken.
Consequences	You must be able to identify the initial impact of the action being followed.
Implications	You should be able to state what the likely outcome of a particular action will be in the longer term, either on a person or on an organisation.

Discuss, **compare**, **justify**, **consequences** and **implications** are the most difficult command words to address. More marks are likely to be awarded to questions using these words – make sure that you know how to respond and do not simply list key points!

HOW THIS STUDY GUIDE CAN HELP YOU

This study guide has been developed to give you the knowledge you need to prepare you for all aspects of your assessments in Higher Business Management.

The guide is presented in a clear and concise way, and is fully supported by the Bright Red Digital Zone (www.brightredbooks.net). We have used case studies, short response questions and specimen exam-style questions to challenge your knowledge and understanding of topics. These activities will also help you to develop the following key skills for business and for life: numeracy, analysis, decision-making, communication, planning, evaluation, research, problem-solving, presentation, ICT and creativity.

This book is suitable either for students progressing from National 5 Business Management or for those starting their studies at Higher level.

 ONLINE

The answers for all of the activities in this book, as well as extra tasks, tests and links, can be found at www.brightredbooks.net

UNDERSTANDING BUSINESS

SECTORS OF INDUSTRY

All businesses in the United Kingdom can be split into four main sectors:

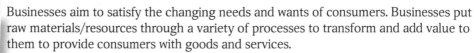

- Primary
- Secondary
- Tertiary
- Quaternary

THE ROLE OF BUSINESS

Businesses aim to satisfy the changing needs and wants of consumers. Businesses put raw materials/resources through a variety of processes to transform and add value to them to provide consumers with goods and services.

Adding value is how goods or services increase in value as they go through the production process. Adding value can be defined as: "the difference between the total cost of production and the final selling price".

Think of a brand-new home in the middle of a housing development which has been released for sale. The final, completed new house has a value which is much higher than the cost of the sum of all the raw materials (bricks, wood and slates etc). Value has been added. How much value is added depends on how much the customer is willing to pay for the house.

PRIMARY SECTOR

Businesses that are involved in exploiting or extracting natural resources – for example, farming, coal mining, fishing, forestry and oil exploration – belong to the primary sector. Some of the outputs from businesses in the primary sector are simply sold to businesses in the secondary sector. For example, a lumberjack business (primary sector) produces wood that is sold to furniture manufacturers (secondary sector) to enable them to produce their products.

SECONDARY SECTOR

Businesses that are involved in manufacturing and construction belong to the secondary sector of industry. They often use the natural resources produced in the primary sector and change them into things consumers need and want. Businesses involved in house construction, car manufacturing, food production, clothing, electronics and household goods belong to this sector of industry.

TERTIARY SECTOR

Businesses that provide a service, as opposed to producing physical goods, belong to the tertiary sector. Shops, banks, hotels, gyms, supermarkets, airline operators, transport (bus and train services) and film production companies are examples of businesses that would be included in the tertiary sector.

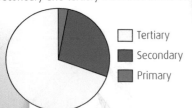

Employment structure for the primary, secondary and tertiary industries in the UK

- Tertiary
- Secondary
- Primary

QUATERNARY SECTOR

The quaternary sector consists of those industries that provide specific information services such as computing, ICT (information and communication technologies), consultancy (offering advice to businesses) and R&D (research, particularly in scientific industries). It is now acknowledged that 'information' is a very valuable resource to business organisations. Indeed, a business can gain a competitive edge if it has access to good business information and advice.

contd

The quaternary sector is sometimes included with the tertiary sector, as they are both sectors of industry providing a service. The tertiary and quaternary sectors make up the largest part of the UK economy, employing 76 per cent of the workforce.

The diagram to the left provides an overview of employment trends within the UK.

The UK has a low proportion of people working in the primary and secondary sectors. The tertiary sector is the main growth area, with most people being employed in shops, schools, hospitals, public services, tourism and hospitality.

What have been the main causes of this trend in employment?
- There has been increased competition from abroad, where many products can be produced more cheaply.
- There have been changes in consumer lifestyles. People have become wealthier, have more free time and so there has been a greater demand for leisure services.
- There has been a lack of investment in manufacturing.
- Many primary resources – for example, coal – have become exhausted.

ACTIVITY: RESEARCH TASK

The secondary (manufacturing) sector in the UK has been in decline for a number of years. Despite this, there are a number of Scottish businesses still operating in the secondary sector. Some of these firms are shown below:

- Linn Products
- Thomas Taylor
- Tunnock's
- Barr's
- Pentland Engineering
- Pringle of Scotland

Try to find out the goods or services that each business manufactures.

ACTIVITY:

Read the short passage below and then answer the question which follows.

Why are call centres keen on Scotland?

BskyB – one of the UK's best-known brands – has three call centre outlets in Scotland. Other well-known organisations that have large call centre sites in Scotland include IBM, NHS 24 and Scottish Power.

So why do some businesses choose to locate in Scotland?

Scotland has a modern infrastructure, natural resources, an entrepreneurial spirit and a world-renowned education system. With English being the third most common native language in the world, Scotland is at the forefront of innovation in industry.

Outline the reasons why you think Scotland is a popular choice of location for call centres.

THINGS TO DO AND THINK ABOUT

Answer the following questions in sentences.

1 Describe the four sectors of industrial activity.   (8 marks)

2 State one example of business activity that belongs to **each** of the four sectors of industrial activity.   (4 marks)

3 Describe which sector of industry is in decline in Scotland.
   Suggest reasons why this might be the case.   (3 marks)

4 State which sector of industry provides most jobs for the Scottish economy.   (1 mark)

5 Explain, using an example, how a business adds value.   (1 mark)

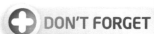

 DON'T FORGET

There are 4 main sectors of industry in the UK!

 VIDEO LINK

Go online and watch the video on sectors of industry at www.brightredbooks.net. For each of the sectors of industry identified in the video, you should try to identify three businesses in the UK that operate in each sector.

ONLINE

Head to www.brightredbooks.net for more about the sectors of industry.

 VIDEO LINK

Watch the video clip 'Primary, Secondary and Tertiary Sectors – Revision' at www.brightredbooks.net. You should now write a short paragraph that clearly explains the difference between the three main sectors of industry.

 DON'T FORGET

The four sectors of industry are primary, secondary, tertiary and quaternary.

ONLINE TEST

How well have you learned about this topic? Take the test at www.brightredbooks.net

TYPES OF BUSINESS ORGANISATIONS 1

The most common type of business organisations in the UK are sole traders, partnerships, private limited companies and public limited companies.

DON'T FORGET

Sectors of industry refer to primary, secondary, tertiary and quaternary. Sectors of business refer to private, public and third/voluntary sectors.

ONLINE

Head to www.brightredbooks.net to revise the advantages and disadvantages of sole traders and partnerships.

ONLINE

One of Scotland's most famous and well-known private limited companies is Tunnock's Ltd, which dates back to 1865. You should study the growth and success of this business by visiting www.brightredbooks.net. Once you have done this, describe the factors that you think have contributed to Tunnock's success.

ONLINE

Read a summary of the terminology you need to know about private limited companies at www.brightredbooks.net

PRIVATE LIMITED COMPANY

The capital of a private limited company (Ltd) is divided into shares, with each member or shareholder owning a number of shares each. A private limited company must have a minimum of two shareholders, and is usually managed by a board of directors (with a minimum of one director and one company secretary). One of the shareholders is usually a director.

A private limited company is not allowed to sell shares to the general public on the stock market.

This type of company is often a family-run business. Examples include Innocent Ltd, Tunnock's Ltd, Baxters Ltd and Arnold Clark Ltd.

To become a private limited company you must register your business with the Registrar of Companies and complete two legal documents – a Memorandum of Association and Articles of Association – which outline the company's details, the responsibilities of directors and shareholders' rights. (These documents are explained in more detail below.)

The main objectives of a private limited company include profit maximisation, sales maximisation, increased market share and developing a good reputation.

Private limited companies are usually financed by:
- issuing shares
- applying for government grants
- borrowing loans
- using retained profits from previous years.

Advantages of operating as a private limited company	Disadvantages of operating as a private limited company
Shareholders have limited liability – shareholders do not risk personal bankruptcy.	Profits are shared among shareholders.
More finance can be raised from shareholders.	More complicated to set up as it involves a legal process.
Shareholders and/or directors bring a degree of expertise to the business.	More difficult to raise large amounts of finance as shares cannot be sold to the public on the stock market.
Control of the company cannot be lost to outsiders.	The company must adhere to the rules and regulations of the Companies Act.
Set-up costs have decreased and the legal process is now much simpler.	Scottish private limited companies must provide Companies House in Edinburgh with a copy of their financial statements.

PUBLIC LIMITED COMPANIES

A public limited company (PLC) must be registered with the Registrar of Companies. It must have a minimum of £50 000 share capital, although in most cases the share capital amounts to much more than this.

The shares of a public limited company can be bought and sold on the stock exchange. There must be at least two shareholders who will own the company, but in most cases an appointed Board of Directors controls and manages it.

All public limited companies must complete a Memorandum of Association and Articles of Association (see below). Public limited companies tend to be very large and, in some cases, employ hundreds of employees. Well-known examples of a public limited company are British Telecom plc, Virgin plc, Stagecoach plc, Microsoft plc, Marks and Spencer plc, Tesco plc, ITV plc and British Airways plc.

The main objectives of a public limited company include profit maximisation, sales maximisation and market domination, while being environmentally responsible.

Public limited companies are usually financed by:

- selling shares (ordinary and preference) to the public
- issuing debentures (long-term loans)
- borrowing bank loans
- applying for government funding
- using retained profits from previous years.

Advantages of operating as a public limited company	Disadvantages of operating as a public limited company
It's possible to raise large amounts of capital by selling shares on the stock market.	The firm can be taken over if a rival firm is able to acquire enough shares.
Larger organisation, which is often considered as less risky by lenders.	Must abide by the rules and guidelines provided by the Companies Act.
Shareholders have limited liability.	There is no control over who purchases shares.
Specialists are usually appointed to ensure the company is run effectively.	A plc must publish its annual accounts.
Shares can be given to employees to motivate them.	Have to share profits – dividends are expected by shareholders.
Death and illness do not affect the operation of the business.	Not all decisions are made by the owners.
Some public limited companies are able to dominate their market.	Set-up costs are high – for example, they might have to produce a high-quality prospectus.

 DON'T FORGET

Public limited companies operate in the private sector.

 VIDEO LINK

Head to www.brightredbooks.net to see an overview of a public limited company.

 **ONLINE TEST**

How well have you learned this topic? Take the test at www.brightredbooks.net

 ## THINGS TO DO AND THINK ABOUT

Answer the following questions in sentences.

1. Describe three advantages to an organisation of becoming a private limited company. (3 marks)

2. Describe three disadvantages to an organisation of becoming a private limited company. (3 marks)

3. Explain, in your own words, an advantage to shareholders of a limited organisation having a legal existence of its own. (2 marks)

4. State the minimum number of shareholders a private limited organisation can have. (1 mark)

5. State who is appointed to run a private limited company. (1 mark)

6. Explain what is meant by 'limited liability'. (2 marks)

7. Describe three advantages to an organisation of becoming a public limited company. (3 marks)

8. Describe three disadvantages to an organisation of becoming a public limited company. (3 marks)

9. State what the minimum amount of capital required is in order to set up a public limited company. (1 mark)

10. For a plc that wishes to expand its operations, describe two external sources of finance that it could use. (2 marks)

TYPES OF BUSINESS ORGANISATIONS 2

MULTINATIONAL COMPANIES

Some public limited companies are so large that they operate on an international scale – that is, they operate in more than one country. These companies are known as multinational companies.

In recent years, there has been considerable growth in the number and size of multinational enterprises.

There are about 500 multinational companies in the world, and most are American. In the United Kingdom, half of the top 20 companies are multinational. Some are British – for example, BP and Vodafone – and some are foreign. Most of the 'incomers' are from the USA – for example, Ford, Apple and Microsoft – although there has been a rapid increase from Japan – for example, Nissan, Toyota and Sony.

WHY DO PUBLIC LIMITED COMPANIES WANT TO EXPAND OVERSEAS?

TO REDUCE PRODUCTION COSTS

Some companies choose to manufacture their products in countries that have lower wage costs. Other companies (such as Ford) produce components of their final product in countries where they can be produced at the lowest cost.

TO REDUCE TRANSPORT COSTS

Components might be cheaper to transport than the bulkier finished article. Also it might be cheaper to manufacture products in a foreign country rather than trying to transport the finished goods from the country of origin. Most Japanese car companies have set up factories in the UK.

TO PENETRATE MARKETS PROTECTED BY IMPORT CONTROLS

A major reason for the presence of US and Japanese firms in Europe is to evade trade tariffs imposed by the EU on goods coming from outwith the EU.

TO TAKE ADVANTAGE OF HOST-GOVERNMENT FINANCIAL ASSISTANCE

Many governments are keen to attract foreign firms and offer various incentives to encourage them to locate in their country – for example, low-cost premises, grants, low-interest loans and labour training subsidies.

TO ESCAPE GOVERNMENT REGULATIONS AT HOME

Many companies are tempted to move from their country of origin if a government imposes restrictions such as minimum wage, or minimum working condition rules.

TO EARN HIGHER AFTER-TAX PROFITS

Many companies move production to countries with low profit taxes to earn higher after-tax profits.

DON'T FORGET

Companies expand overseas to gain economies in or advantages of large-scale production.

VIDEO LINK

Watch the video at www.brightredbooks.net This highlights problems that multinational business can cause for smaller business organisations.

ADVANTAGES AND DISADVANTAGES OF MULTINATIONAL COMPANIES

Advantages of multinational companies	Disadvantages of multinational companies
Employment is created in the 'host' countries.	In some cases, the jobs created in the 'host' country are low-skilled assembly jobs, with the high-skilled research jobs being kept in the country of origin.
Economies of scale can be achieved – countries producing on such a large scale can spread production costs over a larger output and so prices can be reduced.	Profits earned in the 'host' country are usually transferred back to shareholders in the country of origin.
Multinational companies can introduce new management styles in the 'host' countries. Many UK firms have copied the management styles introduced by American and Japanese multinationals. These management styles have increased staff motivation, reduced costs and have developed their businesses into powerful global market leaders.	A multinational company could make demands on the government of its 'host' country and, if these requests are not granted, the company could withdraw from the country. This could cause unemployment in areas of the 'host' country.

contd

ACTIVITY:

Read the short passage below and then answer the question which follows.

It can be easy to forget that Primark first began life in Ireland in 1969 trading as Penneys, because since then the organisation has grown to a whole new level. It has 161 UK stores, 35 Spanish stores, five stores in The Netherlands, three stores in France and is still popping up in other countries throughout Europe. Imagine the excitement, then, when it was reported that Primark is planning to open its first megastore in Boston, USA in 2015. So what lies in store for America?

Describe reasons why you think Primark decided to open a megastore in America, when it is known predominantly throughout Europe.

THINGS TO DO AND THINK ABOUT

Read the passage below and then answer the following questions in sentences:

Coca-Cola

The 'H' on our taps stands for hot water and the 'C' for cold, but Coca-Cola reportedly famously said they would never rest until the 'C' stood for Coke! In consideration of the company's ambition of replacing water with Coke, the thought of an ice-cold Coke will hold universal appeal and the name Coca-Cola is recognised globally.

In fact it is the world's best known expression after 'okay'. However, the only problem that Coca-Cola faces is the low consumption of Coke products in foreign markets in comparison to the USA.

The chart below depicts the issue that in recent years Coke has been trying to resolve.

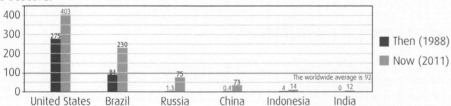

This shows that Russia, China and India are barely drinking any Coca-Cola in comparison to the USA. Although there has been obvious improvement since 1988, it is still below the worldwide average of 92. These countries are among the emerging markets that everyone is rushing to tap into.

For an organisation who over the past three years has reported a $9 billion net income in 2012, sold over 3500 products worldwide, achieved a global 2% increases in sales and prevented 5 million metric tonnes of CO_2 emissions of escaping into the planet's atmosphere, this is certainly helping their cause of becoming more accessible than drinking water.

1 Explain how Coca-Cola could be described as a multinational.

2 Describe how Coca-Cola could benefit from operating globally.

3 Discuss implications that a new entrant into the global soft drink market could face when attempting to compete with Coca-Cola on a global basis.

4 Explain reasons why changes to employment legislation in a foreign country might impact on a multinational company.

 VIDEO LINK

Watch the video clip on how Coca-Cola has been affected by globalisation over the years at www.brightredbooks.net

 ONLINE TEST

How well have you learned this topic? Take the test at www.brightredbooks.net

TYPES OF BUSINESS ORGANISATIONS 3

FRANCHISES

A franchise is a business run by one firm (franchisee) under the name of another (franchiser). The franchiser gives the franchisee a licence permitting them to sell goods or services under the franchiser's brand name, usually in return for a share of the franchisee's annual profits or an agreed annual royalty. The franchisee's licence permits them to use the franchiser's name, publicity materials, branding and uniforms.

Many individuals use franchising as a means of starting up their own business. There is less likelihood of failure because the franchiser provides the franchisee with support and guidance. Examples of businesses operated as franchises include Subway, Kentucky Fried Chicken, McDonalds, Body Shop, Burger King, Pizza Hut and British School of Motoring (BSM).

BUYING A FRANCHISE

Buying a franchise can cost anything from a few thousand pounds for a cleaning business to many hundreds of thousands of pounds for a fast-food franchise, like Subway.

Before you buy a franchise business, you should do your homework, just as you would before purchasing any business. For example, you should carry out your own market research and analyse potential revenue and expenses, look into the background of the franchiser, find out how long the business has been running and how many franchises it has. You should also check how successful its franchises have been – have many actually failed?

You should also check the support and training that you will receive. Examine the terms of the legal agreement closely to find out how long you will have the franchise for, and whether you will have an option to renew it in the future.

VIDEO LINK

View the video link at www.brightredbooks.net for all you need to know about franchising.

DON'T FORGET

There are many examples of franchises in every town centre. Why not visit your nearest town centre and identify business organisations that operate as a franchise, limited company and public limited company?

OBJECTIVES OF FRANCHISES

The main objectives of franchises are profit maximisation, sales maximisation, market growth and the establishment of a well-known brand name. Franchising is financed by the capital invested by the owner of the original business, and also by capital invested and annual fees paid by the franchisees.

Advantages to the franchiser	Disadvantages to the franchiser
It is a quick way for the franchiser to increase market share.	The reputation of the whole franchise is dependent on the success of individual franchisees.
The franchiser will earn a percentage of the franchisee's profits each year.	The share of profit earned from the franchisee could be less than if the franchiser had expanded the business on their own.
Risks and business uncertainties are shared between the franchiser and the franchisee.	The franchiser has to devote time and resources to support the franchisee – especially in the early stages of the business.

Advantages to the franchisee	Disadvantages to the franchisee
The franchisee can set up a business using an established business name, which reduces business risk.	A franchise can be expensive to purchase and set up.
Business risks and uncertainties are shared between the franchiser and the franchisee.	The franchisee might have little control over products, prices and store layout and so they might not be able to use their own initiative.
The franchiser will offer training and business support and advice.	A royalty or percentage of profits must be paid annually to the franchiser.
The franchiser is likely to advertise nationally (possibly on TV) so there is no need for franchisees to advertise individually.	At the end of the franchise agreement period, the franchiser might not renew the agreement or could change the terms of the legal agreement.

contd

 **ACTIVITY:**

Read the short passage below and then answer the following questions in sentences.

Flutter Eyes and Candy Creations

Franchises are seen as a possible way for entrepreneurs to dip their toes into the business waters. Franchises can be agreed in many different types of industries from Papa John's (food) to ChipsAway (automotive) to ChemDry (carpet cleaning).

Newer franchises include Flutter Eyes and Candy Creations. Flutter Eyes provide a mobile eyelash extension and semi-permanent eyelash service whose unique selling point is that they bring their services to the homes of their clients. Candy Creations provide 'sweet tables' for events such as fundraisers and parties. They are famed for their special 'Sweetie Trees' which are particularly popular at weddings.

1 Explain what is meant by 'franchise'.

2 Describe three terms of the franchise agreement that the franchiser might set.

 **ACTIVITY:**

Choose a franchise that you are familiar with and create a short report using the following information:

- History and background of the franchise
- Product/service information
- Success or failure?
- Future for the franchise

You can use the internet to research your information. Your report should be word-processed and should be no longer than two pages.

 **ACTIVITY:**

Copy and complete the table below filling in the details for each type of organisation.

	Definition	Example	Ownership	Controlled by
Private limited company				
Public limited company				
Franchise				
Multinational				

 THINGS TO DO AND THINK ABOUT

Specimen exam-style questions

Now that you have learned about the different types of business organisations, answer the following specimen exam-style questions in sentences.

1 Explain two reasons why an organisation would wish to become a private limited company. (2 marks)

2 Explain the advantages and disadvantages of becoming a public limited company. (4 marks)

3 Many large organisations are now classed as multinationals. Explain the advantages and disadvantages of operating as a multinational company. (4 marks)

4 Describe the main characteristics of a multinational company. (4 marks)

5 Describe three advantages of franchising for the franchiser. (3 marks)

 ONLINE

Head to www.brightredbooks.net for further activities on business organisations.

 ONLINE

Find out more about setting up a McDonald's franchise at www.brightredbooks.net. Have a look through the information provided on franchising including the short case studies on the different franchisees.

 VIDEO LINK

Watch the video clip about the origin of franchising at www.brightredbooks.net

 ONLINE TEST

Take the topic test at www.brightredbooks.net

PUBLIC SECTOR ORGANISATIONS

The overriding aim of public sector activity is to provide services for the general public or to improve local communities. Public sector organisations are managed by the government on behalf of the taxpayer. The public sector is made up of:

- central government
- local government
- public corporations

CENTRAL GOVERNMENT

Central government – for example, the Westminster government (in England) and the Scottish Parliament – are responsible for providing citizens with essential services such as health, defence and transport. Government departments – for example, the Department of Defence – are set up to manage each of these areas under the leadership of a government minister. Although politicians are elected by the public to run and control central government for a fixed term, departments are staffed by paid civil servants.

Finance is allocated to each government department from money raised through income tax, VAT and corporation tax. The finance allocated to each department will reflect government priorities.

The main objectives of central government include providing a cost-effective service, improving society and operating within allocated finance. For example, the public sector provides council housing for those unable to buy their own home. They also provide merit goods such as education and public goods like street lighting which it would not be profitable for the private sector to provide.

LOCAL GOVERNMENT

·EDINBVRGH·
THE CITY OF EDINBURGH COUNCIL

ONLINE

Investigate your local council further by following the link at www.brightredbooks.net

Local government – for example, councils like Glasgow City Council, the City of Edinburgh Council and Highland Council – are set up by central government (for example, the Scottish Parliament) and run on its behalf by locally elected councillors. The day-to-day running of council services is organised by paid managers and employees from each council. A local council aims to meet local needs and will take responsibility for providing services such as schools, environmental health, roads and social housing, and leisure facilities like swimming pools and sports centres.

Recent procurement legislation has meant that local authorities now contract out services such as refuse collection and school meals. This means that private firms are invited to submit bids to the local authority for the right to run a particular service. This is known as competitive tendering. It is argued that this will result in a more cost-effective service for the community, because private firms have an incentive to keep costs low and efficiency high to maximise profits.

Finance for local government comes from central government, business rates and from council tax. Some councils raise additional funding from entrance fees to swimming pools and from parking charges.

The main objectives of local councils include cost-effective services (in some cases through competitive tendering) to make improvements to their local area and to ensure that they operate within budget.

PUBLIC CORPORATIONS

Public corporations are organisations that are regulated by central government.
A chairperson and a board of directors are appointed to manage the organisation on behalf of the government. The British Broadcasting Corporation (BBC) is an example of a public corporation. It exists through the granting of Royal Charter. The BBC is funded by the licence fee, which is set by the government and paid by UK households who watch or record TV as it is being broadcast.

Objectives of public corporations include providing a quality service, serving the public interest and operating within allocated finance and budgets.

Over the past thirty years, most public corporations have been sold by the government and are now public limited companies, with their shares bought and sold on the stock market. Examples include British Telecom plc, British Airways plc, Scottish Power plc and more recently Royal Mail plc.

ADVANTAGES AND DISADVANTAGES OF THE PUBLIC SECTOR

Advantages of the public sector	Disadvantages of the public sector
Provides some of its services to all consumers.	Often considered to be bureaucratic.
As a public sector organisation, it faces little competition.	As there is no profit motive, there is often a lack of innovation.
Provides services that could be unprofitable if provided by firms in the private sector.	A change of government is likely to mean changes in priorities and so changes in funding and spending.
Provides employment for many people.	Can often 'crowd out' private firms.
Provides goods and services for those members of the community who cannot afford them.	

 DON'T FORGET

Public sector organisations are financed from taxation paid by individuals and private sector businesses.

 THINGS TO DO AND THINK ABOUT

Copy and complete the following task.

	Controlled by	Objectives	Sources of finance
Local government organisation – for example, education services			
Central government organisation – for example, NHS			
Public corporations – for example, BBC			

 **ONLINE TEST**

How well have you learned this topic? Take the test at www.brightredbooks.net

THIRD SECTOR ORGANISATIONS

VOLUNTARY ORGANISATIONS

Voluntary organisations – for example, the Scouts, Girl Guides, and amateur football clubs – are run and staffed by volunteers. They are usually set up to bring together people with a similar interest. They are normally managed and organised by a committee of elected volunteers. These organisations can raise finance by applying for grants from the lottery, from sports councils or from local authorities. At local level, they can charge would-be members a fee. They can also organise fundraising activities like bag-packing in supermarkets and sponsored walks.

The main objective of voluntary organisations is to serve people in the local community.

CHARITIES

Charities are set up to help a particular cause. In the UK, the government keeps a register of charities. All credible charities should, therefore, be on this register. Registered charities are usually exempt from paying taxes. Charities are often set up as trusts with no individual owner – the overall management and control is undertaken by a board of trustees, who are usually unpaid for the work that they do. Volunteers often conduct much of the day-to-day work and fundraising. Examples of well-known charities in the UK include Oxfam, Cancer Research, Children in Need and the Red Cross.

Charities are financed by donations from the public, donations from companies, government grants, lottery grants, income from charity shops, raffles, fetes and jumble sales.

The main aims and objectives of charities include helping to relieve poverty, providing funding for medical research and helping to protect the vulnerable.

 **ACTIVITY:**

Read the short passage below and then answer the following questions in sentences.

Oxfam

Founded in 1942, Oxfam, a registered charity, now operates in over 90 countries throughout the world. Oxfam works with poor people, regardless of race or religion, in its struggle against hunger, disease, exploitation and poverty.

1 Oxfam is involved in a wide range of charity work. Name three other charities that you know of.

2 Describe how Oxfam raises money to help support its cause.

3 Describe the main aim of a charity such as Oxfam.

SOCIAL ENTERPRISES

Social enterprises are businesses that trade to tackle social problems, improve communities, people's life chances or the environment. They make their money from selling goods and services in the open market, but they reinvest their profits back into the business or the local community so that when **they** profit, **society** profits.

The term 'social enterprise' was coined to recognise the organisations in the UK and across the world that were using the power of business to bring about social and environmental change.

Social Enterprise UK states that a social enterprise should:
- have a clear social and/or environmental mission set out in their governing documents
- generate the majority of their income through trade – buying and selling
- reinvest the majority of their profits to support their social cause
- be independent of state intervention
- be majority controlled in the interests of the social mission
- be accountable and transparent.

Examples of social enterprises include *The Big Issue* and the Eden Project.

Social enterprises are financed by grants, loans and equity finance (the exchange of capital for part-ownership of the business as in, for example, Dragon's Den). The two main providers of equity finance are venture capitalists and business angels.

The main objective of social enterprises is to generate an income to tackle a social cause.

VIDEO LINK

To find out more about social enterprises you should watch the videos at www.brightredbooks.net

ADVANTAGES AND DISADVANTAGES OF THE THIRD SECTOR

Advantages of the third sector	Disadvantages of the third sector
Social enterprises provide an opportunity for local people to gain employment.	Social enterprises have to compete in the commercial market and so face the same challenges and risks common to all businesses.
Social enterprises bring about a positive change to people and communities – they are not just driven by profit.	Charities and voluntary organisations usually depend heavily on unpaid volunteers or workers.
Charities raise awareness of (and raise funds to support) a particular cause.	Those with a paid role in the third sector usually earn less than they would if they worked in the private or public sector.
Voluntary organisations provide opportunities – for example, clubs and sporting activities in local areas.	Charities and voluntary organisations depend heavily on the generosity of the community for finance – for example, donations and fund raising.

DON'T FORGET

Third sector organisations do not focus on profit.

THINGS TO DO AND THINK ABOUT

The following are examples of third sector organisations:

- Oxfam
- Barnardos
- *The Big Issue*
- Children in Need
- Save the Children
- SSPCA

Select **one** of these organisations and use the internet to research the following aspects:

- background history
- aims and objectives
- sources of finance
- partnership agencies
- achievements to date.

ONLINE TEST

How well do you know this topic? Take the test at www.brightredbooks.net

BUSINESS OBJECTIVES 1

WHAT IS A BUSINESS OBJECTIVE?

Objectives are targets or goals that an organisation strives to achieve. To a certain extent, objectives provide strategic direction for an organisation and its employees – they show what an organisation would like to achieve over time. As such, achievement of objectives can be used to show how successful an organisation has been.

Some organisations will share their objectives with all their stakeholders, via their mission statement, company policies and website.

ORGANISATIONAL OBJECTIVES

Overview of organisational objectives

Private sector objectives	Public sector objectives	Third sector objectives
Profit maximisation.	To provide a service.	To provide a service.
Sales maximisation.	To improve society.	To help those in need.
Market growth.	To operate within allocated finance/budgets.	To raise funds to support a cause.
To produce high quality products/services.	To prioritise spending.	To support the local community.
Social responsibility and good reputation.	To serve public interest.	To be socially responsible.
Survival.	To be open and transparent with the electorate.	To bring people together with similar interests, for example, the Girl Guides.
Managerial objectives.	Satisficing.	To raise awareness of national and international problems.
Satisficing.		Satisficing.

PROFIT MAXIMISATION

One of the main aims of business organisations in the private sector is to make a profit – as big a profit as possible. Certainly in the long run, a business has to make some kind of profit to remain viable. There will also be an expectation from shareholders and other investors that they will receive some kind of return on their investment. Profits that are reinvested in the business will enable the business to grow and increase its market share.

SALES MAXIMISATION

In many large companies, where ownership and control are separated so that the managers are not necessarily shareholders, the size of a manager's salary is often linked to the annual turnover of the business. Therefore, a major aim of the management team in this context would probably be to generate as much sales revenue as possible.

MARKET GROWTH

A private sector organisation might have the objective of growth. Becoming larger could enable such a business to take advantage of economies of scale (large-scale output) and become more efficient through having lower unit costs. A business that grows could also get some degree of monopoly (controlling) power and so be able to charge higher prices.

SURVIVAL

For some businesses, survival is the overriding goal. Small family-run businesses might be more concerned about preventing large enterprises from taking them over than they are about making enormous amounts of profit.

Also, during an economic recession, which can prove fatal for some businesses, the focus might simply be to survive the downturn.

MANAGERIAL OBJECTIVES

Where ownership and control are separated – for example, in a public limited company – managers within a business could choose to pursue their own individual aims. These will vary depending on what individual managers want to achieve, but could include the following:
- responsibility for a large team
- money to spend on perks (for example, expense accounts and company cars)
- budgets to spend on projects that they believe will bring them prestige and status (for example, expansion into new markets).

contd

CREATING A GOOD REPUTATION (CORPORATE AND SOCIAL RESPONSIBILITY)

A firm might want to improve its public image – and hence its chances of survival and market growth – by demonstrating corporate and social responsibility. For example, every month every Waitrose branch donates a total of £1000 (£500 in convenience shops) to three local worthy causes chosen by their customers. Customers are given a token at the checkout and asked to place it in the box that supports the cause of their choice. The more tokens a cause gets, the bigger the donation it receives.

There is now also an expectation that all business organisations will aim to be environmentally friendly. For example, many of the big supermarkets have introduced 'bags for life' to reduce waste.

SATISFICING

For some businesses, the objective is only to make a level of profit that is sufficient to keep all stakeholders satisfied. For example, they will aim to earn a level of profit that will enable them to pay an acceptable dividend to shareholders, or to provide funds for future expansion. This concept is often referred to as 'satisficing'.

PRODUCING HIGH QUALITY PRODUCTS/SERVICES

An objective for some businesses will be to provide a high quality product for consumers. For example, Marks and Spencer tend to focus on producing high quality products and use straplines such as 'This is not just food, this is M&S food' to convey this objective to their customers.

PUBLIC AND THIRD SECTOR OBJECTIVES

The main objective of organisations in the public and third sectors is likely to be provision of a service. They will aim to provide their services to meet the needs of their customers or service users in the best way possible, while staying within budget. A hospital, school or council will probably have this as their primary objective. For example, Glasgow City Council launched the following slogan in 1983 to promote itself as a place to visit and to live.

'GLASGOW'S MILES BETTER'

ACHIEVING OBJECTIVES

In reality, organisations usually aim to achieve more than one objective. In addition, achievement of one objective often leads to the achievement of another. For example, where a firm's objective is to grow and expand or increase sales, then an increase in profits will probably also be achieved as a consequence of that objective.

Setting objectives will depend on the size and age of the organisation, the experience of the management team and the state of the economy. Organisations might re-prioritise their objectives over time as they face different challenges. However, it is clear that private sector organisations are likely to focus on profit.

CONFLICTING OBJECTIVES

There are often conflicting objectives within an organisation. For example, shareholders probably want the business to focus on profit, whereas managers probably want to focus on sales maximisation to earn high bonuses.

Here are three other examples of conflicting business objectives:

GROWTH V PROFIT

If a business has the objective of growth, it will have to spend large amounts of money investing in new buildings and equipment. It will also face rising costs such as wages and advertising. As business costs rise to finance growth, profits could initially fall.

GROWTH V CUSTOMER SERVICE

Many businesses have achieved success as a result of excellent customer service. However, as a business grows into a large (perhaps multinational) organisation, management often becomes more and more removed from the 'shop floor' and has less contact with customers. They can lose touch with customer needs and wants and, as a result, customer complaints increase and sales decrease.

SURVIVAL V PROFIT

If a business objective is just to survive, it is unlikely that it will earn high profits. A business is unlikely to be just surviving and maximising profits at the same time.

 THINGS TO DO AND THINK ABOUT

1 Choose two different organisations within the private sector.
2 Log onto their website and research what their objectives are.
3 Note these down in your workbook.

 VIDEO LINK

Watch the video shown at www.brightredbooks.net on business objectives.

 DON'T FORGET

A business can have conflicting business objectives.

 DON'T FORGET

The achievement of one objective might automatically lead to the achievement of other objectives.

 ONLINE TEST

Want to test your knowledge on this topic? Head to www.brightredbooks.net and take the test.

BUSINESS OBJECTIVES 2

⚙ ACTIVITY:

Copy and complete the table below by stating an example of each type of organisation. You should then suggest 2 possible objectives for each organisation. The first one has been completed for you.

Organisation	Objectives
Public Limited company Example – Tesco plc	1. to offer customers the best value for money and the most competitive prices. 2. profit maximisation.
Franchise	
Multinational Organisation	
Public Sector Organisations	
Third Sector Organisations	

DON'T FORGET ➕

A mission statement shares the business aims and objectives with customers, employees and other stakeholders.

MISSION STATEMENTS

Under both UK and EU law, a company must state what its overall aim is. This can be embodied in a **mission statement** that explains what the organisation is in business to do, and what it wants to achieve. A mission statement can often be found in the front of a company's annual report. It is, effectively, a summary of the organisation's main activities, long-term objectives and underlying purpose and direction.

Mission statements are best when they are simple and informal. This is highlighted in the examples shown below:

Example:

The Body Shop Plc: 'To dedicate our business to the pursuit of social and environmental change.'

Example:

Ford Motor Company Plc: 'Our mission is to improve continually and meet our customers' needs, allowing us to prosper as a business and to provide a reasonable return for our shareholders.'

⚙ ACTIVITY:

The following organisations can be found in most high streets and out-of-town retail parks:

- McDonalds
- Marks and Spencer
- New Look
- River Island
- Next
- Primark

Use the internet to research the mission statements for each of the businesses above. What are their aims and objectives? Record your findings in your workbook.

EFFECTIVE ORGANISATIONAL OBJECTIVES

For a business's objectives to be effective, they must be **SMART**:

S	**Specific** – they need to provide detail about what specifically needs to be achieved – for example, increase pre-tax profits by 20 per cent.
M	**Measurable** – they need to be measurable – for example, an increase in sales of 10 per cent.
A	**Achievable** – they need to be achievable – for example, a 10 per cent increase in sales is not likely to be achievable during a recession.
R	**Realistic** – it has to be possible for the organisation to achieve them.
T	**Time specific** – they need to have a deadline – for example, increase pre-tax profits by 20 per cent in the next financial trading year.

contd

SHORT- AND LONG-TERM ORGANISATIONAL OBJECTIVES

Short-term objectives will often differ from long-term objectives, especially if the business is currently experiencing poor financial performance. A short-term objective might simply be to survive the difficult trading conditions that it is experiencing. Once this has been achieved and the business has stabilised its performance, then it will revert to its long-term objective of diversification into new products and new markets to earn high profits.

 **ACTIVITY:**

The mission statement of Starbucks is 'to inspire and nurture the human spirit – one person, one cup and one neighbourhood at a time'.

Use the internet to research the mission statements of three other organisations.

Do you think these mission statements are aimed at helping the customer (as the Starbucks' one clearly is) or are they aimed at improving the lives of the organisation's employees?

ACTIVITY:

Read the case study below.

Wecyclers

In Lagos, Nigeria, there is a worsening waste crisis that is indicative of the city's soaring population. The overburdened municipal government can only collect 40 per cent of the city's refuse and only 13 per cent of recyclable materials are salvaged from landfills. Those who live in highly populated, slum conditions with no regular waste collection suffer from a multitude of issues such as increased flooding and spreading diseases.

Wecyclers was created to tackle these growing problems. On a weekly basis, cargo bicycles go around people's homes collecting plastics, cans and sachets. The residents will receive points for the weight of the recyclables they collect, which are then redeemable against such items as food, consumer electronics and cash. Wecyclers is just one of a new breed of social entrepreneur making sustainability pay.

While Wecyclers and their competitors are focusing on reusing waste, other businesses are attempting to reduce the amount of packaging used in the first place through modern methods of technology. Unilever is trialling a smaller canister for deodorants.

The organisation claims these new compressed deodorants 'last as long as the big ones, with less packaging'. Indeed it is thought this will save 275 tonnes of plastic in the first year alone.

Use the internet to research other social entrepreneurs and create a short PowerPoint based on your findings.

 ONLINE

Head to www.brightredbooks.net to find out more about business objectives.

 ONLINE TEST

Test your knowledge of business objectives at www.brightredbooks.net

 THINGS TO DO AND THINK ABOUT

Specimen exam-style questions

Now that you are confident with this topic, try answering the following specimen exam-style questions in sentences.

1   Describe four potential objectives of a private limited company.   (4 marks)

2   Explain three reasons why a competitor might decide to take over an established organisation which is not making much of a profit.   (3 marks)

3   Public sector organisations are owned and controlled by central government. Describe two objectives of a public sector organisation.   (2 marks)

4   Compare the objectives of a private sector organisation with those of a public sector organisation.   (4 marks)

INTERNAL FACTORS

ONLINE

Could you fit in with the corporate culture at IKEA? Follow the link at www.brightredbooks.net to try the quiz and see for yourself.

FACTORS IMPACTING ON BUSINESSES

A successful business organisation is one that can understand, anticipate and take advantage of changes within its operating environment.

An organisation's operating environment can by analysed by looking at:

- **Internal factors** – factors within the organisation that impact upon the way it operates.
- **External factors** – factors outwith the organisation's control that impact upon the way it operates.

INTERNAL FACTORS

Internal factors include:

Finance	When a business is unable to access the necessary finance, it will be unable to invest in new assets or finance the research and development of new products. It will also have to look at cutting costs – particularly labour/wage costs.
Staffing	The success of any business depends on a highly skilled and motivated workforce. A capable workforce will increase output and reduce unit costs. Businesses that invest in staff training will gain an advantage.
Management	Effective leadership is vital to the success of any organisation. Strong leaders with clear vision will make decisions that will have a positive impact on a business.
ICT	Effective use of information communications technology (ICT) is likely to give a business a competitive edge. Failure to embrace and invest in new technology could be disastrous.
Change in costs	Rising costs will have a negative impact on a business organisation. Rises in the cost of wages, raw materials and overheads are likely to reduce profit.
Information	A business that has access to up-to-date information will be more successful. For example, a business with accurate market research information is more likely to respond accurately to the needs and wants of consumers.
Corporate culture	An organisation that creates a strong and shared culture that employees embrace will be more successful.
Policies	Clear and transparent company policies provide guidance and direction. For example, all businesses should have policies on health and safety at work and absence management.

VIDEO LINK

Find out more about organisational culture and motivating employees by watching the video at www.brightredbooks.net

Some of these factors can be overcome by:
- training staff to be more efficient
- strict budgetary control
- arranging loans
- motivating employees with incentives.

 **ACTIVITY:**

Copy and complete the table shown below. For each of the internal factors in the table, give an example of how it could affect a business. The first one has been done for you.

Finance	This is necessary to achieve growth, to buy new equipment and remain competitive and to fund training sessions for staff. A lack of finance could mean that costs have to be cut resulting in, for example, redundancies, a delay in new product development or the downsizing of the business.
Staffing	
Information	
ICT	
Management	
Changes in costs	

HOW CAN AN ORGANISATION CREATE A STRONG CORPORATE CULTURE?

An organisation can develop a strong corporate culture by:

- Use of a phrase or motto that can be recognised by customers/used in marketing.
- Offering flexible working patters to motivate staff.
- Offering non-financial motivators such as gym facilities and 'chill out zones' within the business to cater for staff's physical and mental well-being.
- Casual dress codes such as dress down Friday's can create a more relaxed environment in which to work.
- Creating a strong corporate identity through the use of uniforms, corporate language or corporate colours can result in employees feeling part of a team.
- Open plan office layouts can encourage better communication, collaboration and team-working.
- Coffee shops and cafeterias can allow staff to relax in a more social setting.
- Break out areas cater for quick and informal meetings to be held.

ADVANTAGES OF A STRONG CORPORATE CULTURE

- Employees feel part of the organisation
- Motivates staff
- May attract new employees
- Improves the image and reputation of the organisation.

DISADVANTAGES OF HAVING A STRONG CORPORATE CULTURE

- May make it difficult to initiate change
- Discourages creativity and new ideas
- New employees may struggle to fit in to the organisation.

ONLINE

Head to www.brightredbooks.net for another great activity on corporate culture.

ONLINE

A 2013 survey conducted by 'Great Place to Work' has highlighted the top 25 multinational companies to work for. Go onto the link at www.brightrebooks.net and identify five companies that made it into the top 10.

DON'T FORGET

Corporate culture embodies the norms, values and traditional behavior shared by employees in an organisation.

 **ACTIVITY:**

Read the passage below. Describe the strategies that could be employed by managers to remedy a 'toxic corporate culture'.

Corporate Culture – The Toxic Culture

We know that corporate culture can be a marvellous asset which can produce amazing results, an unbeatable competitive advantage and can be a key factor in being a strong organisation with a large slice of the market.

However, if organisational culture is not managed correctly, it can fester over time and become more and more dysfunctional until it is completely toxic. If this happens, it can become a liability hanging around the organisation like a bad smell!

A toxic culture can result in an unhealthy working environment which can damage the emotional, physical or financial wellbeing of its employees. It may have deteriorated to this point as a result of weak leadership; high staff turnover; gossip mongering; the feeling that it is 'us and them'; authoritarian leaders or retaining poor-performing staff which can be very frustrating for those who work hard and have a strong work ethic.

 THINGS TO DO AND THINK ABOUT

1 Define what is meant by 'corporate culture'. (1 mark)

2 Explain the importance of a strong corporate culture to an organisation. (2 marks)

3 State three advantages of having a strong corporate culture. (3 marks)

EXTERNAL FACTORS 1

PESTEC 1

There are a number of key factors in the external environment of a business. All businesses must react efficiently to changes in their external environment – if they don't, they could fail. External factors can be summarised as follows:

Political factors

Economic factors

Social factors

Technological factors

Environmental factors

Competitive factors

DON'T FORGET

The PESTEC acronym will help you remember the external factors that impact on a business.

POLITICAL

Political decisions made in both the UK and the EU can have a direct impact on the way that a business operates. The government's introduction of a statutory minimum wage affects all businesses, as do laws like the Health and Safety at Work Act and the Data Protection Act.

The government has also introduced laws banning advertising tobacco on television (and more recently new laws preventing shops from displaying tobacco products), the purchase and sale of alcohol outwith certain hours and also a smoking ban in public places. Sanctions and penalties are in place for any businesses that do not comply with this legislation.

There is also a free trade agreement between member countries of the European Union that allows countries to export their output to foreign markets without incurring tariffs or taxes.

Government policy can be developed to support certain industries as, for example, when the government placed orders for new defence ships as a way of maintaining shipbuilding in certain areas of the UK.

In addition, government grants can be made available to businesses to help create employment, and rates of corporation tax can also be reduced to help increase profits.

The government also supports business through the development of infrastructure such as roads, airports, schools, colleges and hospitals.

 **ACTIVITY:**

Read the following passage and then answer the questions which follow in sentences.

Political – Primark

The price of cotton increased by over 90 per cent last year. This is potentially damaging news for clothing manufacturers and retailers. Companies such as Next have issued profit warnings as they face not only the rising costs of cotton but also increased wage demands from their factories in China.

To combat this, clothing manufacturers and retailers are seeking alternative suppliers in relatively cheaper countries such as Vietnam, Bangladesh and Laos so that they can remain competitive on the UK high street. However, such a strategy is likely to come under close scrutiny.

Employment legislation exists to protect the legal rights of both employees and employers but Primark found itself under scrutiny when it was accused of breaching employment legislation. For some organisations, the search for cheaper production costs can lead to their products being unknowingly produced in sweatshop conditions, as exposed recently in a series of scandals surrounding retail giants such as Primark and Arcadia.

contd

1   Explain the different effects that two political factors could have on an organisation.

2   Describe four external factors (other than political) that could have an impact on an organisation's success or failure.

ECONOMIC

All organisations are affected by national and global economic factors. Within the UK, factors such as inflation, exchange rates of currency, interest rates and rates of taxation determine the 'climate' of the economy and dictate how consumers might behave.

Where the economy is on the economic trade cycle – whether that's boom, recession or recovery – will also affect consumer confidence and behaviour.

When the economy is at the 'boom' stage, there are likely to be high levels of consumer spending, enabling businesses to increase sales and/or profits. However, the government may use Fiscal Policy (for example, increase taxation and cut government spending), to reduce consumer spending across the economy, if there is a danger of rising inflation (rising prices). This action could mean a fall in sales and profits for businesses.

An economy that is in recession is characterised by high unemployment, low consumer confidence and spending leading to lower profits for businesses. Monetary Policy may be used (for example reduce interest rates and increase bank lending) to encourage consumer spending across the economy to reduce unemployment. Businesses will respond to an increase in consumer demand by increasing the output of goods and services. This action could lead to a rise in sales and profits for businesses.

SOCIAL

Within society, aspects such as family, friends and mass media affect our attitudes, interests, opinions and behaviour. These aspects also shape who we are as people and how we choose to spend our disposable income. For example, within the UK, people's attitudes are changing towards their diet and health. As a result, the UK is seeing an increase in the number of people joining fitness clubs and a massive growth in the demand for organic food. Fast-food businesses like McDonalds are having to expand their range of products to offer healthier options. Other noticeable changes in UK society include:

- an ageing population, with more demand for goods and services for the elderly
- more women being career-oriented and holding management positions within business organisations
- increased concern about the environment
- increased car ownership
- people having more leisure time to eat out and go on holiday
- workers from the European Union choosing to live and work in Britain
- longer opening hours for shops
- development of retail parks in the outskirts of large towns, meaning that many 'high streets' are struggling to attract consumers.

As society and consumer behaviour changes, organisations **must** be able to offer products and services that complement and benefit people's lifestyle and behaviour. Failure to do so could see a business being 'squeezed' out of the market.

 THINGS TO DO AND THINK ABOUT

Using the information here and on the next two pages, outline each of the **PESTEC** factors in the table below giving a brief example for how each one can impact on the business. The first one has been completed.

Political	Factors such as UK and EU legislation – for example, pension laws. Organisations have to adhere to these laws or run the risk of being penalised with fines or – depending on the seriousness – legal action.
E	
S	
T	
E	
C	

 **DON'T FORGET**

Fiscal Policy involves changing levels of government expenditure and taxation to influence economic behaviour.

 **DON'T FORGET**

Monetary Policy involves changing interest rates and the level of bank lending to influence economic behaviour.

 **ONLINE TEST**

Want to check your knowledge of this? Take the test at www.brightredbooks.net

EXTERNAL FACTORS 2

PESTEC 2

TECHNOLOGICAL

The development of technology is changing the way that businesses operate. The internet and the growth of e-commerce mean that consumers can now shop from the comfort of their homes or 'on the move' using smartphones 24 hours a day. Businesses that are slow to embrace progress in technology will 'fall at the first hurdle'.

The technological revolution means a faster exchange of information. This is beneficial for businesses, because they can react quickly to changes within their operating environment.

Technology is being employed in nearly every area of business – for example, e-mail and video conferencing can speed up communication, and databases can be used to store customer and supplier details and to create mailing lists. Businesses can communicate with customers through social media such as Facebook and Twitter. Technology is, increasingly, replacing labour in production line processes – for example, in the production of motor cars. Supermarkets are using technology for inventory control and to replace checkout operators.

Governments are also keen to encourage investment in research and to develop technology that will give their country the competitive edge.

Technology will continue to evolve at a rapid pace, and organisations that ignore this will face extinction.

ENVIRONMENTAL

Environmental factors have become much more significant in recent years, with pressure groups such as Greenpeace and Friends of the Earth becoming much more high profile. As a result, they are able to exert more influence on how businesses behave. For example, Shell Oil wanted to dispose of a disused oil platform by 'dumping' it at sea. Action by Greenpeace in many countries – in particular their strategy of encouraging consumers not to buy Shell petrol – forced Shell to consider other ways of disposing of the platform.

The power of these pressure groups has encouraged most large businesses to adopt corporate or social responsibility as one of their business objectives. Simple measures like employing recycling banks, minimising packaging and encouraging the use of re-usable carrier bags (or 'bags for life') are now all common practice with large supermarkets.

Other environmental factors that affect business organisations include storms, floods and other adverse weather conditions. Some businesses have been severely affected by flooding in recent years. They have had to close and refurbish or even rebuild. Unfortunately, these are environmental factors over which they have little or no control.

COMPETITIVE

Most businesses are likely to face a degree of domestic and foreign competition.

The actions of competitors will influence the operation of a business – if there is a strong degree of competition between firms, then action will have to be taken to protect sales, market share and profits. The higher the degree of competition in a market, the harder individual firms will have to work to keep costs down and produce their products as efficiently as possible.

These 'price wars' will ultimately benefit consumers but they can hit the profits of the companies involved very hard.

contd

Some businesses also have to deal with competitors who make imitations of products that steal market share.

There is also a growing population of experienced people who want to be entrepreneurs and start their own business.

Businesses are now expected to adhere to **ethical competition** and, for example, not exploit child labour. The Coca-Cola Company has recently produced the following code of conduct to shape the future direction of the business:

- Act with integrity
- Be honest
- Follow the law
- Be accountable.

Consumers now expect business organisations to act in the most ethical way possible. This could mean that business organisations face rising costs and reduced profitability. Organisations must highlight to consumers the good work that they do ethically to gain a competitive advantage over those businesses that operate in an unethical manner.

 **ACTIVITY:**

Look at the following factors that can impact upon an organisation and classify each one as political, economic, social, technological, environmental or competitive:

- Regulations regarding disposal of waste electronic components by organisations.
- The average life expectancy of a briton to be in their early 80s.
- A rise in unemployment.
- Encouraging workers to 'bring your own device' to work.
- An increase in national insurance contributions.
- New ways of packaging food stuffs.
- Changes to employment law.
- Changes to working patterns with emphasis on flexibility.

 THINGS TO DO AND THINK ABOUT

Specimen exam-style questions

Now that you are confident with this topic, try answering the following specimen exam-style questions in sentences.

1 Explain two economic factors that can have an impact on a business.   (4 marks)

2 Explain how external factors could affect an organisation.   (3 marks)

3 Manufacturers have to transport goods to retailers. Describe two external factors that might result in transport difficulties.   (2 marks)

4 Discuss how the following factors could affect an organisation's decision to locate abroad:
   - political
   - economic
   - social
   - technological   (4 marks)

5 A confectionery company might have the strategic objective to increase its market share by 10 per cent. Describe the internal and external factors that could prevent the achievement of this objective.   (4 marks)

6 Explain the advantages that a 'corporate culture' could bring to an organisation and its employees.   (4 marks)

7 Describe different methods that organisations can use to develop a corporate culture.   (5 marks)

8 Explain the advantages for an organisation of having a strong corporate culture.   (4 marks)

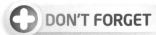 **DON'T FORGET**

The Competition and Markets Authority (CMA) oversees competition in the UK economy.

 ONLINE

Head to www.brightredbooks.net for more information on the CMA.

 ONLINE

Head to www.brightredbooks.net for more activities on this topic.

 ONLINE TEST

Want to check your knowledge of this? Take the test at www.brightredbooks.net

STAKEHOLDERS 1

There are many parties who have a financial or other interest in the performance of an organisation – these groups of people are often referred to as stakeholders.

STAKEHOLDERS BY SECTOR

The main stakeholders are considered to be:

Private sector organisations	Public sector organisations	Third sector organisations
Shareholders	Central government	Board of trustees
Employees	Local government	Volunteers
Customers	Councils	Donors
Suppliers	Voters	Club members
Government	Pressure groups	Office of the Scottish Charity Regulator
Local community	Trade unions	Pressure groups
Directors/managers		
Lenders		
Trade Unions		
Pressure groups		

All stakeholders have a vested interest in an organisation and to some extent are also able to exert a degree of power or influence over the organisation's activities.

PRIVATE SECTOR STAKEHOLDERS

SHAREHOLDERS

Shareholders have a clear financial interest in the performance of a business. They have invested money in the company by purchasing shares on the stock market, and they therefore expect the company to grow and prosper and to get a healthy return on their investment. This return can come in two forms. Firstly, a rise in the price of the shares will enable them to sell their shares at a premium. Secondly, they will expect a share of the annual profits in the form of a healthy dividend.

Ordinary shareholders are able to exert power at an Annual General Meeting (AGM). They are responsible for electing a board of directors, to run the company on their behalf.

EMPLOYEES

Employees also have a financial interest in a business, since their salaries and job security will depend on the performance and the profitability of the company. In addition, employees are looking for job satisfaction, opportunity for promotion and good working conditions. It is the employees who are responsible for the business's output (or service) and so they have a significant input to the workings of the business. However, if workers feel undervalued, stressed, or underpaid it can result in poor quality output and/or a high rate of staff turnover.

Many workers are a member of a trade union and can put pressure on an organisation by taking industrial action that ranges from work-to-rule, go-slow or even strike action, where they completely withdraw their labour.

CUSTOMERS

Customers are vital to the survival of any business, since they purchase the goods and services which provide the business with the majority of its revenue. Customers essentially want high-quality products at the lowest possible price. In addition, customers

DON'T FORGET

Stakeholders have different expectations and can impact on an organisation in different ways.

contd

now expect to receive good customer care service and a high standard of after-sales service. It is therefore vital for a business to find out exactly what the needs of the customers are, and produce an output of goods or services to directly satisfy these needs. This is often done through market research.

All business organisations must try to keep customers loyal so that they return in the future and become a repeat purchaser.

Customers can therefore influence what products and services a business should provide. They can also provide positive or negative feedback to family and friends on the quality of the goods purchased and the customer service and after-sales service received. As such, the reputation of a business is very much in the hands of the customers.

SUPPLIERS

Without flexible and reliable suppliers, the business would be unable to guarantee the necessary high-quality raw materials required to produce its output. It is important for a business to maintain good relationships with its suppliers so that raw materials can be ordered and delivered at short notice. Establishing good relationships with suppliers will also allow the business to negotiate good credit terms and discounts. Suppliers will want a business to be successful to ensure prompt payment and repeat business for them.

Suppliers can influence how profitable a business is by changing the amount that they charge for raw materials provided. They can also change credit terms and withdraw trade and cash discounts.

THE GOVERNMENT

The government affects the workings of a business in many ways:

- Businesses have to pay taxes to both central and local government. These taxes include **corporation tax** on profits, **value added tax** on sales and **business rates** to their local council. A change in any of these taxes can have an impact on profits, sales and business expenses.
- Governments can introduce legislation such as the minimum wage, Health and Safety at Work Act, advertising bans (for example, with alcohol and tobacco) and smoking bans. All businesses must adhere to legislation or face prosecution.
- Businesses are also affected by government economic policies. For example, if the government increases interest rates, this could deter a business from borrowing to finance expansion or replace assets. However, a business can also benefit from government incentives such as job creation programmes and government grants or low-interest loans.

BANKS AND LENDERS

Banks and other lenders are able to support a business by offering or withholding loans to finance expansion, address temporary cash flow problems or to purchase new assets. They also negotiate interest rates and repayment periods. However, before any loan is given, lenders will ensure that the organisation has sufficient funds to make repayments.

THE LOCAL COMMUNITY

A business organisation can create employment for the local community as well as providing goods and services to consumers in their local area. Businesses often sponsor local events and good causes (such as local charities) and this can help establish the business's reputation as a caring and socially responsible organisation. Some businesses will also develop links with local schools and colleges by working on school-based projects or providing resources such as computers for classrooms.

However, businesses can also cause many problems in local communities, such as congestion, pollution and noise and overcrowding, and these negative factors can sometimes outweigh the benefits that the business brings to the local area.

DIRECTORS/MANAGEMENT

Directors and managers are responsible for the successful leadership of an organisation. It is management who make decisions on matters such as hiring staff, product portfolio and target markets. They want the organisation to be successful because this enhances their professional status and promotion prospects and enables them to negotiate higher salaries and bonuses.

 THINGS TO DO AND THINK ABOUT

Choose a business local to you – for example, Asda, Tesco, Morrisons or Waitrose. Think about how three of the stakeholders listed above might affect the running of that business.

 ONLINE TEST

Want to test yourself on stakeholders? Head to www.brightredbooks.net

STAKEHOLDERS 2

OVERVIEW OF PRIVATE SECTOR STAKEHOLDERS

Stakeholder	Main interests	Power and influence
Shareholders	Increased market share, profits, dividends and a rise in the price of shares.	They elect directors at the annual AGM.
Employees	Fair pay, job security, good working conditions and job satisfaction.	They can affect business through industrial action such as strikes, staff absenteeism, staff turnover and the production of poor quality products.
Customers	High-quality products, good customer service including after-sales service, product/service availability and good value for money.	They can buy products from rival businesses and they might or might not recommend the business to family and friends, which impacts on reputation.
Suppliers	Repeat orders, prompt payment for goods supplied.	They can change the price of products provided and can change terms and conditions of – for example – delivery times, carriage charges and trade and cash discounts.
Government	Job creation in local areas, tax receipts and ensuring the business operates legally.	They produce legislation, set tax rates and offer subsidies and grants.
Management	Salary, status, job satisfaction, bonuses, promotion and share options.	They have detailed information, and responsibility for making decisions.
Local community	Local employment, protection of local environment and positive impact on local area.	They can make complaints to local council and can participate in protests, which can damage business reputation.
Lenders	Ensuring all loans and credit given can be repaid.	They can grant or withhold loans, set interest rates and repayment periods.

Examples of conflict between stakeholders	
Management want profit.	Employees want higher wages and job security.
Customers want a good quality product or service at a good price.	Shareholders want reduced costs and higher profits/dividends.
Managers want high levels of sales and expansion of operations.	Local communities want to protect their local environments.
Banks want to charge interest on loans and ensure money lent is secured against assets and repaid on time.	Owners want loans for expansion and for purchasing assets at low rates of interest.
Managers want discounts for bulk buying and favourable credit terms.	Suppliers want prompt payment at high prices so they earn profit.

ONLINE

Head to www.brightredbooks.net for further activities on stakeholders.

PUBLIC AND THIRD SECTOR STAKEHOLDERS

PUBLIC SECTOR

Public sector organisations are also influenced by stakeholders. For example, voters, pressure groups and the local community can all have an impact on the objectives of services such as health, police, education and social housing.

THIRD SECTOR

Third sector organisations like charities are influenced by donors who support their cause, and by members of the public who are willing to act as volunteers to help them achieve their aims.

INTERDEPENDENCE OF STAKEHOLDERS

Sometimes stakeholders need to work together and rely on each other for the business to succeed. For example:

- Owners/Managers cannot run the business without committed, hard-working employees.

- Employees rely on managers making decisions to ensure the long-term survival of the business to secure jobs.

- Government relies on employees paying Income Tax and owners of businesses paying Corporation Tax.

- Local communities rely on businesses to create jobs and provide goods and services.

- Owners/managers rely on suppliers supplying them with raw materials/inventory.

In your workbook, identify whether each of the following stakeholders are internal or external.

- Central government
- Donors
- Banks and other lenders
- Taxpayers
- Managers
- Shareholders
- Customers
- Suppliers
- Trade payables
- Employees
- Local community
- Local government

Read the short passage below and then answer the following questions in sentences.

Stakeholders – General Motors and Marks and Spencer

In recent times, General Motors has been having difficulty with its vehicles in the USA. It has had to take drastic action and recall over 13 million vehicles so far in 2014 due to safety concerns. In fact, GM was fined for failing to address defects within its vehicles, which had linked to 13 fatalities.

The image below shows the impact this recent recall news has had on the share price of the company over the course of one day.

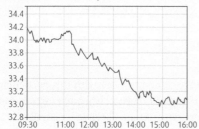

Marks and Spencer, on the other hand, is reporting that managers and employees of the company will receive no bonus after the organisation's profits have fallen for three years consecutively. This will affect all 82 000 Marks and Spencer employees from the boardrooms to the shopfloor.

This shows the impact that this news had on Marks and Spencer's share price over the course of one day.

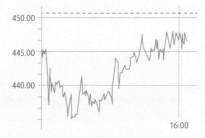

1 In your own words, compare how you think the interests of managers and employees might conflict in a large company such as General Motors.
2 Describe how an organisation such as Marks and Spencer can be influenced by its different stakeholders.
3 In what ways might the stakeholder of an organisation such as Marks and Spencer face conflict?

 ## THINGS TO DO AND THINK ABOUT

Specimen exam-style questions

Now that you are confident with this topic, try answering the following specimen exam-style questions in sentences.

1 Describe how a local council such as East Ayrshire council may be influenced by its different stakeholders.   (6 marks)
2 Employees are one group of Tesco's stakeholders. Describe how three other stakeholders can influence organisations.   (6 marks)
3 Describe how four stakeholders other than shareholders can influence an organisation.   (4 marks)
4 Describe an interest each of the following stakeholders has in an organisation's financial information:
   - employees
   - HMRC
   - trade payables   (6 marks)
5 A large department store in the centre of Glasgow is finding it difficult to maintain profits. A hostile takeover is proposed by one of its main competitors and shareholders have been offered the chance to sell their shares. Describe the ways in which shareholders can influence organisations.   (3 marks)

INTERNAL ORGANISATION: GROUPING

Internal organisation is the term used to describe the way in which a business groups its staff and work activities. Organisations can group their activities in a number of ways, depending on factors such as:

- size of the organisation
- products or services being provided
- target markets.

FUNCTIONAL GROUPING

This is a very common organisational structure where the activities in an organisation are grouped into departments based on similar skills, expertise and resource used. It is widely used by British companies. Functional departments include: Marketing, Operations, Human Resource Management (HRM), Research and Development, Finance and Administration.

An example of an organisation that uses functional grouping.

Board of Directors
Chief Executive
Production — Marketing — Accounts — Human Resource — IT

Advantages	Disadvantages
Staff with similar skills and expertise work together, and so departments become highly specialised.	Functional departments can focus on the aims of their own department, rather than on overall organisational aims.
A clear organisational structure with defined departmental roles.	There can be a breakdown in communication between departments.

PRODUCT/SERVICE GROUPING

Here, the grouping of activities is based around a particular product or service and is usually described as a **division**. Each division is a self-contained unit focusing on a particular product or service. The functional activities needed to produce the single product or service will be grouped together and assigned to work with this particular product/service only. As each division will have its own functional activities, departments are likely to be smaller. In most cases, organisations using this type of structure are very large, producing a variety of products for different markets.

Hewlett Packard uses product/service grouping.

Hewlett Packard
Imaging and Printing Group — Personal Systems Group — Enterprise Systems Group — HP Services — HP Financial Services

Advantages	Disadvantages
Each division can be more responsive to changes in its market.	There can be a duplication of resources – for example, each division can have its own functional departments.
Staff working in each division develop a high degree of expertise in each product/service.	
Senior management can easily identify which divisions are making the largest contribution to the overall success of the business.	Divisions could compete against each other, rather than cooperating to achieve overall success for the organisation.
A strong team culture is developed in each division.	

DON'T FORGET

Organisations will select the most appropriate methods of grouping in relation to their product or service – and this can change over time.

CUSTOMER GROUPING

Organisations structured around customers or groups of clients are more likely to be found in the service sector. They offer a high degree of personalised service to their customers as they are usually customer-focused. They are highly responsive to immediate customer needs and to the anticipation and provision of future customer wants due to the close working relationships they have with their customers.

Managing Director
Customer Type A — Customer Type B — Customer Type C — Customer Type D

contd

Advantages	Disadvantages
Customers receive a service and price suited to their own individual needs.	It can be more expensive because the more customer groupings you have, the more staff you require.
Customer loyalty is developed because staff get to know their customers well and always aim to satisfy their needs and wants.	There can be duplication of advertising and administration costs, especially if each grouping has its own office. This can ultimately reduce profits.

LOCATION/GEOGRAPHICAL GROUPING

With this method, staff are divided into divisions, each dealing with a different geographical area. Many organisations with a broad customer base spread across a large geographical area are structured in this way. Organisations using this method of grouping can meet the needs of customer groups in different countries who might have language and cultural differences. This enables the organisation to acquire specialist knowledge about customer groups and so employ specific marketing techniques.

Hewlett Packard makes use of this method of grouping.

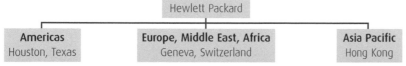

Hewlett Packard

Americas	Europe, Middle East, Africa	Asia Pacific
Houston, Texas	Geneva, Switzerland	Hong Kong

Advantage	Disadvantage
The needs of customers in different geographical locations – for example, in different countries – are more likely to be met.	This method of grouping can be very costly to staff, especially if groups are located around the world.

DON'T FORGET

While functional is the most common method of grouping an organisation's activities, other methods of grouping can be used.

ONLINE

For more on this, follow the link at www.brightredbooks.net

TECHNOLOGICAL GROUPING

Organisations can group their activities along technological lines. For example, in car production there are separate processes or stages that a car has to pass through to get to the end of the production line. It therefore makes sense that the car manufacturer should group its activities around these processes. However, this type of grouping is really only appropriate when there are obvious stages of production, and where these stages flow naturally from one to the next.

Advantages	Disadvantages
Staff become highly specialised and it can be quicker and cheaper to train new staff as they only need to be trained on one technological system.	Work can become very low-skilled and repetitive and so staff lose motivation
When problems occur in the production process, it is easy to identify exactly where they have arisen.	Industries that use technological grouping tend to be very capital intensive, which is very expensive to set up.

LINE/STAFF GROUPING

This is a method of grouping where the organisation is divided up into line departments. Each department has a line manager, responsible for the work of their department, and instructions from the managing director are passed through these lines of communication and chain of command.

With this method of grouping, an organisation can organise its departments into **Core** and **Support** departments. Core departments are directly responsible for the production and selling of the business' products. They carry out the activities that allow the business to generate profits. **Support departments** don't contribute directly to the production of the organisation's goods or services but they do support the **Core departments** and ensure the business operates efficiently.

Advantages	Disadvantages
Staff become specialised and competent in their activities.	As the organisation grows, communication between departments can become a problem.
Each department has a designated manager who is responsible for and oversees the work of the department.	Coordination of activities between departments can be lacking.
Specialist equipment and staff are not spread across different departments, so the organisation saves money.	Line managers might focus on departmental aims rather than the overall aims of the organisation.

ONLINE TEST

Want to test yourself on grouping? Head to www.brightredbooks.net

FORMS OF ORGANISATIONAL STRUCTURE 1

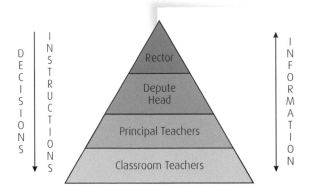

HIERARCHICAL (TALL) STRUCTURE

This is the traditional structure suitable for medium and large organisations. It is also often called a **pyramid structure** because of its shape. Most schools will normally operate this type of structure. The organisation structure of a typical secondary school is shown to the left.

Decisions and instructions are made by senior management at the top of the organisation and are then passed down to middle managers and then on to the general workforce. Information passes back up the organisation in a similar manner.

Position in the pyramid indicates the level of responsibility and authority an individual employee has. Staff at the top of the pyramid have more responsibility and authority. All members of the organisation have clearly defined roles and duties and these are usually outlined in a formal job description. With this type of structure, specialisation of tasks is very common, and this is often combined with a breaking up of the organisation into key functional departments. Specialisation allows the organisation to achieve greater efficiency.

This type of organisational structure has been criticised for its inability to respond quickly to changes in market and consumer demands. Indeed, it is argued that this organisational structure often suffers from time delays, both in communications passing up and down the structure and in the decision-making process, when many individuals on different levels are required to provide input. Some large organisations in the public sector – like the Civil Service, the Armed Services, the Police and the National Health Service – can have over 20 different layers in the pyramid!

VIDEO LINK

Watch the following video clip at www.brightredbooks. net for further information on hierarchical and flat structures.

FLAT STRUCTURE

This type of structure is mainly used by small organisations. In a flat organisational structure there are very few levels in the hierarchy. This offers significant benefits for the organisation – for example, communications are passed quickly from one level to another – and this speeds up the processing of information and any decision-making. Many small organisations such as professional partnerships of doctors, dentists or lawyers use this type of structure.

Example: A doctor's practice

Flat Structure.

The example above shows a flat management structure where each doctor communicates with a practice nurse, who in turn communicates with one secretary/receptionist.

Increasingly, large organisations are moving towards a flatter structure in an attempt to overcome the problems of poor communication and slow decision-making associated with a hierarchical structure. This often involves cutting out some of the layers of the hierarchy – a process known as delayering.

MATRIX STRUCTURE

A matrix (or task-based structure) is formed to complete a specific task or project. It involves bringing people with specialist skills together and placing them in project teams to complete specific tasks. When the task or project has been completed, the matrix structure will become obsolete. As new tasks and projects emerge, new matrix structures will then be created to complete these new projects. Individual members of the matrix structure will have their own area of functional responsibility or remit to ensure the task or project is completed as efficiently as possible. It is often argued that a matrix structure is ideally suited to project-based work as it creates project teams with the most appropriate expertise and skills to complete the task.

A typical matrix structure is shown below.

Example: Shell UK Exploration and Construction

Project	Production	Engineering	Maintenance	Finance and Administration
Project 1 Brent Alpha Manager	2 members of staff	4 members of staff	3 members of staff	2 members of staff
Project 2 Brent Bravo Manager	4 members of staff	6 members of staff	2 members of staff	4 members of staff
Project 3 Brent Charlie Manager	8 members of staff	4 members of staff	3 members of staff	4 members of staff

The example above shows that the organisation has three different projects operating simultaneously. Each project is staffed by a team of employees drawn from different functional areas. For example, Project 1 has a team of 11 employees from four different functional departments.

The main advantage of a matrix structure is that it provides an opportunity for **all** individuals to use their skills and talents effectively. There is no hierarchy as all members of the project team have the same level of responsibility and authority. It is also likely that all individuals will get the opportunity to work in a variety of project teams over a period of time, which should increase job satisfaction and motivation.

The main disadvantage of this structure is that it is costly in terms of providing support staff (for example, secretaries and administration staff) for each project team. When projects are short-term and team membership is constantly changing, it can be difficult to coordinate individuals and create an effective team culture.

DON'T FORGET

Organisations can change their structure over time as they grow and expand.

VIDEO LINK

Watch the video clip at www.brightredbooks.net for more information on matrix structures.

THINGS TO DO AND THINK ABOUT

1 Describe two advantages and two disadvantages for each of the following groupings of activities:

- Functional
- Customer
- Technological
- Product/service
- Place/territory
- Line/staff

2 List the key features of each of the following types of organisational structure and give an example of an organisation that might use each structure:

- Hierarchical/tall
- Flat
- Matrix

ONLINE TEST

Want to test yourself on organisational structures? Head to www.brightredbooks.net

FORMS OF ORGANISATIONAL STRUCTURE 2

ENTREPRENEURIAL STRUCTURE

An entrepreneurial structure is typically found in **small businesses** and in those organisations where decisions have to be made relatively quickly such as in the production of daily newspapers. For example, front page headlines in a newspaper are often decided by the editor at the very last minute, prior to going to print.

In this structure, the owner of the business or a very small group of managers often make decisions without consulting other staff in the organisation, so there is great reliance on a few key workers.

Although this structure allows for quicker decision-making, it can demotivate employees, because their views are rarely considered.

There can be problems with this structure as the organisation grows, because too heavy a workload can be placed on too few individuals who have responsibility for decision-making. This can lead to inefficiency.

CENTRALISED STRUCTURES

Like an entrepreneurial structure, all control and decision-making lies with the most senior directors or managers, or the owners of the organisation. There might be more of them, but all control of the organisation is still held by these key members of the organisation. Subordinates have little or no authority at all. This type of structure is often associated with a hierarchical structure and has several key advantages:

- The organisation can benefit from strong leadership from the top.
- Directors or senior management have control of all aspects of the organisation and so can take a holistic approach.
- Procedures for purchasing and storage of inventory or raw materials can be standardised and so the organisation can benefit from economies of scale.
- Directors or senior management make decisions from the point of view of the business as a whole, not for the particular benefit of one department or another.
- Managers are likely to be more experienced and highly skilled and as such may reach better decisions.
- It is easier to promote a unique corporate image if the organisation adopts a centralised approach, as all external communications can be done in a standardised format.

Although McDonald's has created clear divisions to allow the organisation to grow in different parts of the world, leadership at the top of the organisation is very strong. Senior managers have control over every aspect of the business, including all franchises. Directors and senior managers make decisions for the whole organisation (including all divisions) rather than for individual restaurants. As a result, McDonald's has developed a world-wide corporate image that it can maintain and/or develop through its centralised structure. Consumers can visit a McDonald's in any country in the world and will already know what the products look and taste like.

DECENTRALISED STRUCTURES

In simple terms, this type of structure is the opposite of a centralised structure. If an organisation uses a decentralised structure, decision-making and control is delegated to and carried out by different departments or subordinates. This, therefore, relieves senior management of having to make many of the routine operational decisions required by the organisation.

contd

Business organisations face a constantly changing external environment. This requires them to be highly flexible and be able to make changes quickly. For example, the move towards global free trade and the increasing use of e-commerce has meant that many Scottish businesses must now compete on an international scale just to survive. A centralised structure doesn't offer this degree of flexibility, and many organisations therefore have to adopt a decentralised structure.

This structure is often associated with a flat organisational structure and offers the following advantages:

- Delegation of authority empowers employees and can be a key motivator for subordinates. It also prepares them professionally to take on more senior positions when they become available in the organisation.
- Departmental managers often have better knowledge and understanding of the requirements of their departments or customers, and can therefore make better decisions based on this.
- Decision-making is often quicker and much more responsive to change in the organisation's external environment.

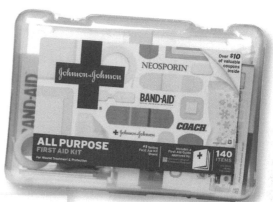

Johnson and Johnson is organised on the basis of a decentralised management structure consisting of three discrete sections – Consumer, Pharmaceutical and Medical Devices and Diagnostics. Each section has its own strategic management team as well as managers in functional departments.

There is no 'right' form of organisational structure. An organisation's structure must reflect and fulfil its aims and objectives, so it has to be flexible enough to change that structure to respond to growth or changes in its external environment.

ORGANISATION CHARTS

These show the structure of an organisation in the form of a diagram. Individual employees are identified in specific positions within the organisation, clearly showing their links to other employees along lines of authority and responsibility.

An example of an organisation chart.

The type of information in an organisation chart includes:

- names and job titles
- departments
- location – for example, room number
- telephone or extension number
- photographs of employees.

DON'T FORGET

An organisation chart is a diagram used to show stakeholders the structure of the organisation and the formal relationships within it.

VIDEO LINK

Head to www.brightredbooks.net to watch a clip about this.

ONLINE TEST

Want to test yourself on organisational structures? Head to www.brightredbooks.net

THINGS TO DO AND THINK ABOUT

List the key features of each of the following types of organisational structure and give an example of an organisation that might use each structure:

- Entrepreneurial
- Centralised
- Decentralised

ORGANISATIONAL STRUCTURES: KEY TERMINOLOGY

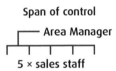

Span of control

Area Manager

5 × sales staff

FORMAL STRUCTURES

SPAN OF CONTROL

This refers to the number of employees or subordinates who report to a supervisor or manager. There is no perfect size for a span of control. It is often suggested, however, that between three and six subordinates is the ideal span of control. Factors such as the calibre of managers and the calibre of subordinates affect a span of control.

Narrow span of control	Wide span of control
Managers might micro-manage (tight management control), which will put employees under pressure.	Staff might make demands on the manager's time and so decision-making by managers could be slow.
Managers might have difficulty solving problems and making decisions because they don't have enough staff to share ideas with.	There could be a greater need for delegation of tasks, which the manager will still ultimately remain responsible for.
Managers might find it difficult to delegate tasks because there aren't enough staff to take on tasks.	Subordinates might have to make decisions by themselves if there are 'queues' for the manager's attention. Managers could lose control of their responsibility as a result.

DOWNSIZING

This involves reducing operating costs of an organisation by reducing its size to save money. This could include:

- Closing an unprofitable division/ department or merging two divisions/ departments together.
- Reducing the scale of operations to meet current market demand.
- Reducing the number of employees to reduce wage costs.
- Halting production of unprofitable products.

Advantages of downsizing	Disadvantages of downsizing
It can cut costs such as rent or wages, allowing money to be spent elsewhere in the organisation.	Valuable skills and knowledgeable staff are lost when redundancies are made.
The business is more efficient (leaner) and so can be more competitive and responsive to changes in the marketplace.	Any remaining staff may feel vulnerable, demotivated and uncertain for the future.
Remaining staff may also feel that their importance has been recognised.	It can sometimes lead to bad publicity and speculation over business difficulties.

DELAYERING

Delayering involves cutting out some of the layers of the hierarchy in an organisation. For example:

Delayering can be advantageous for an organisation as:

- It means money saved on managers wages can be spent elsewhere in the organisation.
- It offers opportunities for delegation and motivation as more authority is passed down the hierarchy when managers are reduced.

Before

Regional Manager
Area Manager
Shop Manager
Supervisors
Shop staff

After

Regional Manager
Shop Manager
Shop staff

- It empowers staff as they have increased responsibility.
- It means quicker decision making and faster communications, making the organisation more responsive to change.
- It encourages innovation.

ONLINE

Head to www.brightredbooks.net for tests, activities and more.

DON'T FORGET

Delayering involves a loss of management jobs.

contd

However, it can result in:

- Fewer promotional opportunities being available for employees. Some employees many seek promotion out with the organisation.
- Experienced managers with valuable skills and knowledge could be made redundant. This is a loss of expertise and experience.
- Any redundancies can cost the organisation a significant amount of money.

ADDITIONAL TERMINOLOGY

Informal relationships	These are the relationships that develop between staff when they interact informally with each other – for example, during lunch breaks. These relationships create an opportunity for employees to share information and support each other.
Delegation	Delegation is when a manager gives authority and responsibility to a subordinate to carry out a particular task. Although the task has been delegated, the manager retains overall responsibility for the work delegated.
Lines of communication	Communication in business is especially important because money, clients and the wellbeing of the business are at stake. Every organisation needs established lines of communication for information to flow down the organisation from senior management to employees and for information to flow up the way too.
Chain of command	This determines how information and instructions are passed vertically down the organisation from senior management to employees. If there is a long chain of command, communication and decision-making will probably be slow.

INFORMAL STRUCTURES

In most organisations, there is also an informal structure, consisting of a network of relationships and communication channels that is often referred to as the 'office grapevine'.

Many people derive a sense of social status and security by contributing to this grapevine. Information passed on in this way is often of a confidential nature and is not usually available to all members of the formal structure. Informal structures often evolve because some staff feel that the organisation's formal structure and lines of communication are inefficient.

Information passed through the informal structure is not always accurate, so managers must be aware of the informal structures within their organisation and the impact they can have. Indeed, some informal structures are so effective that management can deliberately feed the 'grapevine' with information that they **do** want to communicate quickly to staff.

Informal structures can also be destructive to the smooth running of the organisation. In extreme cases, the informal structure can oppose the decisions taken by the formal structure (the management team) and can sabotage management aims and objectives.

 THINGS TO DO AND THINK ABOUT

Specimen exam-style questions

Now that you are confident with this topic, try answering the following specimen exam-style questions in sentences.

1 Describe the benefits to an organisation of grouping their activities by:
   - function
   - product/service   (4 marks)
2 Easyjet has chosen to group its business activities by customer (business and private travellers). Describe the advantages and disadvantages of this type of grouping.   (4 marks)
3 Organisations that operate in different geographical areas might choose to group their activities by territory or location. Describe an advantage and a disadvantage of doing so.   (2 marks)
4 Compare the use of functional grouping with product/service grouping.   (4 marks)
5 McDonald's has branches in most large towns. They operate within a centralised organisational structure. Describe the features of a centralised structure.   (4 marks)
6 Describe the features of a decentralised structure.   (4 marks)
7 Explain what is meant by a 'matrix structure'.   (2 marks)
8 Explain the advantages and disadvantages of an entrepreneurial structure. (4 marks)
9 Describe the effects of increasing a manager's span of control.   (5 marks)
10 Distinguish between a centralised structure and a decentralised structure. (2 marks)
11 Describe factors that can influence the formal structure of an organisation. (3 marks)

 **DON'T FORGET**

Most organisations have a formal communication structure. However, the 'office grapevine' can be more powerful!

DECISION-MAKING IN BUSINESS ORGANISATIO

THE ROLE OF MANAGEMENT: OVERVIEW

- **Plan** – managers must plan for the future survival of an organisation.
- **Organise** – managers bring resources together.
- **Command** – managers instruct others to ensure all tasks are completed.
- **Coordinate** – managers must ensure that all functional departments are working collegiately to achieve strategic aims.
- **Control** – managers must have an overview of the entire organisation and ensure that aims and objectives are being achieved.
- **Delegate** – managers give authority and responsibility to subordinates to carry out particular tasks or roles.
- **Motivate** – managers must encourage others to fulfil their roles and provide opportunities for them to progress in their job.

In simple terms it could be said that a manager:
- works with subordinates to get 'the job done'
- deploys resources effectively and efficiently
- controls and coordinates activities in an organisation
- is accountable to and carries out the wishes of the owner of an organisation
- makes **decisions** about the running of an organisation to meet its objectives.

Managers must make key **decisions** to achieve the organisation's aims and objectives and improve performance. The more important a decision is, the more senior the person responsible for making it will be.

There are three main types of business decision: strategic, tactical and operational.

> **DON'T FORGET** ⊕
>
> If managers are not making good decisions the organisation could fail!

STRATEGIC DECISIONS

What are strategic decisions?	Strategic decisions set out the long-term aims of an organisation, provide focus and direction for the organisation and establish what it hopes to achieve at some point in the future – for example, improved profitability.		
Who makes strategic decisions?	Strategic decisions are usually made by the most senior people in any organisation – in other words, the owners of the organisation or their representatives.		
Examples of strategic decisions	• increase market share • increase profitability	• diversify into a new product range • improve the organisation's image	• decide on a target market • expand the business into a foreign country

TACTICAL DECISIONS

What are tactical decisions?	Tactical decisions set out the medium-term actions required to achieve strategic decisions. They describe, in detail, how resources are going to be brought together and used within the organisation.	
Who makes tactical decisions?	Tactical decisions are made by senior management, middle management or heads of departments.	
Examples of tactical decisions	• choosing whom to give subcontracts to • analysing when and where to open new branches • developing a new marketing campaign	• looking to source cheaper suppliers of raw materials to reduce expenditure • changing the pricing policy by raising or lowering prices

OPERATIONAL DECISIONS

What are operational decisions?	Short-term (day-to-day) decisions usually address problems that arise each day or week. For example, if a secretary has telephoned to say they are ill and cannot come into work, the operational decision might be to transfer another member of the administrative staff to cover their duties until they return.	
Who makes operational decisions?	Operational decisions are usually made by low-level managers, section heads or team managers, although all staff in the organisation could be involved in making them.	
Examples of operational decisions	• considering how to respond to a customer's complaint • considering how to deal with staff absence • working out the best way to organise work rotas	• working out when to pay suppliers to take advantage of cash discounts • deciding how much overtime should be allocated • deciding on a new filing system for customer records

contd

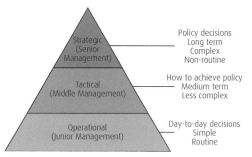

These three types of decision are likely to be interconnected within an organisation. For example, if the **strategic** decision is to increase profitability, the **tactical** decision might be to find cheaper suppliers of raw materials to reduce expenditure. Finally, the **operational** decision might be to decide when to pay suppliers to achieve cash discounts for prompt payment.

All three types of decision focus on achieving increased profitability.

EVALUATION AND REVIEW OF DECISIONS

As well as making decisions, managers or decision-makers have to look at the outcomes of their decisions. What was actually achieved? Was this what we expected? If not, do we have to make any further alterations to the work we are now doing as a result of decisions made?

Facts and figures are a valuable part of this evaluation process – for example:

- increase in profits
- increase in sales
- less staff absence
- positive feedback from customer surveys
- greater market share
- increase in output
- reduction in costs.

Managers must therefore undertake a continuous process of review, evaluation and remediation of the decisions they make at all levels – strategic, tactical and operational. No decision, however large or small, can stand in isolation and fail to affect the organisation in one way or another. The more managers reflect on the decisions they have made, the more successful they will be at adapting to change and improving organisational performance.

Short- and medium-term (operational and tactical) objectives have to be reviewed to assess their performance in meeting the long-term (strategic) targets set by management. Similarly, long-term (strategic) aims also have to be reassessed (and perhaps altered) in view of the achievements made in the medium- and short-term (tactical and operational).

DECISION-MAKING MODELS

SWOT ANALYSIS

This is another strategy used by managers to minimise the risks associated with making decisions within an organisation. A SWOT analysis involves analysing the current position of a product, a department or even the whole organisation, and trying to identify the possible **Strengths, Weaknesses, Opportunities** and **Threats** that could affect its future.

- **Strengths** – the positive **internal** factors that the business is currently experiencing.
- **Weaknesses** – the **internal** areas where the business currently performs poorly.
- **Opportunities** – the **external** activities or circumstances that the business could potentially take advantage of in the future.
- **Threats** – the **external** problems or challenges that the business could potentially face in the future.

A SWOT analysis is simple and easy to follow, and managers can use it to help them:

- build on current business strengths
- gather and analyse information
- address any weaknesses identified
- capitalise on available opportunities
- take measures to protect the organisation from threats
- be proactive rather than reactive.

 DON'T FORGET

Strengths and weaknesses are the **internal factors** that the company currently faces. Opportunities and threats are the **external factors** that the company might face in the future.

 ONLINE

To see an example of a SWOT analysis, head to www.brightredbooks.net

 ONLINE

Other decision-making strategies include POGADSCIE, Thought Showers and PEST Analysis. Read more about these at www.brightredbooks.net

 VIDEO LINK

Visit www.brightredbooks.net and watch a good video on swot analysis.

 THINGS TO DO AND THINK ABOUT

1 Describe what is meant by a SWOT analysis and what it is used for. (3 marks)

2 Explain why it is important for managers to evaluate decisions and how they can do this. (4 marks)

ONLINE TEST

Want to test yourself on this topic? Head to www.brightredbooks.net

FACTORS AFFECTING DECISION-MAKING

INTERNAL FACTORS AFFECTING DECISION-MAKING

There are a number of **internal** factors within an organisation that can impact upon a decision and the quality of that decision. These are outlined in the diagram below.

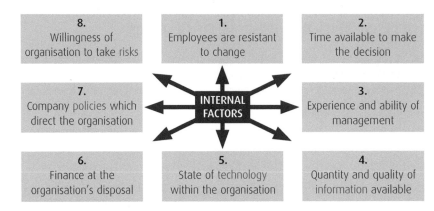

1	When employees do not support certain proposals their actions – for example, industrial action – could impact on the final decision made.
2	When the decision does not have to be made urgently, managers are more likely to take their time, consider all options and make a better-informed decision.
3	A highly skilled and experienced management team is more likely to make more effective decisions.
4	The quantity and quality of information available to managers enables them to make better-informed decisions based on all the facts.
5	Up-to-date technology enables managers to process information quickly, and informs their decision-making. Technology also provides management with more options regarding decisions about the potential to change production processes.
6	Ready access to finance usually provides a manager with more options and therefore impacts positively on their ability to make a decision. Limited finance can often restrict the decisions that a manager can make.
7	Certain policies – for example, policies on pay, human resources and the environment – can restrict which decision is made by management. Decisions usually have to be made in line with company policy.
8	Sometimes you have to take a risk to succeed, and managers or directors who are given more discretion and power – for example, by shareholders – will feel more empowered to do that.

EXTERNAL FACTORS AFFECTING DECISION-MAKING

There are a number of factors in an organisation's **external** environment that can impact upon a decision and the quality of that decision. Organisations have little or no control over changes in their external environment. However, if they are to succeed, they must respond to these changes. These external factors are outlined in the diagram below:

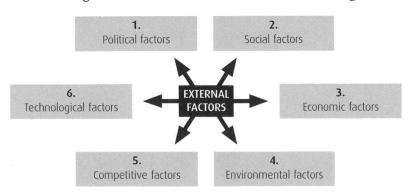

contd

1	A general election can result in a new government and new laws, which can impact on organisations. Organisations must also respond to changes in European Union legislation, because the UK is part of the EU.
2	Organisations must respond to social trends – for example, ageing population, obesity and a raised retirement age.
3	Economic factors such as immigration, unemployment, changes in interest rates and changes in government expenditure and taxation will be taken into account by organisations when making decisions.
4	There is an expectation that all organisations will be environmentally responsible. Decisions that could lead to environmental damage – for example, pollution, noise or congestion – will probably be opposed by the local community or pressure groups.
5	A business must always take account of its rivals, and the way competitors behave will influence the decisions made by an organisation – especially when the market is small, with only a few suppliers.
6	Technology is developing at a rapid pace and organisations that want to remain competitive must keep up with these changes and regularly upgrade their technology, even if it means postponing other projects.

CENTRALISED AND DECENTRALISED DECISION-MAKING

Centralised decision-making means that all control and decisions are made by the most senior managers.

Decentralised decision-making means that control and decision-making is delegated to different departments or subordinates.

DON'T FORGET

The acronym PESTEC will help you to remember the external factors that can impact on decision-making within an organisation

Read the short passage below and then answer the questions which follow.

Decision-making – Tesco

Tesco is launching a massive counter-attack on pound shops as it wages war in a desperate bid to recover its lost customers. The nation's biggest retailer has begun to open heavily advertised 'pound shop' areas within its stores to take on the thriving Poundland and other low-cost chain stores.

In these new zones, a range of products will be sold for as little as 50p including typical household items such as pet food, detergents and washing-up liquids.

Tesco has previously tried to take on pound shops. In 2009 a 'pound shop' strategy for food and non-food items was implemented with a dedicated aisle for these items and a £1 section was rolled out in approximately 50 stores in 2012.

1   Name the type of decision that you think this is.

2   Do you think it will be a success? Explain your thoughts.

THINGS TO DO AND THINK ABOUT

Specimen exam-style questions

Now that you are confident with this topic, try answering the following specimen exam-style questions in sentences.

1   Describe, using examples, the three types of decisions taken by organisations to achieve their objectives. (6 marks)

2   Justify why strategic decisions are generally made by senior managers. (3 marks)

3   Distinguish between a strategic and a tactical decision and give an example of each. (6 marks)

4   Moving operations to another country is an example of a strategic decision.
    Suggest tactical and operational decisions that might be required to achieve this. (4 marks)

5   Describe two tactical decisions that could lead to growth. (2 marks)

6   Distinguish between a tactical and an operational decision. (3 marks)

7   Describe how a manager could evaluate the effectiveness of their decision. (4 marks)

8   Explain internal problems that can arise when managers try to make effective decisions. (5 marks)

9   Explain the role of the manager in effective decision-making. (5 marks)

10 Explain the purpose of a SWOT analysis when making decisions. (4 marks)

THE GROWTH OF FIRMS: METHODS OF GROWTH

A strategic or long-term aim of most business organisations is to achieve growth. Achieving growth enables a business to:

- increase sales and/or profits
- dominate the market by becoming a market leader
- take advantage of large-scale production or economies of scale
- reduce the risk of business failure
- avoid the threat of takeover from rival firms
- develop a well-known business name
- push competitors out of the market.

INTERNAL AND EXTERNAL GROWTH

A business can grow **internally** or **externally**.

Internal growth	External growth
This is often referred to as **organic growth** and means that the business develops over a period of time by increasing output, opening new branches/stores, developing new products, entering new markets and employing more staff.	This is when a business **integrates** with another business to become a larger and more powerful organisation. External growth is usually achieved by means of a **merger** or **takeover.** This is often considered a quicker method of achieving growth.

INTEGRATION: OVERVIEW

Integration is the term used to describe a situation where two firms combine to become larger and more powerful in the market.

MERGERS

If the integration is on equal terms (50:50) it is described as a **merger**.

For example, **Orange** and **T-Mobile** merged their UK operations to create the country's largest mobile phone operator, with 28.4 million customers or a 37 per cent market share.

Another example of a merger in the UK was when the Bank of Scotland merged with Halifax to create the organisation commonly known as **HBOS.**

TAKEOVERS

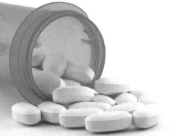

However, if integration is a result of one firm taking control of another so that the latter completely loses its identity, it is called a **takeover.** Such takeovers can be friendly, where both firms realise that this is the best way to survive, or hostile, when a **predatory** firm swallows up another one to gain market share by destroying the opposition. In such a situation the predatory firm can simply sell off the assets of the firm being taken over – often referred to as **asset-stripping.**

For example, UK-based drugs giant AstraZeneca recently faced a hostile takeover bid by American drugs giant Pfizer.

HORIZONTAL INTEGRATION

This is the combining of two firms operating at the same stage of production – for example, the two supermarkets Walmart and Asda engaged in horizontal integration in 1999.

Other examples of horizontal integration include Dixons Retail and Carphone Warehouse, Fyffes and Chiquita and Glaxo Wellcome and SmithKline Beecham, both UK drugs companies, which merged horizontally to form a larger and more powerful organisation.

Advantages of horizontal integration are that the business:
- eliminates competitors
- increases its market share

contd

- can achieve greater economies of scale (such as greater discounts) as a result of being able to buy inputs in larger quantities
- acquires the assets of other firms
- becomes more powerful and, therefore, more secure from future hostile takeover bids.

Disadvantages of horizontal integration are that the business:
- can become a very large firm that dominates a market
- eliminates competitors to the extent that it has more opportunity to exploit consumers and raise prices to earn higher profits
- can also under-cut competitors and push smaller, more vulnerable businesses out of the market.

DON'T FORGET

If the public would suffer as a result of a proposed merger going ahead, then the government has the power to stop it!

DON'T FORGET

Franchising is another method of achieving growth.

VERTICAL INTEGRATION

This is the joining together of firms operating at different stages of production.

BACKWARD VERTICAL INTEGRATION

This is when one firm takes over another firm that is operating at an earlier stage of production – for example, a jam manufacturer might try to take over a fruit farm. This enables the takeover firm to be sure of the availability and quality of its input.

FORWARD VERTICAL INTEGRATION

This is when one firm takes over another firm that is operating at a later stage of production – for example, an oil refinery might try to take over a chain of petrol stations. The main reason for this is to control the distribution outlets for the product.

Backward vertical integration and forward vertical integration are outlined in the diagrams to the right.

Advantages of vertical integration are that the business:
- eliminates the 'middleman' and his profit
- has greater economies of scale
- can link processes more easily
- secures a source of supply
- secures outlets in which to sell its products.

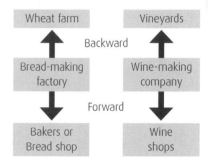

Disadvantages of vertical integration are that the business:

- will have to find and invest huge amounts of money/ equity
- may not have the expertise to oversee both the retailing and manufacturing aspects of the business.

THINGS TO DO AND THINK ABOUT

Read the short passage shown below and answer the following questions in sentences.

Merger – Disney and Pixar

In 2006 Walt Disney agreed a £4.1billion deal which saw Disney merge with Pixar. At that time, the late Steve Jobs was the Chief Executive of Pixar and reportedly claimed 'Disney and Pixar can now collaborate without the barriers that come from two different companies with two different sets of stakeholders'. It's fair to say that his claims made perfect sense. Disney has benefited from the creative and innovative Pixar, who in turn have benefited from Disney's commercial clout and wealth of experience in marketing and advertising.

1 Define what is meant by 'merger'.

2 Explain the difference between a merger and a takeover.

3 Do you think the merger between Walt Disney and Pixar has been successful? Give reasons for your answer.

4 Identify any one stakeholder who would benefit from the merger outlined above.

ONLINE

Head to www.brightredbooks.net for more on the growth of businesses.

ONLINE TEST

Want to test yourself on this topic? Head to www.brightredbooks.net

THE GROWTH OF FIRMS: METHODS OF GROWTH

CONGLOMERATE INTEGRATION (DIVERSIFICATION)

This refers to the combining of firms that operate in completely different markets – for example, an airline company taking over a chain of record shops.

Example:

Mars originally started off as a confectioner that mainly focused on chocolate. However, they have now diversified into supplying the following products:
- **Pet food** – Cesar, Sheba, Whiskas, Pedigree, Kitekat
- **Chocolate** – Bounty, Snickers, Topic, Twix, M&Ms
- **Foodstuffs** – Dolmio, Uncle Ben's
- **Wrigley** – Lockets, Tunes, Hubba Bubba, Orbit, Juicy Fruit
- **Drinks** – Klix, Flavia

Example:

Samsung is best known for its smartphones, tablets and televisions. However, Samsung's business activities and operations are spread much wider than just these two important markets.

The electronics giant also makes military hardware, apartments and ships, and operates a Korean amusement park! The business currently has around 350 000 employees and, in 2011, it reported revenues of $220 billion. Economists estimate that Samsung's revenues account for about 20 per cent of the value of South Korea's economy. Samsung is considered to be the most diversified business in the world.

REASONS FOR DIVERSIFICATION

- It allows the firm to **spread risk** – failure in one area can be compensated for by success in another.
- It enables a firm to overcome **seasonal fluctuations** in its markets and ensure revenue is being earned all year round.
- It makes the firm larger and more **financially secure**.
- The firm acquires the **assets, management** and **expertise** of other companies.

VIDEO LINK

The video clip at www.brightredbooks.net shows the Chief Executive Officer (CEO) of Lego discussing the company's growth and diversified product portfolio.

ADDITIONAL FACTORS AFFECTING THE GROWTH OF A BUSINESS

De-merger	This involves splitting up a conglomerate so that its subsidiaries become new companies in their own right. Shareholders will be allocated shares in the new companies according to how many shares they had in the original one. **Fosters**, who are known for their range of lagers, decided to de-merge their wine production. It is now listed on the stock market as a company in its own right.
Divestment	This involves the selling off of assets, or of one or more subsidiary companies, to raise finance or to address diseconomies of scale (disadvantages for a business of being too large). For example, **eBay** recently sold off Skype.
Asset-stripping	This is when one business buys another and then sells off the profitable sections and assets bit by bit. The sum of the parts can be greater when sold separately. **RBS** faced an inquiry by banking regulators into allegations that it was driving firms to collapse to buy back their assets at rock-bottom prices.
De-integration	This is when a business reduces the scale of its operation or sells minor areas off to focus on its core areas. This also enables the business to raise finance through selling off less profitable sections. For example, in 2014 **Sony** decided to sell off the PC section of its business.
Management buy-in/ buy-out	This involves a team of managers getting together and buying an existing company from its owners. The management team has to raise the necessary finance to buy and run the organisation, which could involve large bank loans. A **buy-out** is when the team of managers comes from **within** the firm, whereas a **buy-in** is when the team comes from **outside** the firm. **Kurt Geiger** shoes and **New Look** clothing have both been subject to a management buy-out.
Retained Profits	Many businesses will finance growth by using retained profits. This is often considered to be more cost-effective because the business does not pay interest. Also issuing shares to raise finance incurs additional costs and there is the danger that issuing new shares could lead to a change in control of the business.

CONTRACTING OUT/OUTSOURCING

This is when an organisation pays another firm to do certain work for them, rather than actually doing the work themselves. Many businesses contract out services like transport, recruitment, catering, printing and publishing, computer technical support, security and cleaning.

ADVANTAGES AND DISADVANTAGES OF OUTSOURCING

Advantages	Disadvantages
The core activities of the business take 'centre stage'.	There could be a risk of losing sensitive data and a resulting breach of confidentiality.
The work is undertaken by another business, which will offer more skill and expertise.	Management might lose control of those activities which are outsourced.
Recruitment and training costs are reduced as there is no need to hire individuals to do the work being outsourced.	The outsourcing provider could work with many customers and they, therefore, might not give 100 per cent attention to any one customer.
In certain cases, the organisation does not have to invest in expensive technology such as IT and photocopiers.	The outsourcing provider might have difficulty meeting delivery time frames and could produce poor quality work, which would reflect badly on the organisation.

 **ACTIVITY:**

Answer the following questions in sentences.

1   Describe four reasons why an organisation might want to achieve growth.   (4 marks)
2   Distinguish between a merger and a takeover.   (2 marks)
3   Describe what is meant by a 'de-merger'.   (1 mark)
4   Describe two advantages of outsourcing.   (2 marks)
5   Describe two disadvantages of outsourcing.   (2 marks)

COMPETITION POLICY

Competition policy in the UK is regulated by the Competition and Markets Authority (CMA) and this body places a number of restrictions on business organisations. Some of these are listed below:

● It is illegal to collude with other businesses to fix prices which would be unfair on consumers.
● Business cannot use their size, status and power to demand unfair prices from their suppliers.
● Businesses are prevented from creating a monopoly situation (one seller in the market).
● Businesses can be forced to change prices if they are deemed to be unrealistically high.
● Businesses can be fined for anti-competitive behaviour.

THINGS TO DO AND THINK ABOUT

Specimen exam-style questions

1   Compare the ways in which divestment and de-merger can aid an organisation's growth.   (4 marks)
2   Moving into new emerging markets (such as one of the BRICS countries) is an example of growth. Describe three other methods of growth.   (6 marks)
3   A large retail group has decided to de-merge into two separate organisations. Explain how this de-merger could affect its stakeholders.   (8 marks)
4   Describe what is meant by diversification.   (3 marks)
5   Describe the meaning of the term 'outsourcing' and its consequences for an organisation.   (6 marks)
6   Discuss the effects of outsourcing on an organisation.   (5 marks)
7   Describe how different methods of growth can lead to increases in profits and sales.   (5 marks)

 VIDEO LINK

The two video clips at www.brightredbooks.net compare and contrast the pros and cons of outsourcing. Watch each clip and then summarise these pros and cons in your workbook.

 DON'T FORGET

Diversification reduces the risk of failure, because it means that the business is operating in different markets.

 ONLINE

Follow the link to the CMA website on the Digital Zone to find out more on Competition Policy. https://www.gov.uk/government/organisations/competition-and-markets-authority

 ONLINE

Head to www.brightredbooks.net for more great activities on this.

 ONLINE TEST

Want to test yourself on methods of growth? Head to www.brightredbooks.net

THE GROWTH OF FIRMS: A CASE STUDY

Every Little Hurts? Tesco's Future Looks Troubled

In recent times Tesco plc, one of the original 'big four' supermarkets, has faced difficulties.

DROP IN SALES

Press reports that Tesco sales have slumped by almost 4 per cent have had an inevitable impact on share prices. This is illustrated in **Exhibit 1**, an extract from the London Stock Exchange that depicts the share price of Tesco from July 2013 to early June 2014.

These latest results have reportedly 'been the worst Tesco has seen for four decades' and are surely a cause for concern for Tesco's executive board of directors. Tesco may still be the biggest UK supermarket with the bulk of the market share, but there are other competitors who are now becoming more of a contender for UK purses.

REINVENTION

2013 saw Tesco trade through difficulties such as the horsemeat scandal where, despite having only a very small amount of affected products, Tesco still suffered from being involved in the negative fallout. It also suffered some difficulty within its US market when the 'Fresh & Easy' chain (only owned since 2007) was put on sale at a loss.

Recovering from negative publicity can be difficult for any organisation, but Tesco has come out fighting in recent times with its three strategic priorities. These are: 'continuing to invest in a strong UK business' 'establishing multichannel leadership in all of our markets' and 'pursuing disciplined international growth'.

Tesco's core purpose is 'We make what matters better, together' and with recent plans underway to improve the customer shopping experience, it clearly still has this at its heart.

Below are some of the ways that Tesco is aiming to refresh and reinvent its larger stores to encourage customers to shop there and enjoy an all-round experience with everything for the family under one roof.

Nonetheless, the fall in turnover is clear, as it was reported in the 2014 company accounts that Tesco profits had fallen by 6 per cent.

For any organisation, setting out strategic priorities is a clear indicator to staff, investors and customers of its long-term aims.

Along with its strategic priorities, Tesco is continuing to make changes and reinvent itself. Recent decisions by Tesco have included the removal of items of confectionery from checkouts in UK stores, the introduction of the grocery home delivery service to Shetland and the adoption of House of Fraser as a 'Tesco Partner'. 'Tesco Partners' is an agreement that Tesco has with approximately 50 other businesses, whereby their items are stocked on Tesco Direct – the Tesco online shopping site. Purchasing these items from the Tesco Direct site allows customers to accumulate Tesco Clubcard points.

CUSTOMER LOYALTY

As customers seem to be leaving Tesco in their droves to shop elsewhere, discount retailers such as Aldi and Lidl are reporting increases in their sales. Aldi and Lidl are direct competitors of each other in the discount supermarket chain, and both seem to be growing in popularity. In the UK, Aldi has won the Which? Supermarket of the Year for two years running, and Lidl has launched bakeries – a common feature in supermarkets such as Tesco and Sainsbury's – in its UK stores.

Neither of these stores run a customer loyalty scheme like the Tesco Clubcard. It is widely recognised that the Clubcard is one of the most generous loyalty schemes available in the UK. Offering one point for every 1p spent in store, the points can then be exchanged for money-off coupons or vouchers that can be used elsewhere in participating restaurants or attractions. The Sainsbury's scheme – Nectar Card – was introduced after the Clubcard, once the then Chairman saw how popular the scheme was.

contd

NO FRILLS

Although Aldi and Lidl have had a slow start in the UK since launching in the late 1980s (Aldi) and mid 1990s (Lidl), the public perception of these discount supermarkets has gradually changed. It is possible this has been partly due to economic circumstances, but it is also due to the fact that the Brits love a bargain and that there are bargains galore to be had at Aldi and Lidl.

Aldi prides itself on making savings by cutting back on its in-store displays and by purchasing in bulk. It then transfers these savings to customers through low prices. Lidl, too, offers quality products at the lowest possible prices in a bid to satisfy all its customers. Both these businesses pride themselves on low-key stores with minimal in-store marketing and point-of-sale displays. Tesco, on the other hand, regularly refreshes its in-store signage and displays, because it believes that this is what the Tesco customer wants.

So despite the plans Tesco has in place to reinvent and refresh its company and its reputation in the eyes of the consumers, why have its sales and share price fallen?

FURTHER INFORMATION

Exhibit 1
Extract from the London Stock Exchange

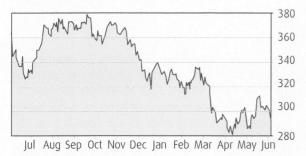

Exhibit 2
Illustration of the % breakdown of the market share held by industry rivals

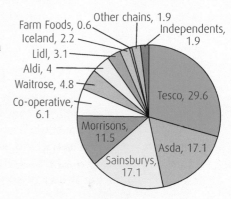

Farm Foods, 0.6
Iceland, 2.2
Lidl, 3.1
Aldi, 4
Waitrose, 4.8
Co-operative, 6.1
Other chains, 1.9
Independents, 1.9
Tesco, 29.6
Morrisons, 11.5
Asda, 17.1
Sainsburys, 17.1

THINGS TO DO AND THINK ABOUT

Answer the following questions in sentences.

1. Tesco is a plc which operates in the UK private sector. Describe two advantages and two disadvantages of operating as a plc. (4 marks)

2. An organisation operating in the private sector will have many objectives, such as maximising its profits. Describe three other objectives that an organisation such as Tesco might have. (3 marks)

3. In recent years, Tesco has suffered as a result of factors outwith its control – for example, the horsemeat scandal. Describe three external factors that might have an impact on Tesco's operations, and give an example of each. (6 marks)

4. Organisations such as Tesco are also at risk of internal factors affecting their operating environment. Discuss four internal factors that can impact on operations and how they can affect the success or failure of an organisation. (4 marks)

5. Many organisations have a mission statement or a core purpose. Tesco's is 'We make what matters better, together'. State a reason why organisations have a mission statement. (1 mark)

6. Tesco has a clear mission statement to ensure that its customers are satisfied. If customers do not shop in Tesco, profits fall. Compare the ways in which three other stakeholders can have an influence on organisations such as Tesco. (6 marks)

7. Tesco has three strategic priorities. Strategic decisions are usually long-term priorities made by senior managers. Justify why strategic decisions are usually made by senior management. (2 marks)

8. Describe two other types of decisions that can take place in an organisation and give an example of each. (4 marks)

9. Describe examples of evidence that a manager at Tesco could use to evaluate the impact of a decision on the organisation. (2 marks)

10. Describe two advantages and two disadvantages of using a SWOT analysis as part of the decision-making process. (4 marks)

THE ROLE OF MARKETING

WHAT IS A MARKET?

A market is a **medium** or meeting place through which **sellers** of a particular product or service can interact with the **buyers** of those particular goods and services. There is the possibility that a **transaction** will take place and the buyer will give the seller money in exchange for a good or service.

The price the buyer is willing to pay during the transaction is usually determined by the factors of **supply** and **demand**. Demand is simply how much of a product consumers are willing to buy and at what price, whereas supply represents how much the market can offer. Price, therefore, reflects supply and demand.

TYPES OF MARKETS

Organisations sell their products or services in different types of markets. A **consumer** market consists of individuals who are buying a product or service for their own personal use, whereas an **industrial** market is one where similar organisations buy products or services to use them in the manufacturing of their own products or services. A durable good which has been sold for the main purpose of being used in the later production of other goods or services is known as a **capital good.**

In some circumstances, the same good can be classified as both consumer and industrial. For example, a car can be purchased by a family as a consumer good, but it will be classed as an industrial good if it's purchased by a company for use by its employees.

MARKET SHARE

When analysing markets, the **market share** can be defined as the percentage of business (total sales) that is held by one product or one organisation in relation to the entire market or business segment. It is usually measured by either the volume of units sold or the revenue made by sales. A high market share can help to create brand loyalty and allow a business to enjoy market growth, and this in turn attracts potential investors.

ONLINE

Learn more about market share by following the link at www.brightredbooks.net

DON'T FORGET

High-growth markets are very attractive to an organisation that wants to increase its market share, because it can be very difficult to build market share in an established market with market leaders once the market growth has begun to slow. For example, many organisations in the soft drinks market find it difficult to build market share, because Coca-Cola and PepsiCo share the bulk of the market between them.

Organisations that hold a large market share have many advantages:

Economies of scale	Organisations with a large market share can afford to buy in bulk, therefore reducing the costs of their raw materials. They can also afford to produce their product at a cheaper price, which can force smaller organisations out of the market.
Cost savings	These organisations can often afford to make special components or ingredients in-house, rather than buying them from a specialist company at a price.
	They can also spread large costs such as advertising over a larger scale of output, which can give them much greater bargaining power than a smaller organisation, which has less influence.
Retained profits	If large profits are made, there is more money available to be reinvested back into the organisation. Retained profits are an important source of long-term finance for an organisation, and can be used in any way the company directors see fit.

MARKET GROWTH

Market growth is an increase in the demand for a product or a service over a period of time. It is usually slow if there is low demand for the product or service. If consumers develop a **product** or **service loyalty**, then market growth will increase. But if the price of the product or service increases, then demand will probably fall and growth will decrease.

An organisation could be selling its products or services in a high- or a low-growth market.

THE ROLE OF MARKETING

TALKING TO CUSTOMERS

Marketing is much more than reminding customers about a product or service. It enables organisations to get close to their customers and build relationships with them.

All organisations need customers to survive. No customers means no sales. The challenge for most organisations is attracting customers and keeping them. Profitable businesses are built upon good customer relations. This can be done through dealing with complaints effectively or reacting to changes in consumer trends.

CONSUMER BEHAVIOUR

All organisations must also understand consumer shopping behaviours. These are outlined below.

Routine/habitual	This is a type of purchasing scenario whereby the purchaser of a product or a service has past experience with purchasing it and automatically makes the decision to purchase again. Brand recognition plays a large part in routine response behaviour.
Impulsive	This is a spur of the moment, unplanned decision to buy made just before a purchase, triggered by seeing the product or upon exposure to well-crafted promotion. Such purchases range from small (chocolate, clothing and beauty products) to substantially large (motor vehicles and holidays) and may lead to financial difficulties.
Informed	With the growth of e-commerce in recent years impulsive shopping on the high street is becoming a thing of the past; today's shopper is seen as the "well-informed shopper", one who spends around 10 hours researching online and visiting several websites before buying online.

MARKETING ANALYSIS

Marketing aims to make a profit for the business by identifying, anticipating and satisfying customer requirements.

- **Identifying customer requirements:** An organisation needs to determine exactly what it is that customers want, because if its products or services don't meet customers' requirements, they won't buy them. Consumer tastes and trends change regularly, so the marketing department needs to ensure that products and services evolve to reflect these changing tastes and trends.

- **Anticipating customer requirements:** The main role of the marketing department is to investigate what customers want now and what they will want in the future. Consumer trends are important in anticipating future desires and marketing departments must ensure they are up to date with market trends.

- **Satisfying customer requirements:** Satisfied customers are essential if a business is to succeed. Organisations aim to satisfy their customers by providing good-quality products and services that offer value for money, by producing well-presented and packaged goods and delivering them promptly, and by providing excellent after-sales service.

 THINGS TO DO AND THINK ABOUT

Look up the CIM paper outlining the role of marketing and how it has changed since the first definition of marketing was published over 30 years ago. The paper: 'Tomorrow's Word: Re-evaluating the Role of Marketing' is available at www.brightredbooks.net

DON'T FORGET

Consumers have three main shopping behaviours:
- routine/habitual
- impulsive
- informed.

DON'T FORGET

Marketing applies to both tangible products and intangible services.

 ONLINE

Head to www.brightredbooks.net for some great activities on the role of marketing.

 ONLINE TEST

Take the test on the role of marketing at www.brightredbooks.net

THE IMPORTANCE OF MARKETING IN THE BUSINESS ENVIRONMENT

WHY MARKETING IS IMPORTANT

Marketing has assumed a key role in business. It's about getting the right **product** or **service** to the customer at the right **price**, in the right **place** and at the right **time.** It also examines consumer attitudes or preferences and competitor weaknesses and strengths.

Marketing is viewed as an essential means of reducing the risk of product/service failure, particularly in a competitive environment.

EXTERNAL FACTORS

There are a number of external forces and factors that can impact on a business. Marketing departments need to examine regularly how they can use these factors to fulfil customer needs.

DON'T FORGET ➕

The acronym PESTEC will help you to remember the external factors that can affect an organisation.

These external factors include:

Government	Waste (Scotland) Regulations came into effect on 1 January 2014. These regulations have strict rules about the recycling and separation of waste. Organisations now need to take this into consideration when designing the packaging for their products, because it has to be easy to recycle.
Economic growth	Economic growth has resulted in an increase in disposable income for many consumers, who are now demanding a wider range of products and services to choose from. To enter markets and increase sales, businesses need to market their products and services successfully.
Society and fashion	Over the past few years, consumers have become more discerning, and are influenced by the latest 'craze' or fashion. Organisations need to be able to respond to this, and to anticipate the next 'big thing'. Marketing has become increasingly important both as a means of identifying consumers' tastes and of influencing them.
Technology	Innovation in technology enables organisations to constantly invent and launch new products or reinvent and adapt existing products to suit the needs of customers. Technology has influenced the marketing methods used by businesses, as can be seen with online advertising.
Competition	Competition among businesses is constantly increasing. Marketing is therefore essential to maintain an organisation's market share and, ultimately, its success.

PRODUCT WARS

The importance of marketing can be seen in some of the more famous product wars that have occurred over the years.

contd

Example:

In the late 1970s and early 1980s, there was a 'videotape war' in the home video market between the Betamax video recorder by Sony and the VHS video recorder by JVC. The main factors were the actual costs of the video recorders and the recording time they offered.

The VHS video recorder was cheaper and the recording time of the VHS tapes was greater, which appealed to consumers.

The Betamax video recorder was a superior piece of machinery and offered better picture resolution, improved sound and less background 'noise' on the videos.

Despite these superior design nuances, consumers opted to stick with the VHS. JVC took full advantage of this and embarked on a clear marketing strategy. They offered licences to any interested manufacturer and were able to create a 'pricing war', as manufacturers competed for sales by offering their recorders at lower prices to attract the consumer.

Sony's decision to limit their recording time also cost them dearly. When VHS was first launched, the recording time was over two hours, which meant that most films could be recorded without needing to change the tape halfway through. By the time Sony changed its marketing strategy so it was in accordance with that of VHS, VHS dominated the market and Betamax was pushed into a niche position with a short shelf-life.

VHS remained dominant until the creation of the DVD.

Example:

Around 2005, there was another 'format war' between Toshiba's High Definition DVD and Sony's Blu-ray discs as a means of storing high definition video and audio. This was won by the Blu-Ray disc.

Example:

Recent press releases have stated that Samsung is planning to stop producing plasma televisions. Samsung are quoted as 'remaining committed to providing consumers with products that meet their needs'. Falling demand for the bulkier plasma television screens has meant that Samsung are focusing on producing thinner, more stylish, curved ultra-high definition (UHD) TVs.

 **ACTIVITY:**

Choose either Samsung or Sony, and research how their products have adapted over the years as technology, fashion, competition and consumer tastes have changed.

Create a short presentation illustrating the history of two of these products. Ensure that you refer to how technology and consumer trends have shaped the product into what it is now.

 ONLINE

For a further activity about product wars, head to www.brightredbooks.net

 THINGS TO DO AND THINK ABOUT

Plenty of products, like Betamax, don't quite make it for one reason or another. Follow the link at www.brightredbooks.net to find out about some innovative yet bizarre products that never quite took off. Cat translator, anyone?

PRODUCT-LED VS MARKET-LED STRATEGIES

VIDEO LINK

Watch the video clip at www.brightredbooks.net about the introduction of the iPod in 2001.

PRODUCT-LED STRATEGIES

A **product-led** or **product-orientated strategy** focuses on producing a technically sound product or service and then, once it's developed, on presenting it to the market. Contact with the consumer is only made at this point, because it is assumed that the product or service being sold is the best or the only version on the market and will therefore sell easily.

The product-led approach was more common in the past when there was less competition and consumers were less sophisticated. For example, when televisions were first produced, their 'novelty' factor and the uniqueness of the product was what sold them.

Similarly, when the iPod was first launched in 2001, the uniqueness of the product's brand made the simple mp3 player a fashion accessory and status symbol.

In a product-led market, the products are usually a new invention, a technically unique product with few alternatives (as in the case of the iPod) or they are at the front of a strong advertising campaign that convinces consumers that they need to purchase them. These products typically have a strong **unique selling point (USP)**, which will be exploited by advertising. Organisations that operate in a product-led fashion can begin to lose sales once competitors enter the market, so they must find ways to retain the interest and loyalty of their customers.

A product-led business has a number of advantages and disadvantages:

Advantages	Disadvantages
Organisations can focus on the quality of their product or service and take their time in production.	The actual needs of the market are completely ignored.
The organisation could invest in technology and apply it to their product or service or a wider range of products/ services.	This technology could be quickly superseded once competitors enter the market and the original organisation could find that its product has become outdated.
The organisation could employ an outsourcing organisation to produce its product, leaving it free to continue its core business in the design of new products.	Any changes in tastes or fashions will not be accounted for.

MARKET-LED STRATEGIES

On the other hand, a **market-led** or **market-orientated strategy** is one that continually identifies, reviews and analyses consumers' needs. The organisation will then modify its products or services in response to any changes in the market. The desire to satisfy the needs of the consumer is at the forefront of this strategy and it is therefore led by the highly competitive market.

Example:

Henry Ford was one of the first industrialists to adopt this marketing approach. Prior to the production of the now iconic Model T car, he examined the market and identified the price at which he believed he could sell the most Model T cars. Ford didn't design the car, produce the car and **then** try to sell it – rather, he made the market his starting point as he followed his dream to create a vehicle that everyone could afford. This resulted in the Model T becoming one of the first 'mass market' products produced using a moving production line, and changed car production from the perception of a luxury toy to an essential part of American society. This shows how customers were intrinsic to Henry Ford's decision-making.

contd

A market-led business has a number of advantages and disadvantages:

Advantages	Disadvantages
The business is better placed to anticipate any dynamic market changes and is flexible enough to react quickly due to its constant use of market information.	Market research is very expensive.
It will be more confident that the launch of the new product or service will be a success, having done the research groundwork and understanding the needs of the consumers.	The future is unpredictable and as business is dynamic by its very nature, there is a high risk of failure.
It will be in a stronger position to deal with the challenges of any rival companies entering the market, as it will be fully aware of the market it operates in.	There will be constant change within the organisation as it strives to meet the needs of the market and stay ahead of competitors.

DON'T FORGET

Marketing occurs in all organisations in all the sectors of industry!

Market Orientation

Product Orientation

INFLUENCES ON PRODUCT-LED AND MARKET-LED ORGANISATIONS

There are a number of factors that can determine whether an organisation will follow a product- or market-led approach.

The actual product	If an organisation exists to create innovative products – for example, as in the communications and pharmaceutical industries – it **needs** to be pioneering and creative to remain competitive and survive. These organisations may conduct some market research but this would be very basic and not geared towards a particular product.
Business objectives	If the organisation's objectives focus on the quality or safety of its products, then it's more likely to take a product-led approach. If its objectives focus on increasing market share and market domination, then it's more likely to take a market-led approach.
Conflicting internal decisions	Within the organisation, different functional areas will have different goals in mind. Finance will be most concerned with cash flow and minimising costs, Marketing with improving customer relationships and conducting market research and Operations with the quality of the product. These could all conflict with each other – for example, Operations might scrap a product three times before it is deemed good enough to pass quality control, while Finance could object strongly to the expense.
The nature and size of the market	If it is going to be very expensive to produce the product then an organisation is more likely to be market-led. The exceptions are organisations that create innovative products – for example, pharmaceutical and electronic/communications companies.
Competition	If an organisation is in a market with little competition, it will probably spend more time carrying out product research, development and production and less time conducting market research. Conversely, if an organisation is in a more competitive market, it will probably spend more time and money on advertising and market research because it doesn't want to lose the market share it does possess.

 **ACTIVITY**

Answer the following questions in sentences.

1   Outline the factors that have made marketing important in today's evolving
    business environment.   (4 marks)

2   Suggest why a product-led approach is important today.   (2 marks)

3   Outline two advantages of a market-led approach.   (2 marks)

4   Outline two disadvantages of a market-led approach.   (2 marks)

 THINGS TO DO AND THINK ABOUT

Create a short presentation that highlights the evolution of the iPod over the years and takes into account the impact of external factors such as society and technology. You can use the internet for research purposes. Can you see how factors such as competition, the market and technology have all had an impact on the product itself?

 ONLINE TEST

Test yourself on product- and market-led strategies at www.brightredbooks.net

TARGETED MARKETING

To be successful, organisations need to know who their customers are, and to target those customers who are going to be most receptive to their products or services.

Undifferentiated
Segmentation

Differentiated
Segmentation
or Multi-Segment
Marketing

Concentrated
Segmentation
or Niche
Marketing

CHOOSING MARKET SEGMENTS TO TARGET

Some products or services – for example, toothbrushes – are marketed towards the entire population. This is known as **undifferentiated marketing**.

Alternatively, the product or service – for example, Barbie dolls – could be aimed at a particular section of the population. This is known as **differentiated** marketing.

In some cases, the organisation has identified a gap in the market and focuses on satisfying customer wants and needs within this context. This is known as **niche marketing**. Examples of niche products could include specialised medical products such as a home oxygen system, or products for specific groups of customer, such as the British retailer Long Tall Sally, which sells clothing for tall women.

An organisation in a niche market provides a specialised product or service that often has a limited demand. However, because the market is smaller and more specialised, there is usually less competition and it can be very lucrative.

ACTIVITY:

Read the following passage and then answer the questions that follow in sentences.

> **Long Tall Sally – Living in a Tall World**
>
> Although being tall can have its perks, it can also be a problem when it comes to finding clothes and shoes that fit.
>   Enter Long Tall Sally, marketed as the 'world's premier tall fashion and footwear destination'. This British retail chain operates in a very niche market, as it offers clothes and shoes to suit women 5 feet 8 inches and above and with shoe size 7–13.
>   This niche market is clearly successful, as Long Tall Sally has grown from one single store in London to multiple stores throughout the UK, Germany, Canada and the USA.

1   Outline what is mean by a 'niche market'.

2   Explain why organisations choose to operate in niche markets.

3   Although trading in a niche market can be rewarding, state what any organisation must do to ensure continuing success.

VIDEO LINK

Watch the video clip at www.brightredbooks.net for a look at mass marketing in the 1930s.

Beautifully tall

DON'T FORGET

Socio-economic groups can be classified into eight categories that are based on the earners in a household. These range from 1 (senior managers) all the way to 8 (those who have never worked or are long-term unemployed).

MARKET SEGMENTATION

Once a market has been identified, an organisation can then choose to break it down into sub-groups of customers who have similar characteristics. The organisation can then target these specific groups and develop products or services for each of them.

The market can be segmented in the ways illustrated to the right:

Geographic	Demographic	Behavioural	Psychographic
Customers within 10 miles of the M25	A Level & University Students	Customers wanting a value-for-money impulse buy	Customers who prefer to buy fairtrade food
Customer location Region Urban/Rural ACORN classification	Age Gender Occupation Socio-economic group	Rate of usage Benefits sought Loyalty status Readiness to purchase	Personality Lifestyles Attitudes Class

contd

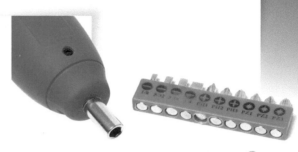
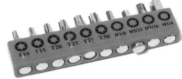

Some organisations, however, can take market segmentation too far!

Market segmentation is a useful strategy because:

- greater knowledge can be gained about customers, so products and services can be **tailored** to satisfy the requirements of the market segment. (More products and services are sold and the profit therefore increases.)
- **prices** of the products or services **can be set** in accordance with the market segment
- it **prevents** products and services being promoted to the **wrong market segment** and in the **wrong place(s)**, which would waste money, time and resources.

 **ACTIVITY**

Complete the table below by giving three examples of products/services that could be targeted at the given market segments.

Market segment	Products/services
Age	1.
	2.
	3.
Gender	1.
	2.
	3.
Income	1.
	2.
	3.
Religion/culture	1.
	2.
	3.

 **ACTIVITY**

Answer the following questions in sentences.

1 Compare what is meant by the terms 'differentiated' and 'undifferentiated' marketing. (2 marks)

2 Define what is meant by 'market segment'. (1 mark)

3 Outline the benefits to an organisation of segmenting the market. (2 marks)

4 State four ways in which the market can be grouped for marketing purposes. (4 marks)

 THINGS TO DO AND THINK ABOUT

Specimen exam-style questions

Now that you are confident with this topic, try answering the following specimen exam-style questions in sentences.

1 Describe what is meant by niche marketing. (2 marks)

2 Holiday companies like First Choice target their products towards particular market segments. Describe four different segments that companies could gear their product towards. (4 marks)

3 Explain why organisations choose to spend large amounts of money on marketing activities. (5 marks)

 VIDEO LINK

The video clips at www.brightredbooks.net illustrate how McDonald's has segmented their market and how other businesses' marketing campaigns are subtly, and sometimes not so subtly, targeted at particular segments.

ONLINE

For further information on market segments and socio-economic groups, follow the Office for National Statistics link at www.brightredbooks.net

 ONLINE TEST

How well have you learned this topic? Head to www.brightredbooks.net and take the test.

MARKET RESEARCH

Organisations survive and succeed by producing products or services that people will want to buy. So to find out what people want to buy, organisations carry out **market research**.

WHAT IS MARKET RESEARCH?

Market research involves researching, analysing and recording what is happening in a market. It also involves analysing information that has already been gathered. Market research is invaluable to any organisation because it provides a source of detailed data about a constantly evolving market, and helps the organisation to maintain a competitive edge.

Market research has many benefits:

- It can help organisations make a more informed decision when it comes to launching a new product or service.
- It reduces the risk of spending a large sum of money on an unsuccessful development and launch of a new product.
- It helps create a link with customers.
- It demonstrates that the organisation is 'listening' to its customers and therefore enhances the company's reputation.

Desk research	Field research
Uses **secondary information** (older information gathered for another purpose from another source).	Uses **primary information** (research carried out specifically by the organisation to gather new information).
Examples of desk research sources include company sales figures; newspapers; specialist marketing magazines such as *Marketing Week*; annual accounts; internet data; government statistical publications or information on competitors.	Examples of field research sources include surveys; focus groups; hall tests; observations and sampling.
As this information has already been gathered by another source, it is available at little or no cost.	This up-to-date information will be very valuable because the organisation can vouch for its origin. Also, because the organisation has carried out the research, it has unique access to it, which will therefore give it a competitive advantage in the market.
The information could be outdated and, because it was gathered for another purpose, could show bias towards another organisation.	This information can be very costly to gather requiring skilled researchers, as well as being time consuming to collect and analyse

 **ACTIVITY:**

Read the following short passage and then answer the following questions in sentences.

ONLINE

Watch the short video clips at www.brightredbooks.net discussing the limitations and giving further detail on desk research.

Broadband Research

A new entrant to the broadband market – Broadband4U – is carrying out desk research before launching its product. It intends to recruit 100 employees to research the industry and its competitors.

1 Explain the type of information that Broadband4U will obtain from carrying out desk research.
2 Suggest why organisations sometimes carry out desk research before using field research.

 **ACTIVITY:**

Read the short passage on page 59 and then answer the following questions in sentences.

contd

Glenskirlie Castle

Glenskirlie Castle in Banknock was built in 2009 with one specific view in mind. The USP of this modern-hotel-with-a-twist is that it was specifically designed to provide a luxury venue and accommodation for weddings and other special functions. In particular, its owners wanted to design opulent suites for guests to enjoy – each with its own elegant theme.

Prior to being built, its owners conducted some desk research into the market. They discovered from the *Scottish Wedding Directory* and some internet searches that there is an increase in both the population and the amount of marriages taking place in Scotland.

1 Explain why the information that Glenskirlie obtained is known as secondary.
2 Suggest possible issues that could arise when using secondary information.

 **ACTIVITY**

Answer the following questions in sentences.

1 Define 'market research'. (1 mark)
2 Suggest two reasons why organisations carry out market research. (2 marks)
3 Outline the two main types of market research. (4 marks)
4 Suggest three reasons why market research might not always be reliable. (3 marks)

 **ACTIVITY**

Organisations such as PepsiCo and Coca-Cola spend millions on marketing.

Write a brief report which supports the need for market research for organisations such as PepsiCo. Your report should be no more than two sides of A4 in size. Include appropriate headings and point out the advantages of market research, justifying the expense involved.

USES OF MARKET RESEARCH

Organisations use market research regularly for the following reasons:
- **Descriptive reasons:** to help identify what is happening in markets – for example, Unilever may want to identify trends in sales of Magnum ice creams over a certain period.
- **Predictive reasons:** to help predict what is likely to happen in markets in the future – for example, Barrhead Travel might research the types of holiday that people are thinking of taking over the next two years, so they can then provide suitable holidays to satisfy customers.
- **Explanatory reasons:** to help explain certain factors that have occurred in markets – for example, First Bus might research why a specific route has seen a fall in the number of passengers.
- **Exploratory reasons:** to help organisations investigate new possibilities in markets – for example, Cadbury could trial a new type of chocolate bar in Manchester to test customer reaction before launching it nationwide.

 THINGS TO DO AND THINK ABOUT

There are some occasions when an organisation needs to carry out more extensive market research. The now infamous marketing disaster of New Coke demonstrates how some successful organisations can still get it very, very wrong.

Head to www.brightredbooks.net to see the clip for more information.

 **DON'T FORGET**

Market research consists of both desk **and** field research.

FIELD RESEARCH METHODS 1

There are a number of different field research techniques that organisations can use.

SURVEYS

Surveys can be conducted over the telephone, online, as a personal interview or as a postal response. Surveys involve the use of **questionnaires** and allow a broad range of data to be collected about consumer attitudes, values and opinions.

TELEPHONE SURVEY

This is when an interview is held over the telephone and a series of set questions are asked.

Advantages	Disadvantages
This is **cheaper** than other methods of surveying such as personal interview, and allows a **wider geographical area** to be covered quickly. Information can be obtained instantly and any confusion over questions can be clarified at the time.	It can be **difficult to persuade people to talk at length** over the telephone: people tend to answer in short responses to get the survey over with as quickly as possible. Times when respondents can be contacted are limited and calling during unsuitable times such as meal times can lead to negative responses. Telephone numbers can be engaged, resulting in the need for call backs.

ONLINE SURVEY

This is when a consumer survey is published on the internet or is emailed to respondents.

Advantages	Disadvantages
This is possibly one of the more **cost-effective** methods of surveying and will not require an interviewer. The respondents input their own data which is automatically stored so that analysis is much simpler. Consumers can be reached **worldwide**.	This method **automatically discounts any respondents** who do not have online access. These harder-to-reach respondents would therefore have to be reached using a more traditional method. Many people automatically ignore 'pop-ups' or messages on screen and can delete the option to complete the survey.

PERSONAL INTERVIEW

This is when an interviewer conducts a face-to-face interview with a consumer using a questionnaire that asks them mainly 'open' questions. The interviewer will fill out the questionnaire on behalf of the interviewee.

Advantages	Disadvantages
This gives the option for interviewees to give more **detailed responses** and any confusion over either questions or answers can be clarified at the time. If necessary, answers can sometimes be followed up if more detail is required.	Respondents might give inaccurate answers because they don't feel comfortable responding in a negative way, or they could give the answers they think the interviewer wants to hear to help them out or to get the interview over with more quickly. This method is also very **time consuming** and **expensive** because specially trained interviewers are required.

POSTAL SURVEY

This is when questionnaires are sent to the public through the post.

Advantages	Disadvantages
This is relatively **cheap** because no interviewer is required. And because there is no interviewer, there should be a completely **unbiased response.** In addition, a **larger area can be covered** more easily. Respondents can complete the survey at their own pace, so it is also more convenient for them.	The response rate is very limited and responses can take a long time to be returned, which can impact on collation and recording times. If this method is to work, the questionnaires must be well-designed and foolproof, so there are no misunderstandings.

DON'T FORGET

You will be expected to describe the advantages and disadvantages of each method of field research.

contd

ACTIVITY:

Answer the following questions in sentences.

1 State an advantage and a disadvantage of using telephone surveys.   (2 marks)

2 State an advantage and a disadvantage of using personal interviews.   (2 marks)

3 State an advantage and a disadvantage of using postal surveys.   (2 marks)

OBSERVATION

Businesses in the retail sector often use this method to 'watch' consumers in their stores. They observe all sorts of things such as the length of time it takes for a consumer to decide on a purchase and how noticeable displays within the store appear to be to consumers. This method is often used in conjunction with others.

Advantages	Disadvantages
This allows for **large numbers** of consumers to be observed during a specific period of time. It is a relatively **cheap** option. It also allows trained observers to watch customers' non-verbal cues (body language and facial expressions) in a real-life situation so that they can assess what customers actually think. Because the customers are unaware of being observed, this is a more reliable source of information.	Consumers cannot be approached and asked why they chose one particular product over another, and questions are therefore left unanswered. It can be time consuming and to address this, organisations can, for example, set up a controlled setting in a laboratory where they can observe consumers during **particular time slots.**

ONLINE

Head to www.brightredbooks.net to complete the activity on observation.

FOCUS GROUP

This is where a group of consumers is brought together to answer and discuss questions that have been developed by market researchers on behalf of particular products/services.

Advantages	Disadvantages
As the groups are small in number and only one interviewer is required, it is a **relatively cheap** and **simple way** to discuss and gather information on customers' views on a particular product/service.	The group of consumers might not be a **fair representation** of the market segment the organisation is interested in, and their views therefore might not be suitable. Also, more vocal group members could influence and colour the other members' views.

VIDEO LINK

Watch the light-hearted look at how focus groups can go wrong if there is not a strong leader at the helm at www.brightredbooks.net

CONSUMER PANEL

This is where a panel of consumers is asked to use a product or service and to give its reactions over a period of time. Consumer panels are often used by TV companies to judge a reaction to a programme.

Advantages	Disadvantages
This builds a strong picture of how reaction to a product changes over time. Respondents are usually given diaries in which they are asked to record their thoughts. This information is used to help research trends.	It is very **time consuming** and **expensive** to maintain. Some panel members might want to leave and organisations usually offer a small financial reward to panel members to discourage this.

THINGS TO DO AND THINK ABOUT

Answer the following questions in sentences.

1 State why a consumer panel is the best method for some organisations to research their product.

2 Explain the value of the information that can be gathered from a consumer panel.

3 Outline any difficulties that could be encountered when using consumer panels.

ONLINE TEST

How well have you learned about field research methods? Head to www.brightredbooks.net and take the test.

FIELD RESEARCH METHODS 2

TEST MARKETING

This is when a new product/service or marketing campaign is made available in a restricted geographical market to gauge the consumer reaction to it.

Advantages	Disadvantages
This allows the organisation to determine the reaction to the product/service or campaign on a small scale before committing to mass market. This also allows any issues to be corrected before a mass launch.	It is a very **time-consuming** and **expensive** process especially if the product doesn't test well in the beginning. Organisations need to be careful as they are exposing their product to potential rivals unless strong privacy is employed and a race may then follow to get the product to the market. As the test market is a **small percentage of the overall population**, it can be very challenging to find testers in the right market segment. Testers could give responses they think the organisation wants to hear, because they don't want to appear rude.

HALL TEST

This is when a group of consumers is gathered together in the same venue. They are asked to try and then give their opinion of a product/service or advertising campaign.

Advantages	Disadvantages
The customers can experience the product or service for themselves and give their opinions. As a group of consumers is being tested at the same time, it is more **time-** and **cost-effective.**	Qualitative information is difficult to analyse. As with test marketing, consumers might give the response that they think the organisation wants to hear, rather than their actual opinion.

EPOS (ELECTRONIC POINT OF SALE)

Some retailers gather information from customers using their debit/credit cards or loyalty cards.

Advantages	Disadvantages
Using this method, the organisation can quickly gather **large amounts** of valuable information about shopping habits, spending patterns and consumer profiles. As the information is quantitative, it is easily analysed and can allow targeted promotions in future.	It is a **very expensive system to set up** and as technology evolves, it can require expensive upgrades. There are no options to gather customer opinions.

SOCIAL NETWORKING (FACEBOOK, TWITTER)

Retailers can use social networking to find out about customers' reactions to products or services, or to obtain their opinions and feedback on different issues.

Advantages	Disadvantages
It can gather **large amounts of** valuable information quickly from large numbers of the public. It allows two-way interaction with consumers, which is an excellent way to build customer loyalty.	It completely discounts those who choose not to use social networking and it relies on customers 'adding' them, which customers might choose not to do. The information put on social networking sites is public, and therefore comments made by customers could be viewed by competitors, to the detriment of the organisation.

DON'T FORGET

To communicate with customers, organisations will use:
- social media
- apps
- text alerts
- on-line surveys
- e-mail
- internet advertising.

SAMPLING

It's not practical for organisations carrying out field research to ask the entire general public what they think about a product or service. They therefore need to carefully select people or groups of people to use as a sample of the population.

RANDOM SAMPLING

People are pre-selected from a list such as the telephone book or the electoral roll, and the interviewer then randomly chooses a number of people from that list to phone. These people must be interviewed no matter what, and if they are unavailable, the interviewer must call again. Costs can therefore start to increase. A sample that is representative of the population will obviously have to be large, and will be time consuming for the interviewer to trawl through.

STRATIFIED RANDOM SAMPLING

Researchers usually prefer this method because the sample is more representative of the population as a whole. The sample is divided or 'stratified' by knowledge about how the population is divided up, and can cover variables such as income or location. For example, if the sample relates to how employment status affects the demand for a car, researchers might stratify the population by different income groups and then choose a random sample from within each of these groups, matching the same proportions in each category with the population as a whole. So if it is known that 10 per cent of the population is in higher managerial occupations, then the sample would have 10 per cent in that same occupation bracket.

QUOTA SAMPLING

With this method, people are selected on the basis of characteristics that they share such as age, gender or occupation. The interviewer must find people who fit the categories required. Once the target has been reached – for example, 10 males between the ages of 18 and 25 – then no more individuals can be interviewed from this group. It is the cheapest method of sampling.

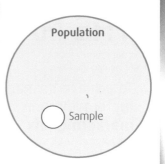

 **DON'T FORGET**

It would take lots of time and effort to investigate the general public, so organisations use carefully selected people or groups of people to use as a sample of the population.

 **VIDEO LINK**

Watch the video clip at www.brightredbooks.net which shows how organisations in the food and drink industry use test marketing.

Why do you think they may use different colours in the taste test room?

 THINGS TO DO AND THINK ABOUT

Specimen exam-style questions

Now that you are confident with this topic, try answering the following specimen exam-style questions in sentences.

1   Organisations use market research to help them gather information about what the customer wants. Discuss the value of field research as a way of gathering information. **(5 marks)**

2   All organisations carry out market research to find out what their customers want. Justify why organisations carry out desk research. **(3 marks)**

3   Outline the use of observations as a method of market research. **(4 marks)**

4   Describe three methods of sampling. **(3 marks)**

5   Distinguish between random and stratified random sampling as a way of selecting participants to take part in market research. **(2 marks)**

6   Describe the advantages and disadvantages of three types of field research that an organisation could use to obtain primary information. **(6 marks)**

ONLINE TEST

How well have you learned about field research methods? Head to www.brightredbooks.net to take the test.

THE MARKETING MIX: PRODUCT 1

To achieve its marketing objectives (maintaining or obtaining a certain market share), as well as the organisation's overall objectives (maximising profits), an organisation must think about its **marketing mix**.

THE SEVEN PS

The marketing mix consists of seven elements – often referred to as the **seven Ps**. As you can see in the illustration below, the elements of product, price, promotion and placement make up the **product** marketing mix, while the elements of people, process and physical evidence (or physical environment) make up the extended **service marketing mix**.

Organisations must get the balance right of **all** these elements in order to be a success.

PRODUCT

The product is the **actual item** – no matter if it's a good or service – that is produced and sold.

THE PRODUCT LIFE CYCLE

A product has a life cycle in that it has a period of time when it appeals to customers. For example, neon hypercolor t-shirts were popular in the 1990s and Troll Dolls were popular in the 1960s, but they have since gone out of fashion. Before a product can be launched onto the market, it needs to go through various stages.

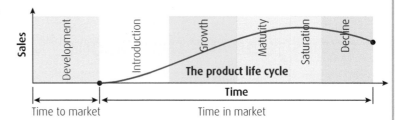

- **Research and development:** the idea behind the product is investigated and developed, finance is raised, a prototype is used to test the market's reaction and feedback is used to adapt the product, where required. Money is invested to develop the product, but as there are no sales at this point, the organisation is making a loss.
- **Introduction:** the product is newly on the market and, as a result, sales are slow. It will probably still not be profitable at this stage. Advertising and promotion campaigns are used to attract and inform consumers about the new product. This can incur high costs.
- **Growth:** the product is becoming more established and sales are increasing due to the growth of consumer awareness so prices may begin to rise. As the product becomes profitable, competitors tend to enter the market.

- **Maturity:** sales are rising more slowly as the product has become established in the market. Sales will eventually reach their peak, as will profits, and substantial amounts of advertising are often used to try to prop up sales. Competition is also reaching its peak, and this will drive down the price of the product.
- **Saturation:** sales have reached their limit and profits are falling due to lowered prices. As more competitors enter the market, it becomes saturated. Some may find themselves forced out of the market because too many are competing for too few consumers.
- **Decline:** the product is no longer fashionable. Technology has improved, consumers' tastes have changed and newer, more advanced products are on the market. Sales fall, advertising stops, prices drop even lower and it is no longer profitable to produce the product.

contd

ACTIVITY

Think of some of the products you know and use in your household.

Draw a labelled product life cycle on an A4 piece of paper and where possible, include an example of a product at each of these stages. You can use the internet for research purposes.

Suggest why these particular products have never entered the decline stage of the product life cycle.

EXTENSION STRATEGIES

Organisations will often use a range of extension strategies to try to extend the life of the product for as long as possible. This can occur during the **maturity** or **saturation** stages. Here are some examples of extension strategies that different companies have used:

- **Introduce new variations of the product:** Since its launch in 1935, Kit Kat has added new varieties to its range. Kit Kat Orange was introduced in 1996, Kit Kat Dark and Kit Kat Mint were added in 1997 and Kit Kat Cookies & Cream was added in 2012.
- **Find new markets for existing products:** Lucozade was first introduced in 1927 as a source of energy for people who were ill. In the early 1980s, Lucozade was rebranded as an energy drink for sportspeople. The slogan 'Lucozade aids recovery' was replaced with 'Lucozade replaces lost energy'. Lucozade now has varieties such as Lucozade Energy, Lucozade Sport and Lucozade Alert.
- **Modify the product's design or packaging:** In 2010 Princes – who are the brand leader in canned ham – launched an innovative ring pull packaging format to improve ease of opening for customers.
- **Sell through a different outlet:** Products marketed or advertised solely on television are often branded with 'As seen on TV!' and can be purchased directly from the manufacturer or in some cases from a few specially selected stores such as Asda. Sometimes these products are only available via the internet – for example, ASOS (As Seen On Screen).
- **Update the product:** Organisations can rename or completely rebrand a product to generate new appeal. For example, Dime bar was rebranded in the UK in 2005 to match with how the product was branded throughout Europe. Other products include Charmin toilet paper, which was rebranded to Cushelle in 2010 and Immac, which became Veet in 2003.
- **Change the product's price:** Discounting a product's price could make it more accessible to a target market which had previously thought it too expensive and therefore out of reach.
- **Use a new advertising campaign:** This could help to make the product more 'visible' to new target markets. For example, a new advertising campaign for Old Spice in 2010 reportedly saw sales for the Old Spice Body Wash increase by over 100 per cent the month after the initial campaign began.

 THINGS TO DO AND THINK ABOUT

Specimen exam-style questions

Now that you are confident with this topic, try answering the following specimen exam-style questions in sentences.

1. Organisations have a range of activities to carry out before they launch a new product on the market. Explain what these activities are. **(4 marks)**

2. Describe the stages of the product life cycle. Use a labelled diagram to support your answer. **(6 marks)**

3. Some organisations change the packaging of their products to make them more appealing to consumers. Explain four other extension strategies. **(4 marks)**

ONLINE

Using the internet, note down some examples of products that have been on the market for over 20 years.

DON'T FORGET

If asked a question regarding the product life cycle, you should always aim to include a fully labelled diagram in your answer as well as explaining the sales and profit situation for each stage.

VIDEO LINK

Watch the Old Spice advert at www.brightredbooks.net

ONLINE

Using the internet, research a product where an extension strategy has been used to prolong its life cycle. Create a short report describing the product and its history and the extension strategy or strategies used.

ONLINE TEST

Test yourself on this topic at www.brightredbooks.net

THE MARKETING MIX: PRODUCT 2

VIDEO LINK

Watch the video clip 'What is branding?' at www.brightredbooks.net for some examples.

BRANDING

A brand is a name, symbol, design or any other feature given to a product that sets it apart from rival products and makes it distinctive to consumers. Brands will try to give a product a positive image. Common brands include McDonald's and Fairy.

Advantages of branding	Disadvantages of branding
It is often associated with quality, so higher prices can be charged. It can build 'snob value', a value of perceived exclusivity.	A poorer brand within a range could result in consumers associating the entire product range with poor quality.
It makes the product easy to recognise, and it's therefore easier to introduce new products with the same brand name.	A brand can often be copied or cheaper fakes produced.
Brand loyalty can be established.	It's expensive and takes time to build a brand.

VIDEO LINK

Watch the video clip at www.brightredbooks.net for a look at the growth of own brands.

OWN BRAND

Some businesses will have **own-brand** products. These were originally aimed at people on a low income but as a result of economic downturns, the own brand product is now popular with the majority of people.

Advantages of own brands	Disadvantages of own brands
They don't require much advertising, so costs are saved.	They are perceived as being of poorer quality.
They are manufactured by another company but the organisation will retain control over the production process.	They can be viewed as a copy or imitation of a brand.

MULTIPLE BRANDING

Multiple branding is when an organisation produces a range of different brand names within its product range such as Unilever.

CORPORATE BRANDING

Corporate branding is when a business uses the name of its company as its brand identity. Examples of corporate brands are Apple, Coca-Cola, Starbucks and Disney.

STRAPLINES

Popular brands are often supported by a catchy strapline. A well-written strapline can encapsulate what a brand is all about.

DON'T FORGET

A generic brand is a trademark that has become associated with a product to the point where the brand name has come to define the product itself – for example, Tipp-Ex, Sellotape and Bubble Wrap.

VIDEO LINK

The video clip at www.brightredbooks.net counts down the top ten rivalries between American brands, but we can recognise many of them in the UK.

PRODUCT PORTFOLIO

Organisations with a wide range of products will have certain products that are aimed at different market segments. This helps to make different types of customers aware of the products and of the brand, and aims to build loyalty from a young age.

An organisation's **product portfolio** or product mix is the range of products it creates. Having a range of products allows organisations to keep their products or brands fresh by bringing out new ones in response to new trends or customer demands, and by retiring any that are in serious decline. It also allows organisations to cater for their different market segments, as well as to increase their profits.

PRODUCT LINE PORTFOLIOS

A **product line** portfolio is when one product's success is then used to introduce 'spin-off' products or closely related products. Disney's 2013 film *Frozen* had success in a wide range of product lines, from video games to dolls to costumes.

contd

x SEGrays

DIVERSIFIED PRODUCT PORTFOLIOS

A **diversified** product portfolio will allow organisations to 'test the water' in other markets that are separate from their core or original business. For example, Richard Branson, the founder of the Virgin Group, has had some successes and some notable failures. Virgin Mobile and Virgin Atlantic Airways are strong brands, but who can remember Virgin Cola? It remains to be seen whether Virgin Galactic and its space flight plans will happen in the future.

Having a product portfolio is a measured business strategy. One failed product can equate to a failed business, whereas having a range means that if one product fails, the business can still survive.

DON'T FORGET

Own-brand labels can have diversified product portfolios too. Asda Smart Price has food, drink, small appliances like kettles and bedroom furniture in its range!

BOSTON MATRIX (PRODUCT PORTFOLIO MATRIX)

If an organisation owns a portfolio of products, it has to choose which products are worth investing in.

A Boston Matrix is a marketing tool used to analyse a product portfolio. It was developed by the Boston Consulting Group, hence its name.

The Boston Matrix splits products into four categories and determines whether the market is one of high or low **market growth** with a high or low **market share**. A balanced portfolio is what many organisations strive for.

ONLINE

Research the Virgin Group website to see the extensive product portfolio they possess.

Stars	These are products with a high growth and a large share of the market. They are strong competitors but require lots of investment to keep them in their strong position. If there are too many stars in a product portfolio, lots of money is spent sustaining their growth. Stars can often become cash cows. The Wii was a star when it was introduced.
Question marks	These are products with a high growth and a low share of the market. They could have future potential but need considerable investment to grow. Not all question marks will become stars, so organisations need to think carefully before investing in them. A new fashion item or a car model are examples of question marks.
Cash cows	These are mature products with low market growth but a high market share of the market. These bring in a steady stream of income which can then be used to sustain stars or question marks. They don't require as much investment and are products that have usually established themselves over the years.
Dogs	These are products with low market growth and a low share of the market. They are usually in decline. For example, DVD recorders replaced VCR recorders but have now themselves been superseded.

Although the Boston Matrix has advantages and is a popular marketing tool, it does have some limitations.

Benefits	Limitations
It can help analyse which products should be pursued, how best company profits should be invested and which products should be removed from the range.	It can only take into account the current market position and does not take into account external factors.
It is simple and easy to understand.	High market share doesn't automatically mean profits all the time.

An organisation can use the Boston Matrix to determine which of its products are more likely to be profitable and, therefore, which to keep in its product portfolio.

	Market share	
	High	Low
High (Market growth)	Stars	Question marks
Low (Market growth)	Cash cows	Dogs

ONLINE

Visit www.brightredbooks.net for an activity on the Boston Matrix.

THINGS TO DO AND THINK ABOUT

Specimen exam-style questions

Now that you are confident with this topic, try answering the following in sentences.

1 Irn Bru has a strong brand identity throughout Scotland.
   Discuss four benefits of having a strong brand identity.   (4 marks)

2 Describe two disadvantages to an organisation of having a well-established
   brand identity.   (2 marks)

ONLINE TEST

Test yourself on this topic at www.brightredbooks.net

THE MARKETING MIX: PRICE

This can simply be explained as 'the amount paid by the consumer to the seller for the product or service'.

PRICE SETTING

Finding the right price

1. Price and availability of substitutes
2. Characteristics relative to competitors
3. Income
4. Price/strength of demand for related products
5. Market environment

We know the price that the buyer is willing to pay during the transaction is usually determined by the factors of **supply** and **demand**. In most cases, as price increases, demand goes down and vice versa. There are some products, however, that don't follow this rule.

When organisations are setting their prices they also need to be aware that consumers will only pay what they are able to **afford** for a product or service, and that many consumers use the price of a product or service as an indication of its **quality**.

Before setting a price, an organisation will need to consider:
- how much profit it wants to make
- how much its rivals are charging
- its target market
- the typical average income of that market
- the position of the product within its life cycle – if it's in the decline stage, the price can be dropped to encourage some last sales.

PRICING STRATEGIES

Pricing strategies will depend on the organisation's objectives and its current business agenda. For example, if an organisation has an objective of 'profit maximisation', it will adopt a pricing strategy to help fulfil this.

COST-BASED PRICING

Cost plus pricing	This strategy involves setting the selling price by calculating the cost of producing or buying the product and adding on a percentage (mark-up) for the organisation's own profit. This is often used in the retail industry as a simple way to set a price. For example, a food outlet could add 50 per cent to a sandwich which cost £1.50 to produce, to make the selling price £2.25. This is not a very competitive pricing strategy
Contribution pricing	With this strategy, the price set takes into account the direct costs of producing the product – for example, raw materials. (This will differ among organisations.) A contribution towards the fixed costs – for example, rent and a profit margin – is then added on. For example, a garden landscaping business has fixed annual costs of £100 000 and it landscapes 100 gardens each year. Each garden landscaped has to generate £1000 towards covering the organisation's fixed costs. This means that £1000 needs to be added to the cost of each landscaped garden for the organisation to simply break even – that is, neither make a profit nor a loss. So if £1200 is added to the cost of a landscaped garden, this generates £200 profit. This strategy is most useful for organisations such as landscapers or builders or those who have a special order or made-to-measure service.

LONG-TERM PRICING STRATEGIES

Low price	This strategy is often used to attract sales of products that have lots of competition – for example, companies lower the price of laundry detergent to sell larger quantities.
Market (competition based) price	With this strategy, prices are set in accordance with those of competitors. Organisations are 'price takers' and not 'price makers'. Petrol stations are an example of this. If one lowers its price, the others are forced to do the same or they will lose customers. Petrol can be described as being **price sensitive**. Because organisations can't compete with their prices, they compete in other ways such as promotions or customer service. For example, Nectar points can be collected at BP stations and at Shell you can buy a Costa Coffee from their Costa Express self-serve machines.
High (premium) price	Luxury products and 'premium' brands are highly priced to appeal to certain consumers. If the price of these items were to drop, their appeal would be lost as their exclusivity would be gone. An example of this is a Ferrari sports car.

contd

SHORT-TERM PRICING STRATEGIES

Market skimming	A new product will initially have a high price and customers will rush out to buy one. As the 'novelty' wears off and competition enters the market, the price will drop to 'skim the cream' off the market. By this stage, many customers will have already purchased this item at the higher price in their haste to be one of the first to own the product. An example of this is the Nintendo Wii.
Penetration pricing	With this strategy, an organisation that is trying to break into an established market with a new product can initially sell the product at a lower price than competitors to attract customers quickly and make sales. When market penetration has occurred and their product has become popular, they can raise the price in line with competitors. This is a common occurrence in the highly competitive breakfast cereal market. Kellogg's recently launched a new cereal product called Special K Granola. They adopted a penetration pricing strategy by selling the cereal at an initial low price. As the product penetrated the market, sales and profitability increased and the price crept up.
Destroyer pricing	With this strategy, an organisation enters an established market and sells their product at a very low price – sometimes even at a loss – to destroy any competitors and force them from the market. This pricing strategy has been used by airlines such as British Airways to prevent smaller airlines from competing in the lucrative shuttle route market.
Promotional pricing	This strategy is used when organisations are trying to boost sales in an established product or to create interest in a new one. Prices will be lowered for a short space of time to drum up attention for the product.
Loss leader	These are products that are priced very low to entice customers into a shop – the idea being that once the customer is in the shop they will then buy more profitable products. No profit is made on loss leaders.
Discriminatory pricing	This refers to selling the same product but at different prices to different groups of consumers. For example, tour operators and airlines vary the prices of their products at different times of the year: school holidays and peak summer season prices are generally a lot higher then off-peak months like November.
Psychological pricing	Organisations that price a product at £79.99 rather than £80 are using this strategy to psychologically influence those customers looking for value for money.

 **ACTIVITY**

Answer the following questions in sentences.

1   Identify two factors that an organisation must consider when
   deciding how much to charge for a product.   (2 marks)

2   Explain what is meant by penetration pricing.   (2 marks)

3   Describe what is meant by a loss leader.   (2 marks)

4   Suggest why premium pricing tends to be used for designer brands. (1 mark)

 **ACTIVITY**

The next time you are in a supermarket, try to spot some 'loss leaders'.

 THINGS TO DO AND THINK ABOUT

Specimen exam-style questions

Now that you are confident with this topic, try answering the following specimen exam-style questions in sentences.

1   Justify why organisations use market skimming as a pricing strategy.   (2 marks)

2   Describe other pricing strategies that could be used by an organisation. (6 marks)

3   Explain why organisations use loss leaders as a pricing tactic.   (2 marks)

4   Describe three pricing strategies that could be used when an organisation attempts to
   break into a new market.   (6 marks)

 **DON'T FORGET**

External factors such as government regulations, supplier prices, time of year or seasonality and the current economic climate can also impact on price.

 VIDEO LINK

Watch the short video clip on psychological pricing at www.brightredbooks.net

 ONLINE

For another great activity, head to www.brightredbooks.net

 ONLINE TEST

How well have you learned about price? Head to www.brightredbooks.net to take the topic test.

THE MARKETING MIX: PROMOTION 1

Promotion is the way in which organisations draw attention to their products or services.

DON'T FORGET

Promotion is not just advertising!

TYPES OF PROMOTION

ABOVE-THE-LINE PROMOTION

This is promotion through independent media such as television and newspapers or through mass media such as cinema and online media. Above-the-line promotional campaigns can help an organisation reach a wide audience.

BELOW-THE-LINE PROMOTION

This is promotion that is controlled by the organisation. It can come in various formats such as direct mail, trade fairs or in-store sales promotions. Below-the-line promotion is aimed at certain market segments, so it is usually differentiated.

The illustration below gives examples of both types of promotion.

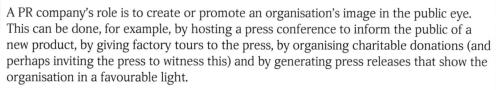

Mobile (SMS)	Internet	Television	Print	Outdoor	Radio	Cinema	Above-the-line
Public relations	**Material**	**Relational**	**One shot**		**Consumer relationship marketing (CRM)**		**Below-the-line**
Awards	Merchandising	Point of display	Sampling		Mail/email		
Endorsements	Packaging	Events	Offers		Branded website		
Sponsorships	Promotions	Brand/retail			Phone prospecting		
Placement	Point of sale	Adviser			Interactive TV		
Word of mouth					Loyalty		

PUBLIC RELATIONS

A PR company's role is to create or promote an organisation's image in the public eye. This can be done, for example, by hosting a press conference to inform the public of a new product, by giving factory tours to the press, by organising charitable donations (and perhaps inviting the press to witness this) and by generating press releases that show the organisation in a favourable light.

Bad publicity has to be dealt with effectively and damage control is key here, because a bad press story can have a destructive influence on an organisation's reputation. The PR company might deal with it by taking the perspective that 'any publicity is good publicity'. But in some cases this is just not possible, and the organisation might have to hold up its hands and accept responsibility publicly, with lessons being learned.

ETHICAL PRACTICE IN PUBLIC RELATIONS

Public Relations departments are used as an interface and point of contact between the public and the media. They promote the organisation's existing products and services and publicise its new products, services and objectives to the general public and the media.

As PR companies work for clients who represent all sorts of different – and sometimes controversial – things, the business of PR can create challenging ethical issues. In a world where ethics is central to our moral core, it is important that a PR department encourages ethical corporate social responsibility.

The general public can influence an organisation and its method of business practice through **pressure groups**. These groups are often members of the general public who have no political powers, but who get together to influence local governments, businesses or the media. Examples include Greenpeace and Friends of the Earth. They can try to persuade the public to boycott an organisation or they might involve local councillors or the media as a way of drawing attention to an organisation's perceived unethical business practice.

VIDEO LINK

The video clip at www.brightredbooks.net shows how PR had a negative effect on a product which was extremely popular at that time.

ONLINE

Head to www.brightredbooks.net for an activity on bad publicity.

contd

Society today has many forums through which thoughts and opinions can be shared and commented on. A business needs to take its reputation seriously, because negative stories relating to unethical practices can have major repercussions on customer relations.

ADVERTISING

This type of promotion raises consumers' awareness of a product or service and encourages them to buy it. Advertising can come in different forms. It can be **informative** (to increase awareness), **persuasive** (to convince consumers to buy it) or act as a **reminder** about the existence of a product or service.

PRODUCT ENDORSEMENT

Organisations often use celebrities to wear or use their product/service to raise customer awareness. If the latest celebrity is seen with a product, it will make the product seem more credible, extend the life of the product or simply influence the customer into wanting to buy it. It's important for an organisation to choose the right celebrity. Examples of successful celebrity endorsement partnerships are Gary Lineker and Walkers crisps and Jennifer Aniston and Aveeno moisturiser. Whenever we see Gary, we think of Walkers crisps (and vice versa) and fans who want to emulate Aniston will be encouraged to try this moisturiser.

Unfortunately, choosing the wrong celebrity can have repercussions for the brand. For example, David Beckham endorsed too many different brands and become overexposed, while Britney Spears signed a multi-million dollar deal with Pepsi in 2001, but was photographed drinking Coke.

PRODUCT PLACEMENT

Organisations can supply branded merchandise to be used in films or television programmes. Sometimes an organisation will pay for this to be done, but at other times the organisation will provide complimentary products or services to television or film production companies in a bid for exposure. Product placement has been used in cinema for decades and is famously used in James Bond films.

Ofcom (the Office for Communications) is an independent regulator and competition authority for the UK communications industries. It has strict rules on the use of product placement and indicates that when a product is used in this way, it has to be advertised.

 **ACTIVITY:**

Look out for the product placement symbol the next time you are watching a television programme. Did you spot the product(s) that was being promoted?

 THINGS TO DO AND THINK ABOUT

Specimen exam-style questions

Now that you are confident with this topic, try answering the following specimen exam-style questions in sentences.

1   Explain the importance of good public relations to an organisation.   (2 marks)

2   Describe two methods an organisation could use to improve its public relations.   (2 marks)

3   Describe what is meant by product endorsement.   (1 mark)

4   Discuss the costs and benefits of product endorsement to an organisation.   (6 marks)

 VIDEO LINK

Watch the video clips at www.brightredbooks.net for examples of informative, persuasive, alternative and reminder advertisements and analyse their differences.

 **DON'T FORGET**

Advertisements can communicate lots of different messages – some obvious, others much more subtle!

 VIDEO LINK

Watch the video clip of *Wayne's World* with an amusing look at product placement at www.brightredbooks.net

 ONLINE TEST

Head to www.brightredbooks.net to take the topic test.

THE MARKETING MIX: PROMOTION 2

VIDEO LINK

Watch the video clips at www.brightredbooks.net to see how advertising online makes money by targeting customers.

ADVERTISING MEDIA

The choice of which advertising media to use can depend on a number of factors:
- The cost involved and any legal restrictions in place.
- The target market to be reached.
- How competitors use advertising to promote their products.
- The actual product itself, its technicalities and the impact that the manufacturers want it to make.

Medium	Advantages	Disadvantages
Television	Gives exposure on a national or global scale.	Very technical products can't be explained easily in a short advert.
	The advert reaches all socio-economic groups and is a common method of mass marketing.	Competition is fierce between companies who want their product to be shown during popular TV programmes or at Christmas time.
	Creative advertising can make a huge visual impact.	Most people do not watch advertisements, so marketing campaigns could include billboards and press articles to 'advertise' a TV advertising campaign, which is time consuming and very expensive
	Advertisements often feature demonstrations of the product in action so consumers can see what it does.	There might not be nationwide interest in the product, so TV advertising would not be appropriate.
National newspapers	Some organisations can take out full-page advertisements which can really grab the reader's attention and give lots of information.	In a newspaper where there could be lots of different advertisements, making one stand out against the crowd can be difficult.
	Different newspapers tend to have different, clearly defined market segments, which allows for more effective differentiated marketing.	
	They have greater attention value as people can take their time to read them when convenient, cut out any advertisements that interest them or even refer back to them.	There is no option for video or sound to demonstrate the product in a newspaper.
	They have a large circulation nationally and newspaper readers tend to be brand loyal.	It can be expensive (especially for full-page advertisements).
	There can be the option to advertise in special colour supplements.	
Local newspapers	They are less expensive than national newspapers.	Local papers don't have the quality of nationals.
	They have a 'captive' audience who are interested in local businesses.	They have a smaller audience because they're local.
Magazines	They are printed in colour, so have high visual impact.	Magazines are not printed as often as newspapers are, so advertisements have a shorter shelf life.
	Readers are more likely to retain magazines than newspapers because they want to refer back to them.	As in the case of newspapers, there is no sound or video option to demonstrate the product so the advertisement needs to be clear.
Radio	It's cheaper than advertising on TV.	It relies on messages being communicated by voice and so advertisements must be creative and attention-worthy to hold the listener's attention and fire their imagination.
	It can target specific market segments during particular shows – for example, the GBX show on Clyde 1 which appeals to clubbers.	It's difficult to target specific segments during peak times.
	There is a captive audience as many people listen to the radio in the car and tend not to change channels especially while driving.	There is no option to rewind or refer back on radio.
Cinema	Colour and sound can be used in creative adverts.	There is limited market coverage.
	Market segments can be targeted via film genre – for example, Disney animation or the latest romcom.	Some cinema goers prefer to arrive in time for the film and use the 'trailer time' to buy refreshments.
	There is a captive audience.	It's expensive to produce 'quality' adverts.

contd

Medium	Advantages	Disadvantages
Outdoor media – for example, billboards	They can be placed in busy locations to widen the audience.	They can go unnoticed and people might not notice any new advertisements – they become part of the scenery.
	They can have a strong visual impact.	They can be vandalised and therefore need to be replaced, which is expensive.
	They are useful for short, sharp messages – for example, Donate Blood advertisements.	Due to their size and the impact that the advertisement needs to convey, only a limited amount of information can be used, so imaginative slogans need to be created which can take time and cost money.
Internet/ websites	It's inexpensive to create and set up, and sound and video can be used.	Technical issues can arise for internet users.
	If the advert is placed on certain websites, market segments can be targeted.	There are a growing number of advertisements on the internet, and people surfing the internet might ignore them or use pop up blockers to stop them.
	It can be updated and refreshed regularly and more easily than other media.	
	Customers can be targeted worldwide, 24/7.	
	The number of times the advert has been 'hit' can be monitored, which is useful for market research feedback.	
Mobile text alerts	These can be sent to existing customers – for example, banking customers – to inform them of new products.	Customers might change their contact details and forget to update all the organisations who send them mobile notifications.
	One text can be sent to many customers at once.	
Direct mail	This is useful for easy-to-target market segments through the use of mailing lists.	Customers can view it as 'junk mail' or an invasion of their privacy.
	It's effective for exclusive products.	If the target audience isn't selected carefully, it can yield a poor response.

THE MARMITE EFFECT

Consumers can have a love/hate relationship with certain promotional campaigns on radio or TV. Marmite cleverly incorporated this into their *Love it or Hate it* campaign, launched in 1996.

The campaign had such a strong impact that the popular phrase 'the Marmite effect' has now become part of our everyday language, and relates to anything that can cause strong, contradictory feelings.

The advertising campaign is still remembered today, so as far as the marketing team behind it is concerned, this is mission accomplished!

 VIDEO LINK

Watch the video clip at www.brightredbooks.net to find out how gender recognition technology can benefit advertising. Then watch the clip from the 2002 Tom Cruise film *Minority Report* where his character (John Anderton) is recognised either through retina scanning or facial recognition, and advertisements are tailored to him. Hollywood's take on personalised advertising might be commonplace before we know it!

 THINGS TO DO AND THINK ABOUT

Watch TV advertisements and note down those that you think used good promotional and selling techniques. Then ask your friends to watch them and compare notes.

 ONLINE TEST

Test yourself on this topic at www.brightredbooks.net

THE MARKETING MIX: PROMOTION 3

ONLINE

Follow the link to the ASA website at www.brightredbooks.net to see what advertisements have been subject to an ASA ruling.

DON'T FORGET

An eye-catching advertisement alone will not sell large amounts of products or services.

ADVERTISING REGULATION

The Advertising Standards Authority (ASA) is a body that monitors advertising in the UK and that has major links with Ofcom (Office of Communications) and Trading Standards.

The ASA deals with many types of advertisements including:

- magazine and newspaper adverts
- television shopping channels
- internet banner adverts
- radio and TV commercials.

The ASA:

- acts on any complaints raised by the public
- constantly checks media outlets for any misleading, harmful or offensive advertisements
- monitors the media to ensure that any rulings they have passed have been adhered to.

SALES PROMOTIONS

Sales promotions are processes and incentives used by organisations to encourage sales of their products rather than those of a competitor. These processes often comprise short-term tactics to improve sales.

There are two main types:

INTO-THE-PIPELINE PROMOTION

These are methods that are used to sell more products into the **distribution system**, so they tend to focus on how a **manufacturer** can attract **wholesalers** and **retailers** into buying and stocking their products.

- **Point-of-sale materials:** These could be promotional sales videos, posters or display stands – any item that draws the eye to the product.
- **Dealer loaders:** These are special offers given to the wholesaler/retailer when buying a product to encourage them to buy more – for example, buy so many boxes and get one free.
- **Dealer competitions:** These offer prizes to the most successful dealer to encourage them to sell more of the manufacturer's product rather than a rival's.
- **Promotional gifts:** These can be special limited edition items – for example, alcohol or diaries/calendars published by the manufacturer.
- **Staff training:** The manufacturer can train retail staff so that they are knowledgeable in the product and can promote it in a self-assured manner – particularly if the product is technical.
- **Extended credit:** This can encourage retailers to stock more of the product because they can buy now, pay later.
- **Sale or return:** This encourages a retailer to buy products from a manufacturer with a safety net attached. If anything does not sell, it can be returned so they are not left with old, unsold inventory.

OUT-OF-THE-PIPELINE PROMOTION

These are methods that are used to sell more products to consumers, so they tend to focus on how a **retailer** can attract **customers**.

- **Buy one, get one free (BOGOF):** This, or other special offers, can be used for a limited time to encourage selected inventory sales. (This could include inventory that is older and therefore less valuable.)
- **Free samples:** This can encourage customers to purchase, because they can taste or smell a product before they buy it.

contd

- **Free offers**: This could be a free gift with purchase, and is a common method of promotion by breakfast cereal manufacturers.
- **Bonus packs**: These could be packs that offer – for example, 15 per cent extra free – but will be at the same price as the original item.
- **Credit facilities**: This is where customers are offered payment plans that allow them to pay at a later date. They are often used when customers are buying 'big ticket items' or retail goods with high-selling prices like washing machines and cars.
- **Loyalty schemes**: These are schemes that allow customers to collect points for purchases. Examples are Nectar, BA, Avios reward currency, Boots Advantage and Debenhams Beauty Club Card. Points can then be swapped for discounts.
- **Vouchers and discount coupons**: These are sometimes included in direct mail, newspapers or, occasionally, on product packaging itself to encourage re-purchase
- **Demonstrations**: These encourage customers to try something to encourage them to buy it – for example, test-driving a new car.
- **Competitions**: This is where customers have to purchase a product to be able to enter a competition and win a prize.
- **Point-of-sale materials**: Retailers often use posters or end-of-aisle displays to attract customers to a particular product.

 DON'T FORGET

Make sure that you know the difference between the two types of sales promotions.

VIDEO LINK

Have a look at the video clip at www.brightredbooks.net which explores how promotion has had an impact on different industries.

PROMOTION AND SOCIAL MEDIA NETWORKS

The main objective of promoting a product or service is to gain and retain customers. Social media is a quick, easy way to promote to an audience across the globe.

Media sharing such as YouTube	Media such as videos and photographs can be shared on platforms like YouTube. This gives organisations an opportunity to promote their new products through short advertisements that run before the video starts.
Microblogging such as Twitter	Updated regularly, corporate Twitter accounts can reach thousands of followers with product and service news. Customer complaints can be publicly resolved in this way, too. However, companies need to remember to keep their tweets professional at all times, as Tesco found out to its cost when a pre-scheduled Tesco tweet stating 'It's sleepy time, so we're off to hit the hay' went viral in the middle of the horsemeat scandal.
Social networks such as Facebook	Companies can post Facebook updates that link to particular products and push particular items such as seasonal produce.
Mobile apps	Mobile apps can help businesses in many ways – examples are customer service (banking apps), apps for catalogues to help sales (IKEA) and a table reservation service (OpenTable).

 **ACTIVITY**

1 Describe reasons why the Advertising Standards Authority exists and describe the influence it can have on an organisation. (3 marks)
2 Outline two methods of into-the-pipeline promotions. (2 marks)
3 Outline two methods of out-of-the-pipeline promotions. (2 marks)

 **ACTIVITY**

Try to spot all the sales promotions you can see when you are next in a shop. Which method(s) do you think encourage the most sales?

 THINGS TO DO AND THINK ABOUT

Specimen exam-style questions

Now that you are confident with this topic, try answering the following specimen exam-style questions in sentences.

1 Describe two short-term promotional measures that manufacturers use to boost the sales of their products or services to retailers (into-the-pipeline promotions). (4 marks)
2 Describe two methods of promotion (other than altering prices) that organisations use. (4 marks)
3 Describe three methods of promoting Scotland's tourist industry overseas. (3 marks)
4 Suggest two appropriate promotional activities that could be used to promote a new watch. (2 marks)

 ONLINE TEST

Head to www.brightredbooks.net to take the topic test.

THE MARKETING MIX: PLACE 1

Place is about **how** the product gets to customers at the right time and in the right quantities.

VIDEO LINK

Watch the video clip at www.brightredbooks.net which discusses the channels of distribution that M&Ms can take.

CHANNELS OF DISTRIBUTION

A **channel of distribution** is the route the product takes to get to the customer from its manufacturer. Some of these channels are illustrated below.

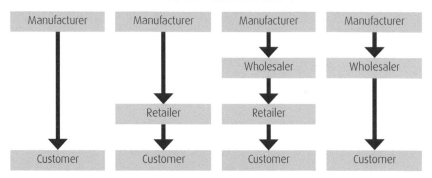

Note that the channel always begins with the **manufacturer** and ends at the **customer**.

FACTORS INFLUENCING CHOICE OF DISTRIBUTION CHANNEL

- **The product itself and its life cycle:** Perishable products such as fruit need a fairly direct channel of distribution so customers can buy them when they are still fresh. Technical goods such as ICT or medical equipment need to maintain a link between the customer and the manufacturer in case of future faults, but they are usually sold direct from the manufacturer.

- **Finance available to the organisation:** If it is too expensive to have retail outlets, manufacturers might use wholesalers who can save them the expense of labelling and packaging.

- **Legal restrictions:** Certain pharmaceutical products can only be sold via prescription in a pharmacy and cannot be purchased any other way.

- **Reliability of wholesaler and retailers:** If past experience has shown these channels to be unreliable, manufacturers will probably sell direct to customers.

METHODS OF PHYSICAL DISTRIBUTION

This is how the product **actually gets transported** from the manufacturer to the customer. It could be via **road**, **rail**, **air** or **sea**.

	Advantages	Disadvantages
Road	• Cheap method. • Customers can have the product delivered directly to them.	• Not very environmentally friendly due to carbon emissions. • Delays or road works can impede delivery times.
Rail	• Can transport large items easily by freight.	• Rail links can cause deliveries to be restrictive. • Rail services can be disrupted.
Air	• Products can be transported across the globe quickly.	• Expensive method. • Larger items can't be transported as easily by this method.
Sea	• Large products can be transported worldwide.	• Takes a long time.

METHODS OF SELLING

WHOLESALERS

Wholesalers act as a connection between the manufacturer and retailers such as Costco. They will buy in bulk from manufacturers and then sell on in smaller quantities to retailers or directly to the public.

There are many advantages to using wholesalers. Wholesalers will sometimes label products for manufacturers, saving them both time and money. By buying larger quantities and then breaking them down to retailers on behalf of the manufacturer, the manufacturer can then concentrate on production.

Wholesalers typically have good relationships with retailers, which means a better chance of the product being purchased by a wider range of retailers, which is good for the manufacturer. By using a wholesaler, the manufacturer can distribute all its products to one location instead of having to transport them to various retail locations nationwide.

Wholesalers such as Makro usually operate from a large warehouse and therefore have plenty of storage space to hold large quantities of inventory – something that a manufacturer will not have. They can also provide manufacturers with invaluable feedback on sales, a useful market research tool.

However, there are some downsides to using a wholesaler. If there are many manufacturers with similar products operating through a wholesaler, some firms might feel as if their product is not being marketed as strongly as their competitors, to the detriment of their sales. A wholesaler is also likely to take a percentage of their profit.

RETAILERS

Retailers sell the product to the customer on behalf of the manufacturer. Manufacturers sometimes prefer to use retailers because retailers can attract large numbers of customers from lots of different target markets over a large geographical distance. Many retailers such as Marks & Spencer already have an established loyal customer base and others such as John Lewis offer the customer extras such as free delivery, guarantees or credit facilities. Here are the different types of retailers.

Supermarket	Large stores selling a wide range of products, not just food and drink. They are often found in populated areas and conveniently offer everything under one roof to the customer. Many manufacturers will sell their products directly to a supermarket and this allows them to exercise economies of scale and buy in bulk. These savings are sometimes passed onto customers because supermarkets have a wide range of products for sale – both branded and own label.
Department store	These stores offer a wide range of products for sale in different product categories such as sportswear and homewear. They are often found in city/town centre locations where footfall of customers is guaranteed.
Chain store	Chain stores are retailers with many stores in many different locations nationwide. They are often found in city/town centres.
Discount retailer	This type of retailer offers products at a discounted price. They try to keep costs low to keep their prices low and probably have cheaper promotional displays in store. They tend to not spend a great deal on advertising and are sometimes found in out-of-town sites such as Matalan.
Independent retailer	This is a smaller business that might be owned by a sole trader, and relies on wholesalers or agents for its inventory. This could be a small fashion boutique or corner shop.

 THINGS TO DO AND THINK ABOUT

Specimen exam-style questions

Now that you are confident with this topic, try answering the following specimen exam-style questions in sentences.

1 Explain the benefits to a retailer of sourcing their products from a wholesaler. (2 marks)

2 Explain the advantages of using a wholesaler for a manufacturer. (4 marks)

3 Explain the disadvantages of using a wholesaler. (2 marks)

 **DON'T FORGET**

Agents are used to brokering a deal on sales on behalf of a seller. Travel agencies will act as an agent for the customer and the seller. They will earn commission on the holidays they sell so they often carry out promotional activities to attract customers to make sales.

 VIDEO LINK

The video clip at www.brightredbooks.net demonstrates a new way to distribute pizza to customers. Is it the future of retail?

 ONLINE TEST

Want to test your knowledge of this topic? Head to at www.brightredbooks.net to take the test.

THE MARKETING MIX: PLACE 2

DIRECT SELLERS

Direct sellers come in different forms. Direct sales are made without an intermediary such as a shop. Examples include e-commerce or teleshopping.

Internet selling/ e-tailers	An e-tailer is a retailer selling goods via the internet. Customers can view their products and place orders online. The customer will pay the e-tailer and the e-tailer will then arrange for the product to be delivered to the customer from the manufacturer or wholesaler. Many e-tailers such as Next offer home shopping in conjunction with their retail stores, but others such as Amazon do not, therefore saving on expensive high street store outlets and other related expenses.
Direct mail	Promotional materials such as brochures are posted directly to homes and workplaces. This method is often used by charities such as Cancer Research to promote awareness and raise money. Sometimes personalised letters can be used by organisations to improve their sales and target specific segments, but many customers don't want to receive lots of 'junk mail' and don't reply to it in case they continue to be targeted in this way.
Personal selling	Organisations use their sales people in various ways to sell products face-to-face to customers – for example, via door-to-door sales, or in department stores at cosmetic counters. This allows customers to view, ask questions about and trial the product, which is a huge advantage. It can, however, be difficult to sell products this way because people often doubt the authenticity of products sold door-to-door, and only one person can be served at a time at cosmetic counters, so this limits sales.
Direct response advertisements	Some organisations place advertisements in specialist or trade magazines to advertise their products. By using specialist magazines, they are targeting their target market. Direct response advertisements are also found in newspapers/ magazines and these advertise to the mass market. There is often a coupon to complete and post, a telephone number, an e-mail address to use or a means of ordering via social media.
Mail order/ catalogues	Catalogues are issued to customers who can buy the goods via mail order. Orders can be made in writing or via the telephone or e-mail. This is still a popular method of direct selling due to its convenience for customers. Mail order companies can offer credit facilities, allowing customers to buy 'big ticket' items and pay in instalments. It is easy to get into debt if accounts are not paid in full as the rate of interest charged is high. For example, Next Directory has an APR of 25.99%.
Direct response television/ teleshopping	This is a way of advertising and selling products via the television. Customers are given a special number to phone when they want to make a purchase. Some television channels such as QVC and JML Direct TV have been specifically created for teleshopping, and target consumers at home.
Telephone selling	Here, companies telephone customers at their home or in the workplace to sell their products or services. This is often used for marketing financial products, but it isn't often received well by customers who find the idea intrusive.
E-mail marketing	In this case, the retailer promotes their product or service via an e-mail marketing message. It is becoming increasingly simple for organisations to send out mass marketing e-mails at any time of the day. In some cases, retailers try to tempt an existing customer to buy their new product by using a more personal touch: they send out personalised e-mails using customer details held on their database.
Mobile marketing	Where an organisation has customer mobile number details, they can send 'push notifications' detailing other products or services that the customer might be interested in. Mobile phone companies such as Vodafone send texts to their customers to inform them of new products.

 **ACTIVITY:**

1   Suggest why a manufacturer would use a retailer as a distribution channel.   (2 marks)

2   Identify two factors that can affect the choice of channel of distribution.   (4 marks)

E-COMMERCE

E-commerce is simply a transaction that takes place online. The internet is a common market place for all types of products and services.

Advantages to the customer	It's convenient – customers can shop 24/7.
	The choice of items is vast, and global markets are available.
	Online stock checker, FAQs and contact details are available.
	Customer reviews and videos on the products can be viewed online, which helps with decision-making.
	Shoppers can compare prices to get the best deal.
Disadvantages to the customer	Customers might be concerned about the security of the site or connection problems mid-transaction could cause problems.
	Websites could be faked to obtain bank information.
	Returning goods can be difficult, with some businesses only accepting courier returns. The customer might be expected to pay for the cost of the return.
	Customers might think that they are getting a great online deal without realising that VAT isn't included.
	There is no option to interact with sales assistants and ask questions about the product, or to try it before buying.
Advantages to the seller	There is no need for an expensive retail outlet and this saves on overheads such as staff wages.
	Setting up the website is fairly inexpensive.
	E-commerce allows the option to retain customer details and gather market research information.
	It's available 24/7 to shoppers worldwide, which will increase the seller's market share opportunities
Disadvantages to the seller	It can be expensive and time consuming to have the entire product range available online. The website will need to be regularly updated.
	Staff turnover can impact on the customer service provided, because staff need to be trained to know what stock there is, and stock items can change regularly.

 **ACTIVITY:**

Which distribution channel would be used for each of the following and what are the factors influencing the choice? Copy and complete the table with your answers.

Product/service	Channel of distribution	Influencing factors
Farmer selling fresh strawberries		
A network of computers		
A made-to-measure suit for a man who is 6 feet 5 inches tall		
Marc Jacobs perfume		
Catering-size bags of rice		

 THINGS TO DO AND THINK ABOUT

Specimen exam-style questions

Now that you are confident with this topic, try answering the following specimen exam-style questions in sentences.

1 Describe the advantages for an organisation of selling online. (2 marks)

2 Describe three methods of direct selling that could be used by an organisation. (6 marks)

 DON'T FORGET

E-commerce refers to the buying **and** selling of products and services over the internet.

 VIDEO LINK

Watch the short video clip explaining e-commerce at www.brightredbooks.net

 VIDEO LINK

Pop-up shops are becoming a more common way to trial products/services. They are also a common seasonal method of temporary retailing – for example, Christmas shops such as Hawkin's Bazaar literally pop up and then disappear again after Christmas. Watch the video clip at www.brightredbooks.net on pop up shops and mobile technology.

 ONLINE TEST

Head to www.brightredbooks.net to test yourself on this topic.

THE MARKETING MIX: PROCESS, PEOPLE AND PHYSICAL EVIDENCE

PROCESS

This element of the marketing mix looks at the systems used to deliver the service. Fast-food restaurants are given this name because they deliver food – fast.

Another example of an efficient business process is when banks automatically send out credit cards to customers a few months before their card expires. This requires an efficient process to identify expiry dates and renewal times, and it's this type of service that will foster consumer loyalty and confidence in the company.

At McDonald's, the processes go on behind the scenes up until the last minute when the customer can see the finished product being sent down to the waiting serving staff. In an age where the customer is king and wants to be fully aware of the product/service they are buying, then why is this not the case at McDonald's? McDonald's processes are clearly tried and tested and are able to complete the crucial goal, which is delivering the product to the customer without loss in quality. Ultimately, customers are not interested in what is happening behind the scenes – they are only interested in receiving a good service.

Implementing systems to minimise waiting times, dealing with complaints professionally, communicating more effectively with customers and providing an efficient delivery service are all vital to keeping customers happy. It is important that everyone involved in the organisation knows what to do, and how to keep processes moving smoothly.

PEOPLE

People are an important part of an organisation. From marketing department personnel to shop-floor staff, each has a role to play – whether directly or indirectly involved. Whenever employees come into contact with a customer, an impression is being formed in the customer's mind.

Staff provide the interactive link between the customer and the manufacturer and as such should be equipped with the necessary skills to provide good customer relations. Organisations can ensure that customers are left with a good impression by having properly trained, well-motivated staff with a good attitude, because the reputation of the company rests in their hands.

Training and motivating staff enables them to provide good customer service, be creative and innovative when providing a service and have an awareness of the influence they have on the target market. Many customers make judgements on service provision based on the people representing the organisation.

Excellent customer service delivered by a happy workforce can give a company just as much of a competitive edge as an excellent promotional campaign. And, most importantly, this will encourage customers to return and tell others about the experience they have had.

Also, customers are more likely to be loyal to organisations that provide memorable customer service – from the way a complaint over the telephone is handled, to direct face-to-face interactions. The staff can help towards making or breaking an organisation.

PHYSICAL EVIDENCE

This is the physical environment of the organisation. A service can't be experienced until it has been delivered. A service might be intangible but there are many other elements involved that **are** tangible and that can create a better customer experience. For example, beauty salons offer spa treatments like massages and facials in delicately perfumed individual rooms with luxurious towels and comfortable beds. They have relaxing music and special ambient lighting. Imagine if you had a facial on a hard table with strong lighting alongside four or five other customers. It certainly wouldn't be quite as enjoyable an experience. Smelly or dirty restaurants with an unfriendly atmosphere would result in some customers walking out before they had even ordered food and experienced what that service was like.

Factories, office environments or retail spaces should be clean and tidy with an air of professionalism. This will help to reassure customers that this is a business that will provide an efficient service. Customers expect well-laid-out shops with clear presentation around the shopfloor – for example, New Look has all its sections covered with signage indicating where ladieswear, shoes and menswear are. Customers expect a well-lit, well-furnished and well-designed retail space, as well as branded carrier bags.

Environment can also include the online environment of an organisation. Customer reviews, recommendations and sharing of stories can give evidence of good or bad service and can be very important to customers. Testimonials are often included in corporate websites or corporate publications to show new customers the type of service they can expect to receive.

Each element of the product and service marketing mix should work in harmony so that the organisation can produce, market, price and sell the product or service to the correct target market.

MARKETING MIX

Finally, one element of the marketing mix can impact on another. For example:

- Spending money on training staff (people) may mean less finance available to upgrade the physical environment (place).

- Deciding to sell online (place) may mean having to charge a lower price to compete. The business may decide to use cheaper materials which may result in a lower-quality product.

- Promotion can be very expensive, leaving less finance available for developing and improving processes.

To be effective an organisation must ensure it manages all seven elements of the marketing mix.

 THINGS TO DO AND THINK ABOUT

Think about the shops that you like and feel most comfortable in. What is it that you like most about them?

Make a list of the key factors in your workbook.

 **DON'T FORGET**

The physical environment should:
- be well designed
- be clean and tidy
- be well-lit
- have ambience
- make use of signage.

 ONLINE

Head to www.brightredbooks.net to try out the Case Study, which will test your knowledge of this unit.

 ONLINE TEST

Test yourself on this topic at www.brightredbooks.net

 **DON'T FORGET**

The online environment should:
- be user-friendly
- be updated regularly
- include customer reviews
- include customer recommendations.

OPERATIONS DEPARTMENTS AND INVENTORY MANAGEMENT SYSTEMS

VIDEO LINK

Watch the video clip at www.brightredbooks.net which illustrates how adding value to corn is big business in the cereal industry.

DON'T FORGET

The more value added to a product/service, the more a business will build a competitive edge.

VIDEO LINK

Head to www.brightredbooks.net to have a look at how operations are managed in an Amazon distribution centre on one of their busiest days.

ONLINE

Revise the purchasing mix at www.brightredbooks.net

WHAT IS OPERATIONS?

Operations is an important core function within an organisation.

The operations department takes raw materials (**inputs**) and puts them through a variety of procedures (**processes**) to turn them into the finished product/service (**outputs**). As the inputs go through the processes, this adds value, turning them into high-quality products or services that the organisation will then sell. This is known as an **operating system**.

Input	Processing	Output
Materials, components, labour, research and development	Production lines, assembly lines, management and skills	End product

This earns the organisation a profit and creates wealth.

THE ROLE OF OPERATIONS

The operations department needs to make important decisions.

These include:
- **Purchasing:** What inventory do we need to purchase; how much should we buy and who from?
- **Systems:** How and where should we produce the product; what staff do we need and what method of production should we use?
- **Inventory control:** How can we ensure that adequate inventory is available; how can we best store it and how can we facilitate it?
- **Quality:** How do we ensure that the quality is consistent throughout?

INVENTORY MANAGEMENT SYSTEMS

Organisations hold an assortment of **inventory** for different reasons:

Raw materials	These are purchased from suppliers and stored by the organisation to allow a flexible response to customer orders. Having a supply in stock can allow production to continue while awaiting new deliveries.
Work-in-progress	These are partly finished goods that require longer stages between production cycles due to their nature – for example, whisky or cheese.
Finished goods	This allows the organisation to meet any sudden changes in customer demand.

DON'T FORGET

An inventory check will allow any outdated items of inventory to be identified and older items of inventory can be rotated to the front to be used first.

INVENTORY CHECKING

Organisations usually perform an annual **inventory check** to count items of inventory held on the shelves. This is done to record the amount of inventory held physically by the organisation so it can be compared to what should be held according to inventory system records.

contd

It also clearly identifies any inconsistencies between system inventory records, system transaction records and physical inventory records. Any discrepancies could indicate theft.

 **ACTIVITY:**

Read the short passage and then answer the following questions in sentences.

Tesco and Business Information Systems

Tesco currently enjoys its status as one of the top four supermarkets in the UK. Tesco prides itself on its efficient systems, both on the shop floor and behind the scenes.

For Tesco to monitor sales and order supplies, and to ensure that its inventory is at an optimum level, it implemented an information system for use in its warehouses known as the GOLD (Global Optimisation for Logistics and Distribution) Warehouse Management System (WMS).

GOLD manages the inventory held in Tesco warehouses. It can monitor inventory levels and alerts staff when inventory is low. It helps staff to identify and locate the low inventory quickly, so the level and quality of the inventory can be assessed quickly. It also means that older inventory can be identified and rotated to eradicate the risk of inventory perishing before it can be sold.

Staff use handheld computers to check inventory on the shelves and to check that prices are accurate. Tesco claims to have improved its in-store inventory control by 40 per cent after introducing the web-enabled handheld computers.

The checkouts are also an important part of Tesco's information system exchange. These EPOS (Electronic Point of Sale) tills are all connected to the branch computer, which records all transactions. The product's bar codes are scanned and these products are then removed from a real-time inventory level program.

This allows inventory replenishment to occur through EDI (Electronic Data Interchange).

It identifies the overall daily sales figures as well as top sellers from each different branch, which helps Tesco to gather a geographical picture of which products sell best where. This information is then sent on from all the branches to Head Office.

The system can also identify poorly performing items, which could mean the non-renewal of these contracts in the future, with the eventual removal of those products from the shelves.

These systems are all linked to provide Tesco with a strong inventory management system. This helps Tesco to keep its edge over competitors and keep a close eye on customers' shopping habits so it can satisfy their demands.

1   Explain why it is important for an organisation such as Tesco to have systems in place to monitor its inventory.

2   Suggest reasons why Tesco would want to ensure that any empty shelves are replenished straight away.

3   Describe the importance of inventory rotation.

4   Justify why you think Tesco uses electronic systems to manage its inventory.

 VIDEO LINK

Watch the video clip at www.brightredbooks.net for a glimpse into what the future could hold for inventory management and what future supermarkets could be like.

THINGS TO DO AND THINK ABOUT

Answer the following questions in sentences.

1   Explain the stages of an operating system.   (3 marks)

2   Describe what is meant by the purchasing mix.   (1 mark)

3   Describe three factors that make up part of the purchasing mix.   (6 marks)

4   Describe the types of inventory that can be held by an organisation. (3 marks)

 ONLINE TEST

Test yourself on this topic at www.brightredbooks.net

INVENTORY LEVEL AND CONTROL

INVENTORY LEVELS

One of the most important tasks for inventory control is to ensure that organisations have the correct level of inventory for their operations.

Too much inventory can be difficult to manage, while too little inventory can mean running out, so the optimum inventory level needs to be maintained.

Inventory levels must be kept at a manageable level – neither too low nor too high.

Too much inventory	If an organisation holds too much inventory, it can result in high storage costs including heating, lighting, insurance, expensive refrigeration units and security costs.
	It can be risky if an organisation buys more inventory than it requires: if it is perishable and it doesn't sell, it will have to be destroyed because it will deteriorate over time and become spoiled.
	Money that is tied up in too much inventory is money that can't be used to invest in other essential aspects of the business.
	Too much inventory is difficult to manage, which means that it is vulnerable to pilfering by staff.
Too little inventory	If an organisation has too little inventory, it will have to make lots of little orders and pay for each of these orders from its suppliers.
	Holding small amounts of inventory can be risky, because if customer demand can't be fulfilled, customers will probably go elsewhere and not come back. The business's reputation is therefore at stake.
	If an organisation holds too little inventory, it will have to halt production while it waits for inventorys to be replenished – but it will still have to pay staff.

Organisations have to manage their inventory levels to meet customer demand by using the following measures:
- **Setting a maximum inventory level**: This is the level that inventory is set at, and it should not be exceeded. This level is restricted by factors such as space and cost.
- **Setting a minimum inventory level**: This is the level that inventory should not fall below, or it will prevent a shortage in resources.
- **Setting a reorder level**: Once inventory reaches this level, an order is automatically placed and inventory is reordered. When considering reorder level, organisations need to take **lead time** into account. This is the time it takes between placing an order, receiving the order and checking it before it is available for use. The longer the lead time, the higher the reorder level needs to be.
- **Setting a reorder quantity**: This is the standard amount of inventory that is ordered each time an order is placed to replenish the inventory level back to maximum.

These inventory levels can be seen in the inventory control illustration below.

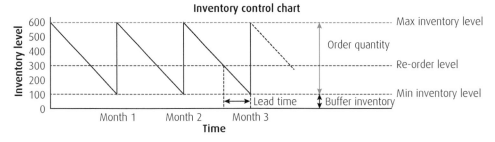

Inventory control chart

DON'T FORGET

Any volume of inventory should be carefully stored, because it is a business resource with great value to an organisation.

ACTIVITY:

Answer the following questions in sentences.

1 Explain why it is important for organisations to manage their inventory effectively.
(2 marks)

2 Describe what is meant by minimum inventory level. (1 mark)

3 Describe what is meant by reorder level. (1 mark)

4 Describe what is meant by reorder quantity. (1 mark)

INVENTORY CONTROL

Some organisations still use a inventory record card system, but it's now more common for organisations to use a computerised system to manage their inventory, using bar codes.

This allows deliveries to be recorded as **received inventory** and any transactions recorded as **reorder inventory**.

 **VIDEO LINK**

Watch the video clip at www.brightredbooks.net which demonstrates how technology allows 30000 different products to be stored under one roof at a Tesco.com store.

INVENTORY STORAGE – WAREHOUSING

Many organisations hold their inventory in one large central warehouse – this is called centralised inventory. Other organisations simply do not have the space, so their inventory is held in lots of different areas. This is called decentralised inventory. Here are the advantages and disadvantages of each.

	Centralised inventory	Decentralised inventory
Advantages	• The handling and management of inventory is considerably improved, because it is stored in one location, and is easier to control. • Once inventory has been delivered and checked over, it is moved to the centralised inventory area and monitored by staff there. They keep a clear note of the type and level of inventory, so the likelihood of theft or loss is lessened. • There is a clear procedure in place for the allocation and control of inventory. Staff working in the centralised inventory area will only issue the inventory when they are presented with a signed, authorised inventory request. • It is often more economical to hold a central stock of resources (such as printer paper and toner cartridges) for use within the organisation as a whole rather than for each individual department.	• Each department has its own inventory area, so staff from different departments don't have to go to the centralised inventory area, which could be in another part of the building. It allows staff to be more productive. • Having several areas where each has a small amount of inventory means that inventory is being used and replenished more frequently, which means that there is less chance of it deteriorating. • Any inventory reorders will reflect what is actually being sold, which is useful information for the business.
Disadvantages	• It can be expensive to retain and train staff who specialise in monitoring and controlling the inventory. • Having a large enough area or warehouse to store inventory is expensive, and there are other running costs such as heating, lighting, refrigeration, security and insurance.	• There is less control and supervision of inventory, therefore theft is common. • Decentralised inventory takes up more space within lots of different areas within the building.

 **ACTIVITY:**

Answer the following questions in sentences.

1 Explain two reasons why organisations should ensure that they don't hold too much inventory. (2 marks)

2 State one reason why organisations should not hold too little inventory. (1 mark)

3 Describe what is meant by 'lead time'. (1 mark)

4 Discuss the benefits of both centralised and decentralised inventory control. (2 marks)

 ONLINE

Read how McDonald's manages its inventory at www.brightredbooks.net

DON'T FORGET

Inventory must be kept at an optimum level – not too high and not too low.

THINGS TO DO AND THINK ABOUT

Specimen exam-style questions

Now that you are confident with this topic, try answering the following specimen exam-style questions in sentences.

1 Outline the key factors in selecting an appropriate supplier of raw materials for an organisation such as a restaurant. (5 marks)

2 For any organisation, describe the problems of:
   • understocking
   • overstocking. (6 marks)

3 Discuss the factors that must be taken into account when setting a inventory reorder level. (4 marks)

4 Discuss the advantages and disadvantages of a centralised inventory control system. (6 marks)

ONLINE TEST

Test yourself on this topic at www.brightredbooks.net

LEAN PRODUCTION TECHNIQUES

Lean production is an approach to production that first originated in Japan. The main aim of lean production is to ensure that the amount of resources used in production is minimised and kept 'lean' so it is more efficient. Waste is reduced and quality is maximised. Lean producers use less factory space, raw materials, stocks, labour and time. The reduction in these factors results in a more productive and cost-effective organisation. There are a range of different lean production practices, including:

- avoiding overproduction
- eliminating waiting times
- avoiding errors
- avoiding inefficient processes
- avoiding unnecessary movements
- lowering inventory levels
- reducing transport.

VIDEO LINK

Watch the video clip at www.brightredbooks.net to see Kaizen in practice.

KAIZEN (CONTINUOUS IMPROVEMENT)

Kaizen is one of the most important concepts of Japanese lean production. It means continuous improvement. The Japanese apply it to their home life, social life and, of course, business life.

KAIZEN

Customer orientation
Total quality control/Six sigma
Robotics
Quality circles
Suggestion system
Automation
Discipline in the workplace
Total Productive Maintenance (TPM)

Kanban
Quality improvement
Just-in-Time (JIT)
Zero defects
Small-group activities
Cooperative labour-management relations
Productivity improvements
New-product development

It is a method that focuses on teams and promotes team spirit as well as celebrating individual contribution. It continuously works towards eliminating waste and improving work techniques.

Kaizen is said to be an 'umbrella concept' that encompasses a range of different working techniques which are necessary for lean production to be achieved.

JUST IN TIME (JIT)

VIDEO LINK

Watch the video clip at www.brightredbooks.net to see how JIT works from a supplier's point of view.

Just in Time (JIT) is an operations approach that aims to cut down on the level of inventory or work-in-progress (WIP) stocks held and the costs associated with them – for example, storage, insurance and security. The JIT method of inventory control has been successfully adopted by mass manufacturers such as Toyota and Dell.

Organisations hold small amounts of inventory and rely instead on their suppliers to deliver components when they are required. The orders of materials are delivered 'just in time', and this ensures continuous production. JIT has several advantages and disadvantages.

Advantages	Cash flow is much improved because money is not tied up in vast amounts of inventory.
	By its very nature, waste and damaged inventory are reduced and cost savings can be made as a result.
	Because less space is required for holding inventory, more space is provided for actual production.
	Any costs involved in holding large amounts of inventory are reduced.
	For JIT to be successful, relationships with suppliers are strong and dependable.
	Organisations can be more flexible and adapt to changes in tastes and fashion.
Disadvantages	Confidence is placed in suppliers delivering when they say they are going to.
	A breakdown in deliveries or in technology can leave the organisation and its reputation in a precarious position.
	The costs involved with ordering – for example, administration and delivery – are increased.
	If the organisation receives large amounts of orders, it can find it difficult to fulfil them.
	Bulk buying discounts cannot be taken advantage of, so it can be an expensive method of ordering.
	It can be time consuming to constantly check each delivery for quality before allowing materials to be used in production.

contd

 **ACTIVITY**

Read the short passage and then answer the following questions in a sentence.

Aldi and JIT

Aldi uses a Just in Time (JIT) method of inventory management by only holding the amount of inventory it requires and no more. Using a JIT system, inventory is only ordered when it is required and delivered just in time for it to be incorporated into the production process.

This ensures that Aldi does not have too much money tied up in inventory, and that it doesn't have to store that inventory before it sells it.

1   Aldi uses JIT as a method of inventory management. Describe what is meant by JIT in your own words.
2   An advantage of using JIT is that there won't be lots of money tied up in inventory. Describe two other advantages of JIT.

ACTIVITY

Read the short passage and then answer the following question in a sentence.

JIT and supply issues

Japan suffered a series of environmental blows in 2011 with an earthquake and subsequent tsunami. Following the aftermath of these disasters, Toyota and Honda had to halt production because suppliers were unable to deliver parts due to the difficult conditions.

This cost the companies millions of dollars a day, and also meant that until their supply chains were rectified, they could not operate at full speed.

1   The passage mentions supplier problems due to environmental factors. Describe two other disadvantages that manufacturers such as Toyota and Honda might face when using JIT as an inventory control measure.

ACTIVITY

You have recently joined a new company which produces electronic components for mobile phones.

Your previous employer was a firm believer in lean management and successfully introduced a Just-in-Time inventory system. Your new line manager has been listening to your experiences with JIT and wants to pitch the idea of adopting it to shareholders.

Write a short report giving a balanced discussion on the use of Just in Time as an inventory control measure.

THINGS TO DO AND THINK ABOUT

Specimen exam-style exam questions

Now that you are confident with this topic, try answering the following in sentences.

1   Explain the advantages of Just-in-Time inventory control.   (5 marks)
2   Explain the disadvantages of 'Just-in-Time' inventory control for an organisation such as Coca-Cola.   (4 marks)

 **DON'T FORGET**

Lean production is largely about eliminating waste and improving quality.

 VIDEO LINK

Watch the video clips at www.brightredbooks.net for a discussion on lean production at Toyota and Atlas Copco.

 VIDEO LINK

For a short explanation on the main principles behind lean management, watch the video clip at www.brightredbooks.net

 ONLINE TEST

How well have you learned this topic? Head to www.brightredbooks.net to take the test.

METHODS OF PRODUCTION 1

Organisations need to have an efficient method of production to meet the demands of their customers.

LABOUR-INTENSIVE OR CAPITAL-INTENSIVE PRODUCTION

Production can be labour intensive or capital intensive.

	Description	Advantages	Disadvantages
Labour intensive	Products are made using labour (human effort). Often the business is smaller and produces smaller quantities of products.	Employees can use their own skills and initiative, which gives them job satisfaction.	Wages are higher because specialised skills are required.
		It is cheaper for the organisation than buying expensive machinery.	It is costly to recruit and train employees.
		Products can be tailored to suit customer requirements.	If a member of staff is absent, production might have to wait until they return.
			Accuracy and quality can vary because human beings and not machines are doing the work.
Capital intensive	Products are made using technology (machines and equipment). The initial set-up of this type of production is very expensive.	A large volume of identical products can be made in this way at a more economical cost.	Individual requirements can't be met.
		Machinery can work 24/7 so production can keep going 24/7.	Breakdowns can be very costly, and idle time can be an additional financial drain.
		Quality and accuracy will be standardised as it is programmed into the machinery.	Employees manning the machines can find their job monotonous and this can lead to lack of motivation.
Automation	Machinery has completely replaced the need for labour.	Production time is quicker and can be repeated constantly with no errors.	There is no flexibility as the machinery can only do what it is programmed to do
		Accuracy is far greater because there is no human error.	More machinery to complete production means more pollution and, in some cases, environmentally unfriendly fumes.
		There is no requirement for workers to man the machinery, so this saves money.	It causes unemployment to increase, which has an economic impact on a country.
		The work environment is safer as employees will not be in automated work areas while production takes place.	Machinery breakdowns are expensive.
Mechanisation	Production requires a mix of both machinery and labour to operate it.	Standardisation can be pre-programmed, allowing production to be consistent.	The initial set-up costs are high.
		Machinery improves the accuracy of work and completes difficult tasks for the worker.	Machinery could break down and idle time is a negative factor.
		Using labour allows for production issues to be flagged up quickly.	Machinery needs to be updated and upgraded every so often, which can be expensive.
		Labour can be trained in becoming expert at operating machinery.	Labour needs to be trained, which is an expense. They will probably also require training whenever machinery is upgraded.

contd

The best method of production for an organisation can depend on various factors such as:
- the actual product being produced
- the quantity of the product to be produced
- the methods of checking quality
- the size of the market in which the organisation exists
- the actual size of the organisation
- the finance the organisation has available and
- the technology available to the organisation.

Organisations need to consider all of these before deciding on a method of production.

There are three main methods of production: job, batch and flow.

JOB PRODUCTION

Job production is when a product is completed from start to finish by a single worker or a team of workers. Typically, one job is completed before moving onto another. This process is very **labour intensive**.

Examples of job production are custom-made jewellery, designer wedding cakes, bespoke tailors or a larger project such as building a house.

Advantages	Disadvantages
The items being produced can be personalised to suit each individual customer's requirements and often include one-off products.	Labour costs are high as workers are highly specialised and production is time consuming and labour intensive.
Customers can still make changes to the design during the production process.	Specialist tools could be required. This involves expensive equipment which might need replaced more often.
Workers are highly skilled and it can be highly satisfying for them to work on a product from start to finish.	As the products are custom ordered, bulk buying of raw materials cannot take place so the benefit of economies of scale won't be possible.
Quality can be carefully checked on a regular basis to ensure it is of a high-enough standard.	The entire process can take a lot of time, especially if specifications change during the process.
Managing the production process is much simpler.	The finished product is expensive.
Due to the degree of skill and time spent, higher prices can be charged.	

THINGS TO DO AND THINK ABOUT

Head to www.brightredbooks.net and watch the following two video clips:

In the first clip, automated systems have been implemented in a German restaurant. Consequently, there is now no need for waiting staff.

The second clip shows a Chinese restaurant that goes one step further and eliminates the need for a chef.

Having watched both clips, do you think automation is a good thing for a country's economy?

VIDEO LINK

Watch the video clips at www.brightredbooks.net to see the ways in which these types of production are being used.

DON'T FORGET

Often factories will use a combination of these types of production because there is still the need for labour (for example, machine operators).

VIDEO LINK

Watch the time-lapse video clip at www.brightredbooks.net showing the construction of a house from start to finish.

ONLINE TEST

Take the test on this topic at www.brightredbooks.net

METHODS OF PRODUCTION 2

BATCH PRODUCTION

This method of production is typically used when a group of similar or identical products has to be produced at the same time. Once that batch has been produced, another identical batch is produced, and so on. All the products in that batch move through the production process together.

This process could be described as having a **mechanised** nature.

Cakes and bread, wallpaper and clothes are examples of batch production.

Advantages	Disadvantages
Because groups of similar products can be made at the same time, they have a standard appearance and quality.	Workers often have to wait in between batches – for example, while machinery is being cleaned and prepared for a new batch. These delays cost the organisation money.
Organisations can take advantage of bulk-buying cost savings, and can therefore enjoy economies of scale.	Motivation and job satisfaction are lower due to the repetitiveness of the job. One impact of this can be seen in higher labour turnover.
Staff members become more expert as time goes on and the level of productivity increases.	If a fault is found in a product, then the entire batch must be recalled and either scrapped or recycled where possible.
There is the possibility to change the specifications of the batches for customers, but the entire batch will be altered, and not just a single unit.	The machinery required can be expensive.
As the same machinery is used for each batch, savings can be made.	Holding large stocks of raw materials can be expensive to store and insure.
Highly specialised workers are not required, so savings can be made in wages.	If only small batches are produced, the running costs of making them are high.

FLOW PRODUCTION

Flow production is used in mass manufacturing where an item goes from stage to stage on an assembly production line, with parts being added to it at each stage. Once it has reached the final stage, the product should be fully assembled. This process is heavily **automated** and is **capital intensive**.

Common examples of flow production can be seen in the production of bottled goods like Coca-Cola, on a car assembly line or on electronics production lines.

Advantages	Disadvantages
This method allows large quantities of products to be produced to a standardised formula.	Technology might have to be updated to keep up with competitors, which can be expensive.
Machinery can reduce the cost of labour and human error.	The initial cost of the machinery and any subsequent breakdowns is expensive.
The use of automation allows constant production 24/7.	No personalisation is possible in flow production.
Raw materials can be bought in bulk, so economies of scale can be an advantage.	Job satisfaction is low because employees have routine, low-skilled duties.
Quality can be checked as the item moves along the assembly line, so the assembly line can be halted and any faults can be rectified as soon as they are identified.	

 **ACTIVITY:**

Read the short passage and then answer the following questions in sentences.

China – the New Car Giant?

Great Wall Motor Company Ltd is China's largest SUV and pickup manufacturer. China is upping their game when it comes to competing within the world's car

contd

industry. Increasingly, in car showrooms near you could be a range of Chinese-branded cars from Great Wall Motors such as the Great Wall Steed S, Great Wall Coolbear and the H6 SUV.

These cars are likely to be cheaper versions of the cars offered by the market leaders such as Toyota and Ford. However, in recent times with the global economy suffering a downturn, potential customers might possibly be more attracted to a lower-priced Chinese car.

1 Which method of production will the Great Wall Motor Company use for producing their cars?

2 Explain any disadvantages that the Great Wall Motor Company could experience by using this method.

DON'T FORGET

All types of production can be supported through the use of different types of technology such as CAM and CAD equipment (Computer Aided Manufacture) and (Computer Aided Design).

VIDEO LINK

Watch the video clip at www.brightredbooks.net to see how cars are produced on the assembly line at a Japanese Nissan factory.

EFFICIENCY OF METHOD OF PRODUCTION

Organisations must ensure that they are producing in the most organised way that they can. They can check this by conducting work studies.

A work study will try to find the most efficient method of using labour, equipment and materials. There are two approaches to work studies: the **method study** and **work measurement**.

METHOD STUDY

This enables an organisation to gather information about the ways in which tasks are currently completed so that it can determine future improvements.

The procedure for a method study is as follows:

Select the task to be examined

Record the way it is currently completed

Examine the facts that have been gathered

Develop an improved method of completing this task

Install it as the new standardised practice

Maintain the new and improved method, checking it regularly

Human factors and **ergonomics** should also be considered when conducting a method study, because workstations need to be carefully organised to enable the worker to perform to the best of their abilities. Workers who are expected to work in a poorly ventilated, cramped space will clearly not be able to work at their optimum level.

WORK MEASUREMENT

This measures how long the tasks should actually take, so that standard times can be determined. This measurement is then compared to the time it takes employees to complete the tasks, so that the fastest and most efficient method can be established.

Work study

Method study	Work measurement
to improve work method	to evaluate human effectiveness

Resulting in more effective use of the resources	Improve planning and control

Productivity improvement

 THINGS TO DO AND THINK ABOUT

Specimen exam-style questions

Now that you are confident with this topic, try answering the following specimen exam-style questions in sentences.

1 Compare job production with flow production. (4 marks)

2 Describe the main features of batch production. (3 marks)

3 Explain the advantages and disadvantages of using job production. (6 marks)

ONLINE TEST

Take the test on this topic at www.brightredbooks.net

QUALITY

Quality is important to organisations. Customers today have a wealth of products and services to choose from, and quality is often a key factor when they come to make a purchasing decision.

QUALITY FOR CUSTOMERS

From the point of view of the customer, good quality can mean lots of different things. Customers will probably consider:

- the actual **physical appearance** of the product in comparison with others – if it looks more appealing and feels sturdier than a rival product, customers will probably think it's better quality
- the product's **durability** and **reliability** – depending on its usage, a washing machine is expected to last at least five years, so one which breaks down irreparably before then would be thought to be of poor quality
- the **after-sales service** – if problems arise with a product, customers will expect there to be a professional response to a complaint, and for the problem to be resolved in an acceptable manner
- the **company's reputation** – if an organisation is well known and trusted for its quality products, customers will probably prefer it to a lesser-known company that sells cheaper products
- **value for money** – customers want to feel that they are getting a quality product or service for their hard-earned money.

Some customers look for a symbol of quality on an item, so that they know it has passed a certain standard.

QUALITY STANDARDS

Many industries have their own set of quality standards and guidelines that they must adhere to when producing products and services. These cover areas such as health and safety and trading standards, and help organisations to measure their quality. Seeing a product or service stamped with a recognised quality standard allows customers to see that the items are as described, and are of a certain quality.

Here are some of the more common quality standards:

VIDEO LINK

Watch the video clip at www.brightredbooks. net for a discussion about trading standards and the importance of how the public can be misled or endangered by faulty products and services.

British Standards Institution (BSI) and the International equivalent (ISO)		BSI awards their logo (a 'kitemark') to certain products and services. This indicates that they have met a specified quality specification.
BS5750/ISO 9000	QUALITY ASSURANCE OBSERVE BS 5750 QUALITY ASSURANCE PROCEDURES	This is a British Standard for quality systems and its International Standards Organisation equivalent is ISO 9000. All products must satisfy these standards or else they are deemed not fit for purpose.
CE Mark	CE	This is shown in electrical products and signifies that EU safety legislation has been adhered to.
Royal Warrant		A product that is endorsed by Royal Appointment quite literally has a royal seal of approval for its quality.
Company or trade branding	British Lion eggs	The British Lion mark on eggs indicates that the eggs have been produced to the highest standards of food safety. Other foods such as meat are stamped with a quality assurance sticker.
Investors in People	INVESTORS IN PEOPLE	This is a framework used in organisations to help improve their performance and effectively manage and develop their staff.

contd

 **ACTIVITY:**

Read the short passage and then answer the following questions in sentences.

Maintaining quality through standards

The British Standards Institution (BSI) is the UK's national body in charge of creating standards. It also plays an important role in global standards.

Having strong standards of quality in place allows an organisation to have a competitive edge over rivals as well as to maintain a name for producing reputable products and services. Having standards in place gives everyone in the organisation a common goal to work towards.

BSI provides certification to products and services in the form of a 'kitemark' symbol.

The kitemark acts as a quality assurance and proves that the product or service has met exacting standards and been tested satisfactorily for safety and performance. The symbol has come to be trusted by the general public as a guarantee of quality and safety. We expect to see it on many different items that we take for granted on a daily basis.

A quality product or service is one that meets the requirements of the customer. There are a number of ways in which an organisation can generate quality products and services.

Market research: Organisations must conduct market research to find out what customers want in a product or service. If feedback indicates that customers feel a particular product is lacking in quality, then organisations need to take this on board and rectify it.

Best practice: BSI works with industry specialists to create these standards, and organisations work towards these industry-best practices.

Quality management: All staff within the organisation have a responsibility for quality systems and should ensure that they check for any defective items.

1 Suggest two things that customers might look for in a quality product or service.

2 Explain why it is important for a motorcycle helmet to have the BSI kitemark on it.

 ONLINE

For a more in-depth look at quality standards, visit the BSI website linked from www.brightredbooks.net

QUALITY FOR ORGANISATIONS

An organisation's products and services **must** be of a high quality. Good-quality inputs (from raw materials to staff) are essential. A poor-quality item simply will not sell.

Quality is important to organisations because:

- It gives them a **good reputation** for quality brands, and customers will be loyal and continue to buy.
- For some it is a **legal requirement** – for example, where legislation has been passed regarding specific requirements for labelling of foodstuffs.
- **Retailers will be happy** to stock a good quality product and will want to continue to do so.
- It allows them to **remain competitive**.
- A better-quality product can be **priced higher** than products that are perceived to be lower quality.
- A better-quality product should be **more durable** so **fewer returns** should be made, which means reduced costs.

- A quality product should mean **few customer complaints** and a good reputation, whereas substandard goods could result in lots of complaints, with the organisation's reputation being brought into disrepute.
- Using suppliers who deliver consistent good-quality materials should help **reduce waste** and reassure organisations that their products will remain of consistently high quality.
- They need to ensure they have a **workable quality system** in place, because if it fails, it will need to be reworked at a huge expense.

 DON'T FORGET

We discussed the methods of physical distribution in a previous section. Go to the Marketing chapter to refresh your memory!

 THINGS TO DO AND THINK ABOUT

Using the internet, research the quality standards that organisations in the following industries strive towards:
- Travel
- Food and Drink

Prepare a short PowerPoint presentation detailing these standards and what they mean for the industries.

ENSURING QUALITY

There are many different measures that organisations use to ensure that they manage the quality of their products or services.

ONLINE

Learn about payment systems and find a great activity at www.brightredbooks.net

VIDEO LINK

Watch the video clip at www.brightredbooks.net which shows how quality assurance is used at Toyota.

VIDEO LINK

Watch the video clip of quality circles in use at Honda at www.brightredbooks.net

ONLINE

W. Edwards Deming is known as the American creative thinker behind quality and continuous improvement who had a huge influence on Japanese industrial quality development. He is often referred to as the 'quality guru'.

As part of his legacy, he introduced the 14 key principles for management to follow when seeking to improve the quality and efficiency of an organisation. Read about Deming and his principles at www.brightredbooks.net

QUALITY CONTROL

This is when the product's quality is **inspected** and **checked at the end of the production process.** Quality inspectors test each product or a sample from a particular batch. These inspectors are specially trained to detect a faulty product before it reaches a customer. This method will inevitably have some wastage because any products that do not meet the necessary standard will either have to be scrapped or recycled.

QUALITY ASSURANCE

This is when the product's quality is **checked at various points in the production process.** All staff have responsibility for checking that the products meet the agreed standard of quality. This method tries to **prevent** any defects from occurring in the product as early as possible and to keep any waste low. Any products that do not conform to the standard will either be scrapped or recycled if possible.

QUALITY MANAGEMENT (QM)

This is when the **entire organisation** has a responsibility for the management and preservation of quality.

This procedure has some important principles which need to feature in any QM policy:

- The commitment to **setting and sticking to quality standards** should be part of that organisation's culture.
- **Continuous improvement** (Kaizen) is important and employees are encouraged to constantly suggest ways to improve or give feedback.
- **Team working** (Quality Circles) is important, customer satisfaction is key.
- The aim is to 'get the product right first time' with zero defects **through constant checking at ALL stages of assembly.**
- **Regular and ongoing staff training** is held to ensure that staff are highly skilled and more efficient.
- There is a clearly defined **quality policy** that all staff are made aware of. All work processes are scrutinised.

The goal of this is to end the production process with a faultless product that can be sold to customers with the knowledge that it is the 'perfect product'.

QUALITY CIRCLES

Quality circles are groups of workers who come together at regular intervals to discuss how to resolve any problems and suggest where improvements could be made within the production process. Employees from different levels of the organisation's hierarchy are involved voluntarily, and it allows them to feel more motivated and empowered as they have been a part of this important process. Employees experience a feeling of **job enrichment** as they are encouraged to use their skills, abilities, knowledge and experience in their jobs.

Advantages	Disadvantages
Team work is encouraged and encourages all workers to feel equal.	When employees are meeting in their quality circles, they are not producing, which costs the organisation money.
Employees feel more positive and valued in the workplace.	A steering committee needs to be set up to oversee the entire programme and team leaders need to be appointed, all of which requires training.

contd

Advantages	Disadvantages
It allows employees to learn new skills and could give them the opportunity to advance their career.	Everyone must show commitment to the quality circle or it will not succeed.
It harmonises the workplace.	Organisations need to account for the fact that time is often needed for successful resolutions to be achieved.

BENCHMARKING

This involves comparing one organisation to other, similar organisations to research the 'best practice'. Often the organisations being compared to will be market leaders and this best practice benchmark is upheld as the standard to equal or, if possible, to exceed.

VIDEO LINK

Watch the video clip at www.brightredbooks.net to see how McDonald's takes its quality measures seriously.

Advantages	Disadvantages
Studying how competitors produce their products or services can identify how savings can be made. This can then be adopted by the organisation.	It's not always easy to gather information about other organisations' procedures because these can be closely guarded. The process can therefore take time.
Studying competitors can identify opportunities for other functions to be improved – for example, marketing and promotions.	Benchmarking can reveal the standards that organisations should strive for, but it doesn't give the full story behind how they reached those standards themselves.
This could be used as a method of motivating workers' performance and showing them ways of making their jobs easier.	Organisations need to ensure that they don't become complacent once they feel they have met the standard.
It can help monitor change more easily in the organisation.	What is best for one organisation might not be suitable for another, due to internal constraints.

MYSTERY SHOPPER

This involves employing someone (for example, in a retail outlet or restaurant) who will pose as a customer and report back to customer service about their experience of the product or service.

The mystery shopper can assess quality in a number of ways – for example, by visiting the establishment, monitoring a transaction when purchasing an item, completing an online survey, sending a letter with a 'customer' request or reporting the level of customer satisfaction they experienced as a result of a telephone query.

DON'T FORGET

Quality is important in all aspects of the organisation's operations, whether in the raw materials used, the way staff are selected or in the methods used to train staff.

Advantages	Disadvantages
It should give an impartial account of the quality of the experience through fresh eyes.	For this method to be ethical, organisations must inform their staff that mystery shoppers will be used from time to time.
It should help rejuvenate and motivate jaded workers and instil the practice that every customer has to be treated equally well.	Some staff might feel threatened by this method, and might not view it as an opportunity to learn and grow.
Procedures could be improved following feedback on performance.	It can be an expensive measure.

THINGS TO DO AND THINK ABOUT

Specimen exam-style questions

Now that you are confident with this topic, try answering the following specimen exam-style questions in sentences.

1 Describe the benefits of a quality standard to both an organisation and its customers. (2 marks)

2 Outline the benefits of using quality circles for:
   • the organisation   • the employee. (4 marks)

3 Discuss the importance of quality inputs in the operations process of an organisation. (3 marks)

4 Describe quality management systems that could be used within an organisation. (6 marks)

DON'T FORGET

The Operations Department will review their processes and systems with a view to continual improvement.

ONLINE TEST

How well have you learned about quality? Take the test at www.brightredbooks.net

ETHICAL FACTORS

Ethical factors can impact heavily on the way that organisations operate.

ONLINE

For further information on how Primark trades ethically click on the link at www.brightredbooks.net

VIDEO LINK

Watch the video clip at www.brightredbooks.net on ethical trade and businesses.

ETHICAL TRADE

Ethics are **moral values** or **beliefs** that influence how an individual or society behaves. The Ethical Trading Initiative (ETI) is a leading alliance of companies, trade unions and NGOs that promotes respect for workers' rights around the globe. Its vision is a world where all workers are free from exploitation and discrimination, and enjoy conditions of freedom, security and equity.

Ethical Trading Initiative
Respect for workers worldwide

Primark is part of the Ethical Trading Initiative. It has lots of different ethical partners such as The Carbon Trust and Self-Employed Women's Association (SEWA).

 **ACTIVITY:**

Research organisations such as Primark that are involved in the Ethical Trading Initiative. Choose two of these organisations and create a short PowerPoint presentation detailing the ways in which they are involved.

UNETHICAL TRADING

Unfortunately, some organisations are guilty of back-pedalling when it comes to promising to be socially responsible and environmentally aware. For example, they use landfill and dump their waste rather than recycle, or increase their packaging rather than minimise it.

 **ACTIVITY:**

Read the short passage and then answer the following questions in a sentence.

Otona and Ethical Decisions

Otona is one car-manufacturing organisation who made a huge unethical decision in 2008 when they appeared to ignore concerns over safety which were raised over their vehicles in the USA.

Instead of instantly recalling the vehicles as one would expect for an organisation where the safety of their customer is of utmost importance, Otona apparently delayed their investigations into the issue.

Otona were ordered to appear before Congress and explain themselves, but Otona didn't seem to grasp the severity of the situation despite there having been some deaths as a result of the fault in the vehicle.

Their global managing director stated at the time 'we can win back the customer's confidence, we're doing a better job'.

Fast track to 2014 and it was reported in the news that Otona told some of its American dealers to stop selling its cars due to a seat heater malfunction. It was reported the 'firm wanted to address the issue quickly to avoid a big recall later on'.

VIDEO LINK

Watch the video clip at www.brightredbooks.net which illustrates unethical trading and living conditions for a factory owner and a worker in India.

1 Describe reasons why you think Otona may have delayed investigations into the safety issue of 2010.

2 Explain why you think Otona responded in such a different way four years later.

FAIRTRADE

Fairtrade is a global movement that works to ensure better prices, decent working conditions and improved terms of trade for farmers and workers in developing countries. It is half owned by the producers who also participate in setting and agreeing Fairtrade standards. Fairtrade promotes sustainable livelihoods by providing producers with access to credit and long-term trading relationships.

The FAIRTRADE Mark is a certification label for products sourced from producers in developing countries. Products that carry the FAIRTRADE Mark must meet economic, social and environmental standards set by Fairtrade International. When a consumer chooses to buy a product with the FAIRTRADE Mark they are supporting farmers and workers to improve their lives and their communities.

Benefits of Fairtrade activities	Costs of Fairtrade activities
Payment of the Fairtrade Minimum Price protects producers from low and volatile market prices.	Fairtrade benefits specific farmers and their businesses and communities, but does not change the structural trade practices that work against them.
Fairtrade Standards protect workers' and farmers' rights, ensure decent working conditions and prohibit child labour.	Fairtrade works with farmers in relatively developed countries rather than with the poorest producers.
Fairtrade Premium is an additional payment for the producers to invest in education and healthcare, farm improvements to increase yield and quality, or processing facilities to increase income.	There are concerns that Fairtrade has resulted in a disproportionate production of certain items such as coffee, which has resulted in a decrease in the price of coffee.
Fairtrade Standards promote sustainable agricultural practices and protection of the environment.	There are concerns that some producers can find it difficult to raise the fees to become Fairtrade certified.

 **ACTIVITY**

Research the subject of Fairtrade. Write a short, objective and balanced report describing different Fairtrade activities that organisations in the UK are involved in. Include your views on Fairtrade.

 THINGS TO DO AND THINK ABOUT

Answer the following questions in sentences.

1 Describe what is meant by ethical trade. (1 mark)

2 Describe the key features of Fairtrade. (2 marks)

3 Describe two benefits of Fairtrade. (2 marks)

4 Describe two costs of Fairtrade. (2 marks)

 DON'T FORGET

Fairtrade coffee was one of the first products to carry the FAIRTRADE Mark.

 **VIDEO LINK**

Watch the video clips at www.brightredbooks.net for a balanced picture of Fairtrade.

 VIDEO LINK

The video clip at www.brightredbooks.net is a documentary about Fairtrade coffee and gives an insight into the life of the farmers who produce it.

 ONLINE TEST

Take the test on ethical factors at www.brightredbooks.net

ENVIRONMENTAL FACTORS

Environmental factors can also impact heavily on the way that organisations operate.

ENVIRONMENTAL RESPONSIBILITY

Organisations have a legal responsibility to be aware of the negative impact their business operations have on the environment.

Some negative impacts include:
- **air pollution** caused by exporting goods all over the world
- **water pollution** caused by not disposing of waste materials safely
- **contaminating land** caused by excessive waste packaging being dumped
- **traffic congestion** caused by delivering goods 24/7
- **noise pollution** caused by the manufacturing process in factories
- **natural habitat destruction** caused by building more and more factories and not taking preventative measures for protecting flora and fauna.

VIDEO LINK

Watch the video clips at www.brightredbooks.net for information about how the UK aims to keep recycling.

WASTE MANAGEMENT

According to a *Science Direct* article, waste management can be defined as 'the generation, prevention, monitoring, treatment, handling, reuse and residual disposition of solid wastes' – that is, how businesses deal with waste materials.

These solid wastes can include household wastes, sewage sludge, agricultural waste and commercial wastes. There are a few methods of waste disposal that an organisation can use. These are outlined below.

	Features	Advantages	Disadvantages
Landfill	With this method, waste material is disposed of either by burying it (**landfill**) or dumping it on the ground (**landraising**). Landfill sites can be either hazardous, non-hazardous or inert.	Most waste is inert. This means that it won't react with other rubbish or the environment. It is therefore safe enough to be disposed of using landfill. Examples include soil, brick rubble and non-recyclable household rubbish.	When biodegradable waste begins to decompose, it produces bacteria which can then produce toxic liquid. This type of liquid is known as leachate and must be collected and disposed of safely to prevent contamination of nearby streams or water sources.
		It is a safe way for households to dispose of any waste that they cannot recycle.	Noxious fumes are also produced and contain explosive gases. Some landfill sites burn them off.
		Some landfill sites have landfill gas extraction systems in place to extract any landfill gases. This gas can then be used to generate electricity.	Landfill sites need to be properly managed and designed. They generally cannot be situated close to households or areas of natural water.
Incineration	Solid, liquid or gaseous waste is disposed of by incineration, or burning. Hazardous medical waste is often disposed of this way.	For some countries like Japan, space is limited and so incineration is common. This allows them to convert waste into heat, gas, steam and ash.	Incinerators can be very expensive to build and run and require large amounts of waste to be economically viable.
		Incinerators can be operated in any weather and, compared to a landfill site, tend to have less of an odour issue.	Vermin might be attracted to the waste in an incinerator, much like landfill sites.
Recycling	This is the collection and reuse of waste materials, which can then be processed into new products. Items can be taken to a recycling centre or collected from the kerbside by refuse collectors.	Many recyclable items are clearly marked so it is easy to identify them. This helps to keep the amount of waste being landfilled or incinerated to a minimum.	It can be difficult to separate recyclable and non-recyclable materials for household kerbside collection.
		Many councils have successfully introduced recycling collections alongside their refuse services and households.	Some materials such as incandescent light bulbs, nappies or batteries can be recycled, but due to the materials they are made of, they need to be handled with care and can usually only be recycled at specialist sites and at considerable cost.

SUSTAINABILITY

Organisations try to manage their waste more efficiently. Just as the ISO 9000 is an international standard for quality, ISO 14000 is a set of standards that relate to environmental management.

There are a number of ways in which organisations can attempt to manage waste more sustainably by recycling or by practising 'resource recovery' or waste minimisation.

	Features	Advantages	Disadvantages
Biological reprocessing	In this case, recyclable organic materials such as food scraps and paper are composted, allowing the residual matter to be recycled as mulch for agriculture.	Waste gases can be extracted and utilised as energy and heat.	It requires households to be careful when recycling household waste.
Energy recovery	This converts non- recyclable waste materials into energy – mainly electricity – via incineration.	The emissions from incinerators is very limited, due to specific built-in devices that neutralise toxins.	Some people argue that the constant use of energy recovery incinerators will demotivate people to recycle.
Reuse	This involves reusing an item that was intended to be disposed of more than once.	Items have an extended life and fewer new items therefore need to be manufactured, so raw materials and energy are saved.	Not all waste can be reused. Items that can be reused many times include glass bottles, wooden pallets and toner cartridges.

 **ACTIVITY:**

Business in the Community (BITC) have created a Corporate Responsibility (CR) Index that examines how organisations are sticking to responsible business practices.

Read the report at www.brightredbooks.net. Choose one of the top ten scorers and conduct some research into their ethical and environmental processes.

Create a short presentation explaining how they practise sustainable business.

RENEWABLE ENERGY

There are many sources of renewable energy and businesses should try to make use of these in order to reduce emissions and environmental damage as well as reducing business costs. Two of these sources include:

- **Solar** – using a solar collector, such as a solar panel, sunlight can be collected and converted into energy.
- **Wind** –wind turbines can pump water or generate electricity to produce significant amounts of energy for factories.

Long-term benefits of investing in these renewable energy sources include:

- The possibility of endless energy.
- Reduced running costs which frees up finance to be invested in other business areas.
- Surplus energy generated can be sold for additional income.
- Shows the business is taking social responsibility seriously.
- Creates a positive reputation for the business.
- Gains a competitive advantage over rivals.

 VIDEO LINK

Watch the video clip at www.BrightredBooks.net on how plastic bottles are recycled into new clothing.

 DON'T FORGET

Organisations which practise effective waste management can benefit from a reduction in their overall running costs.

 ONLINE

For further reading on recycling and sustainability, head to www.brightredbooks.net

 ONLINE TEST

Take the test on environmental factors at www.brightredbooks.net

THINGS TO DO AND THINK ABOUT

1. Name three negative impacts that business operations can have on the environment. (3 marks)
2. Describe two disadvantages of using landfill sites for waste disposal. (2 marks)
3. Describe one advantage and one disadvantage of recycling waste. (2 marks)
4. Explain why reuse is an effective method of achieving sustainability. (1 mark)

TECHNOLOGICAL FACTORS

Technology has seen many dynamic changes over the years, from the dawn of the industrial revolution in the eighteenth century to the digital revolution of the twentieth century and the knowledge age of the twenty-first century. To stay competitive and ensure that they identify, anticipate and satisfy consumers' needs, organisations need to be constantly evolving through **invention** and **innovation**. Technology can help make this happen.

DON'T FORGET

Turn back to the 'Marketing' chapter to refresh your memory about how technology can be used in the marketing department.

Technology can also be used very effectively within the operations department.

VIDEO LINK

Watch the video clip at www.brightredbooks.net to see how technology has had a massive impact on a small bakery.

ELECTRONIC POINT OF SALE (EPOS) AND BARCODES

This is more commonly known as an 'electronic checkout'. The EPOS system is controlled by computer and allows a receipt to be given to the customers, with all the details of the transaction listed. This acts as proof of purchase.

The EPOS system scans the barcodes on the products, which then looks up the price of the item and deducts the item from the total inventory balance.

This means that at the end of the trading day, the business has an up-to-date list of all items sold. This also allows for automated inventory control as the system can be set to automatically re-order items if it reaches a particular level. It also acts as a deterrent to theft by staff.

HAND-HELD SCANNERS

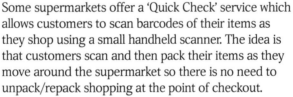

Some supermarkets offer a 'Quick Check' service which allows customers to scan barcodes of their items as they shop using a small handheld scanner. The idea is that customers scan and then pack their items as they move around the supermarket so there is no need to unpack/repack shopping at the point of checkout.

This is much more convenient as it saves time for the customer and money for the organisation, as they do not need to provide as many checkout assistants. Customers simply pay and go! Inventory levels within the business are also automatically updated when customers scan products.

DATABASES

These can be used to record supplier details or items of inventory. Databases can consist of thousands of records that can then be easily searched and sorted to enable the user to locate particular items. Databases can also create reports that can be used to list top-selling items – useful for sales departmental meetings.

COMPUTER-AIDED DESIGN (CAD)

This system is used to design an item before it is manufactured. This used to be done by hand in a technical drawing.

contd

Advantages	Disadvantages
The accuracy of the drawing has increased significantly, and human error – for example, in drawing measurements – have been reduced.	The initial expense of purchasing the necessary equipment and software is high.
Ideas can be saved, modified, printed and shared, which saves time and allows clients to see a 3D visual concept of their design. It's also easier at this stage to see where changes need to be made, therefore saving valuable time.	Staff must be trained in how to use the software and hardware
It reduces space as hard copies of drawings no longer need to be stored.	Less people are now required to create CAD drawings so it can have an impact on unemployment.
Standard layouts or templates can be created and saved as a time-saver.	

COMPUTER-AIDED MANUFACTURE (CAM)

This system uses machinery that is controlled by computers.

Advantages	Disadvantages
It produces consistent results.	The expense of the machinery is high.
It can produce highly accurate results.	It can take time to programme the machinery with the operating code.
It can run efficiently 24/7.	Staff need to be trained in how to use the system.
Difficult shapes can be created because CAM is so precise.	

ROBOTICS

This is when production is completely automatic and conducted by *machinery/ robotics*. This allows for a consistent approach within production and a standardised product to be created meaning no quality differences. This can be, although an expensive method of production for an organisation, a more efficient method as human error is removed so no mistakes are made. Production can run 24/7 with no need for breaks, unlike human workers who require time off.

 DON'T FORGET

To support routine administrative procedures, all departments will make use of:
- e-mail
- Internet
- Word processing.

THINGS TO DO AND THINK ABOUT

Answer the following questions in sentences.

1   Name one advantage of using CAD.   (1 mark)
2   Name one disadvantage of using CAD.   (1 mark)
3   Name one advantage of using CAM.   (1 mark)
4   Name one disadvantage of using CAM.   (1 mark)
5   Outline two advantages of using robots in the production process.   (2 marks)

VIDEO LINK

Watch the video clips at www.brightredbooks.net for further ways in which innovation and technology invention are having an impact on operations.

TECHNOLOGICAL FACTORS: A CASE STUDY

Read the following case study and then answer the questions that follow.

Self-service checkouts – a help or a hindrance?

The advance of technology is evident wherever you look and technological changes keep industries fresh and innovative.

One particular area of change has been the introduction of automated or 'self-service' checkouts in supermarkets up and down the country. In spaces where supermarkets once had one or two checkouts with checkout assistants, they are now able to fit in perhaps six or more self-service checkouts with one checkout assistant to aid shoppers in the self-service area.

The self-service checkout system is simple enough to operate. Customers scan and then pack their own items into bags. Most systems will use voice commands to guide customers during the process, such as 'scan the next item' and 'put the item in the bagging area'. To prevent fraud or shoplifting, the systems can detect the exact weight of the item once it is placed in the bagging area, and will alert the checkout assistant if this does not match.

Many supermarkets such as Tesco, Waitrose, Asda and Sainsbury's have increased the number of self-service checkouts they now offer, in as many of their stores as they can. Other retailers such as B&Q have also successfully installed self-service checkouts.

Advantages of self-service checkouts

Reduction in wage costs

There is no need to have a checkout assistant standing by each individual self-service checkout. One person can do the job instead. This cuts wages costs and allows savings to be made.

Customers will benefit from these savings through cheaper prices on staple goods, and shareholders will benefit from higher sales and profits by receiving a higher dividend. These savings could be reinvested into the organisation in other ways, or could perhaps create more self-service checkouts!

Customer service

With an average of six self-service tills replacing one or two checkouts, queues go down more quickly, and this improves the service for customers.

Disadvantages of self-service checkouts

Effects on staff

As the self-service checkouts become increasingly popular and prevalent in our shops, fewer and fewer checkout staff are required.

Shops may redeploy their staff in different areas within the store such as shelf-stackers, self-service checkout assistants or other shop-floor positions. However, there will be some checkout operators who will be out of a job and there is no alternative post available for them.

Customer satisfaction

It is becoming clearer through customer polls and surveys that not everyone is in favour of the self-service checkout. Some customers dislike the temperamental nature of the checkout and feel that it is actually quicker for them to go to a manned checkout.

Some customers also feel that this method is more 'clinical', with no social interaction. This can, for some, make their shopping experience less satisfactory. In the UK, our population consists of many elderly people, and for many of them, shopping can be their main social interaction.

Environmental implications

Checkout assistants can control the amount of carrier bags used by offering them in stages. Many customers, however, prefer to use their own shopping bags or recycled carrier bags.

The layout of the original checkout allows lots of packing space at the bottom, which is ideal for bigger transactions. The self-service checkout, however, has less packing space available and so the customer could end up using more plastic carrier bags – which is what many shops are trying to stop. To get around this, some self-service checkouts have an option for customers to use their own bags. But the customer has to hang

contd

around until this has been verified by the assistant, because they cannot progress past this point.

Theft and fraud

The self-service checkouts are set up to detect the weight of bagged and scanned items. However, some items such as greetings cards are very light and virtually undetectable and the assistant is usually required before the transaction can progress. This all leads to frustration for the customer. Theft is an extra cost for shops, and shoplifters use the fact that one assistant is overseeing six checkouts to their advantage.

'Big ticket' items are a major temptation for thieves. In 2007 a customer was arrested after he attempted to buy a plasma screen TV at a self-service checkout after he swapped its bar code with one from a £3.99 DVD.

Conclusion

Most retailers are in agreement that operating self-service checkouts leads to a choice for customers. Market research indicates that customers either like them and use them happily enough, or dislike them and are forced to use them during busy periods. However, what is true is that, as customers become more used to self-service checkouts, they become second nature, and it appears that the trend for self-service checkouts will continue.

But with retailers offering fewer manned checkouts and more self-service checkouts, the question still remains: are customers finding this operating system a help or a hindrance?

 THINGS TO DO AND THINK ABOUT

Answer the following questions in sentences.

1 Self-service checkouts are an operating system that more and more retailers are using.
   Describe the three stages of the operating function.   (3 marks)

2 Retailers such as Tesco and Sainsbury's must carefully consider which suppliers to use.
   Describe what is meant by the 'purchasing mix'.   (6 marks)

3 Self-service checkouts can help with inventory management.
   Suggest why inventory checks are important procedures for an organisation. (2 marks)

4 Suggest the inventory management advantages that self-service checkouts could provide. Discuss the implications for an organisation such as B&Q of holding too much or too little inventory.   (6 marks)

5 Retailers such as Tesco must hold their inventory in an accessible area.
   Distinguish between a centralised and a decentralised inventory system.   (4 marks)

6 Using self-service checkouts requires fewer staff and could be described as 'mechanisation'. Explain what is meant by the terms 'mechanisation' and 'capital intensive'.   (2 marks)

7 Bakery departments in supermarkets often make large amounts of baked goods at once. Explain the features of the method of production that they would probably use to produce these items.   (2 marks)

8 As well as receiving a good customer service, customers are keen to receive the best quality product possible. Explain three factors that customers might look for in a good-quality product.   (3 marks)

9 Describe why customers would feel reassured to see an item on the shelf marked with a quality standard.   (1 mark)

10 Retailers such as B&Q use quality measures in their stores. They also use quality circles as a quality method. Describe an advantage and a disadvantage that B&Q could face when using quality circles within the organisation.   (4 marks)

11 Supermarkets stock different types of products – including some Fairtrade products. Discuss two advantages and disadvantages for producers who get involved in Fairtrade.   (4 marks)

12 Using self-service checkouts can result in more plastic bags being used by customers.
   Describe the negative impacts that this could have on the environment.   (2 marks)

WORKFORCE PLANNING

INTRODUCTION

Human Resource Management (HRM) can be defined as that part of an organisation's activities designed to recruit, train, develop and maintain an effective workforce.

The most valuable resource to any business is its workforce. Without efficient and effective workers strategic aims and objectives cannot be assured.

Just as buildings, machinery and other non-current assets need to be maintained and repaired to ensure that they work properly, time and care must also be taken by an organisation to retain and develop the human resources that it employs.

Human Resource Management is not carried out solely by the HRM department. Line managers, such as heads of departments or team leaders, will also have responsibility for the activities of the workforce that they work closely with on a day-to-day basis. For example, line managers would be expected to be involved in training new staff.

The HRM department in an organisation is likely to fulfil a number of different roles:

Facilitator	It will provide training to other members of staff in the organisation.
Auditor	It will monitor how other departments and employees within these departments are following HR policies and procedures.
Consultancy	It will provide information and guidance on HR matters to departmental heads or team leaders.
Executive	It is seen as the 'expert' in matters relating to Human Resource Management and makes decisions about what should be done in this area.
Service	It will ensure that all managers and staff are kept up to date with changes in HR information, policies and law.

Staff within a Human Resource Management department usually undertake the following activities:
- human resource planning
- drawing up job descriptions and person specifications
- organising interviews and recruiting staff
- training staff and encouraging professional development
- implementing the organisation's performance appraisal system
- ensuring safe working conditions
- promoting positive employee relationships
- handling grievances between staff members
- developing and implementing HRM policies and procedures – for example, equal opportunities.

WORKFORCE PLANNING

Workforce planning is the continual process of forecasting the workforce requirements of the business for future years.

For most business organisations, staffing will change each year for a number of reasons:
- **Retirement** – some employees will have reached the end of their working lives.
- **Promotion** – some employees will have been promoted creating vacancies elsewhere in the organisation.
- **Maternity leave** – some employees leave temporarily to start a family.

DON'T FORGET

Human Resource Management is the responsibility of all managers, irrespective of their job title or functional responsibility.

DON'T FORGET

Use the acronym 'FACES' to remember the role of Human Resource Management.

contd

- **Work-life balance** – some employees may reduce their contractual working hours to seek a better work-life balance.
- **Resignation** – some employees may resign from the organisation as they have found employment with another organisation.
- **To meet increasing demand for new products/services** – as organisations achieve growth or increase their product portfolio, they may need to recruit more staff.

STAFFING FORECASTS

This looks at **how many** employees the business will require in the future, as well as the **type** of employee that will be required, for example graduate trainees, manual workers or supervisors. Forecasting should ensure that the 'right' employee is in the 'right' job to ensure maximum efficiency and effectiveness of the workforce.

Forecasting can be done in a number of ways:

- **Using past data** – if the workforce has grown at 2% per year over the past four years, this trend may well continue.
- **Analysing the expected levels of customer demand and sales** – for example more employees may be required if the number of customer orders is estimated to rise significantly.
- **Estimating the level of labour turnover** – for example, if the number of employees that are expected to leave the business next year is 20, then the business will have to recruit new employees to replace those that are leaving.
- **The views of management** – management are often in the best position to estimate the number of new employees that will be required in their department or division.
- **Conducting a skills analysis of current workforce** – if there are gaps in specialist areas of knowledge which may occur due to retirement, for example, or if skills need to be developed in current staff, the decision to recruit may be taken.
- **Expected changes in working practices** – for example, if a business decides to make greater use of technology and robots to produce its products, then less labour will be required.

It will always be difficult for a business to accurately forecast the number of new employees it requires, because the business world and the internal requirements of the organisation are constantly changing.

THINGS TO DO AND THINK ABOUT

Workforce planning is the process of analysing an organisation's future needs in terms of numbers, skills and locations of staff. It allows the organisation to plan how those needs can be met through recruitment and training. It is vital for a company like Tesco to plan ahead. Because the company is growing, Tesco needs to recruit on a regular basis for both the food and non-food parts of the business.

The workforce planning process at Tesco runs each year from the last week in February. There are quarterly reviews in May, August and November so that Tesco can adjust staffing levels and recruit where necessary. This allows Tesco sufficient time and flexibility to meet its demands for staff and allows the company to meet its strategic objectives – for example, to open new stores and maintain customer service standards.

Tesco seeks to fill many vacancies from within the company. It recognises the importance of motivating its staff to progress their careers with the company. Tesco practises what it calls 'talent planning'. This encourages people to work their way through and up the organisation.

1 Outline why you think workforce planning is an ongoing process throughout the year for Tesco.

2 Describe the factors that HRM at Tesco should take into account when they are planning to fill vacancies from outside the organisation.

3 Outline the main advantage of operating a 'talent planning' policy at Tesco.

DON'T FORGET

Workforce planning allows managers to plan ahead for staffing changes.

DON'T FORGET

Workforce planning can make use of outsourcing and subcontracts to reduce costs.

DON'T FORGET

Workforce planning can avoid overstaffing an organisation.

VIDEO LINK

Head to www.brightredbooks.net to watch some great videos about this.

ONLINE TEST

Want to test your knowledge of this section? Head to www.brightredbooks.net and take the topic test.

RECRUITMENT

THE RECRUITMENT PROCESS

The recruitment and selection process begins when the business realises that there is a vacancy in the organisation which needs to be filled. It is extremely important that it invests time and money on the recruitment process to employ the most suitable employees. The recruitment process can be split into five main stages:

Stage 1 Identify a job vacancy

A job vacancy occurs when:
• an existing employee leaves the organisation
• existing employees are experiencing an overwhelming increase in their workload
• the business expands and more employees are required.

Stage 2 Conduct a job analysis

A job analysis has to be conducted to identify whether a position is needed at all. The job analysis highlights the tasks, duties, skills and responsibilities associated with the vacancy. At this stage, the organisation might actually decide that the position is no longer required. During a recession, for example, organisations will look for ways of making cost savings.

Stage 3 Prepare a job description

If the vacancy is to be filled, a job description is then written. This outlines the job title, the location, tasks and the responsibilities that will be covered by the successful applicant. The job description also includes information on hours of work, rate of pay, holiday entitlement and any fringe benefits such as a company car.

Stage 4 Prepare a person specification

A person specification is written next. This describes the 'ideal' person for the job and lists the qualifications, experience, skills and personal attributes that are desirable or essential for the successful applicant.

Stage 5 Advertise the job vacancy

The HRM department then writes an advertisement for the job and places it in a variety of media (including newspapers, job centres, job agencies, the internet, radio, and internal noticeboards) to attract as many people as possible to apply for the post.

ONLINE

Head to
www.brightredbooks.net
to see an example job
description and an example
person specification.

INTERNAL AND EXTERNAL RECRUITMENT

The job might be advertised within the business (so only open to internal applicants) or advertised through external media (so open to both internal and external applicants). Internal and external recruitment both have their advantages and disadvantages, and these are outlined in the table below:

Internal recruitment	
Advantages	**Disadvantages**
• Shorter training and induction period is necessary. • Internal applicants are known to the organisation and are likely to have demonstrated that they would be competent to do the job. • Employees are motivated and feel valued when given the opportunity for promotion. • Existing employees are familiar with company policies and procedures. • Vacancies can be filled more quickly. • The organisation can save money on advertising, recruiting and selecting employees.	• No 'fresh blood' is introduced to the organisation. • Filling one vacancy from within the organisation simply creates another vacancy elsewhere in the business. • Existing employees might not have the necessary skills or knowledge to carry out the job. • When a vacancy arises, promotion must be earned and employees must compete against each other and against external candidates.

contd

External recruitment	
Advantages	**Disadvantages**
• The organisation has a larger pool of applicants to select from. • Talented employees with new ideas can be introduced to the organisation. • It could prevent resentment and jealousy between rival internal applicants.	• Internal applicants might feel that they are not valued – especially if they do not get the job. • External recruitment can be more expensive to organise. • External applicants are unknown to the organisation and there is the possibility that the wrong person could be selected.

External vacancies are usually advertised in national or local newspapers; specialist magazines and journals; job centres; recruitment agencies; colleges and universities and on the internet.

Selection is the process of **selecting the right person** for the job from the list of applicants. Unsuitable candidates are removed from the process, this is known as **short listing**.

The more methods of selection used, the greater the chance the organisation has of selecting the best candidate for the job.

APPLICATION FORMS AND CVS

An **application form** is created by the organisation and has questions relating to the skills, experience and qualities necessary for a position. It can be more useful than a **curriculum vitae (CV)** which simply lists the skills, employment history and education qualifications of the applicant. A CV is specifically created by the applicant to 'sell themselves'. However, application forms give all applicants the same questions, so they have the same opportunity to sell themselves for the job. It is matched with the Person Specification to decide whether or not the candidate will progress further in the selection process.

INTERVIEWS

VIDEO LINK

Check out the clip on the recruitment process at www.brightredbooks.net

Most interviews have standardised questions in a specific order, are led by trained interviewers, are a certain length of time and have a standardised response evaluation format. If a candidate is invited to attend for an interview, this means they have been placed on a **leet**.

Interviews can take different formats:

- with a single manager (**one-to-one**)
- with a single manager, one after the other (**successive**)
- in front of a number of people (**panel**)
- in a group with other candidates (**group**)
- over the **telephone**.

DON'T FORGET

Filling a vacancy from within the organisation could simply create another vacancy elsewhere.

THINGS TO DO AND THINK ABOUT

The external recruitment process at Marks and Spencer is as follows:

1 Vacancies are advertised on the M&S website.

2 Recruitment of employees is conducted through the website or through the hotline.

3 Application forms are available online.

4 Information relating to specific jobs is also available online and applicants can use the query facility to ask questions about the jobs on offer.

5 A confirmation e-mail is sent to applicants on receipt of application forms.

6 Applications can be tracked and monitored online.

7 The recruitment process takes into consideration applicants with a disability or learning difficulty and assistance is offered via a contact telephone number.

Outline the advantages to both Marks and Spencer and external applicants of this online recruitment process.

ONLINE TEST

Test yourself on this topic online at www.brightredbooks.net

THE SELECTION PROCESS

FINDING THE RIGHT PERSON

Once the job has been advertised, the next step is to filter out the people who are simply **not suitable** for the job by comparing the information in the application form or CV to the essential and desirable skills and qualities outlined in the person specification. It's essential to do this because it would be too expensive and time consuming to put all applicants through the selection process. A short list of potential candidates is then drawn up using a number of selection methods.

TESTING

Applicants undergo one or more selection tests to assess their suitability for the vacant position. The main tests used by Human Resources Departments include:

GENERAL ABILITY TESTS

These measure verbal, mathematical, reading and reasoning skills, which are fundamental to success in many different kinds of jobs, especially where cognitive activities such as reading, computing, analysing or communicating are involved.

SPECIFIC ABILITY TESTS

These measure specific physical and/or mental abilities – such as reaction time, written comprehension and mechanical ability – that are important for certain jobs and occupations.

ATTAINMENT OR PROFICIENCY TESTS

Attainment tests (also known as proficiency tests) are frequently used to measure knowledge or skills that are important to a particular job. These tests are generally:

- **Knowledge tests** which involve specific questions to determine how much the individual already knows about particular job tasks and responsibilities. For example, an applicant for a legal secretary position may be asked to take a test to assess their knowledge of contract law. Knowledge tests tend to have relatively high validity.
- **Work-sample** or **performance tests** which require the individual to actually demonstrate or perform one or more job tasks. These tests generally require a high degree of job-relatedness. For example, an applicant for the post of office-machine repair person could be asked to diagnose the problem with a malfunctioning machine. These tests can be expensive to develop and administer.

PSYCHOMETRIC TESTS

These are used to assess an applicant's personality to find out whether they would be suitable for the job. It's essential that applicants give truthful answers, although they often give answers they think the organisation wants to hear, affecting the validity of these tests.

MEDICAL TESTS

A doctor or nurse carries out a medical examination to assess whether there are any medical conditions that could affect the applicant's ability to undertake the duties associated with the job. Some jobs – for example, police officers, fire fighters and soldiers – are required to meet strict medical conditions.

INTELLIGENCE TESTS

These are sometimes called IQ tests and are designed to assess the mental capability of the applicant. Questions in these types of tests centre on problem-solving and thinking skills, numeracy and literacy. Each applicant is given a score at the end of the tests and this enables a comparison to be made with other applicants.

contd

PHYSICAL FITNESS TESTS

These tests assess candidate's physical fitness to perform the duties associated with a job – for example, as a member of the police or as a firefighter.

ASSESSMENT CENTRES

Many large organisations have their own assessment centres, where candidates can be asked to attend – sometimes for several days. This allows the organisation to observe applicants over a period of time and in a range of different scenarios.

Applicants are usually required to take part in role-play exercises, team-building activities and to create and deliver presentations. They will be observed and monitored closely to assess their communication, team work, social, leadership and problem-solving skills.

Some of the activities candidates are asked to undertake are outlined below.

- **In-basket tests** where the candidates are asked to sort through a manager's 'in-basket' of letters, memos, directives, and reports, all of which describe different problems and scenarios. Candidates are asked to examine them, prioritise them, and respond appropriately with memos, action plans, and problem-solving strategies. Trained assessors evaluate the candidates' responses.
- **Leaderless group discussions** are group exercises in which a group of candidates is asked to respond to various kinds of problems and scenarios, without a designated group leader. Candidates are evaluated on their behaviour in the group discussions. This might include their teamwork skills, their interaction with others, or their leadership skills.
- In **role-play exercises**, candidates are asked to pretend that they already have the job and have to interact with another employee to solve a problem. The other employee is usually a trained assessor. The exercise will involve providing a solution to a problem that the employee presents, or suggesting some course of action for a hypothetical situation. Candidates are evaluated on the behaviour they display, solutions they provide, or advice they give.

Assessors must be appropriately trained. Their skills and experience are essential to the quality of the evaluations they provide.

It can be costly to set up an assessment centre. While large companies often have their own assessment centres, mid-size and smaller firms often send candidates to private consulting firms for evaluation.

ONLINE

For more information on assessment centres and reference checks head to www.brightredbooks.net

DON'T FORGET

Candidates might have to undergo a range of different tests for just one part of the selection process.

ONLINE

There are several different types of interviews such as one-to-one, panel, successive and group interviews – learn more about each of these at www.brightredbooks.net

OFFER OF APPOINTMENT

The organisation now has to decide which candidate should be offered the appointment.

The successful applicant will be formally offered the position (subject to reference checks) and the unsuccessful candidates will be informed – usually in writing. It is normally good practice to offer the unsuccessful candidates feedback on their performance in some or all aspects of the selection process.

 THINGS TO DO AND THINK ABOUT

To become a police officer with Police Scotland, applicants have to undergo a series of tests at an assessment centre. Follow the link 'How to become a police officer' at www.brightredbooks.net and make a list of different tests that applicants can expect to undertake during the selection process.

ONLINE TEST

Want to revise your knowledge of this? Head to www.brightredbooks.net and take the topic test.

TRAINING 1

A business organisation needs to offer its employees training and continuous personal development opportunities (CPD) on an ongoing basis. A well-trained workforce with up-to-date skills will help to achieve its strategic aims and objectives.

If a business is seen to be 'investing in people' it will gain a good reputation and attract the best applicants for any vacant positions. Indeed, both the UK and the Scottish governments are encouraging organisations in both the public and private sectors to encourage and support lifelong learning.

DON'T FORGET

Induction training is likely to be the first training a new employee undertakes

TYPES OF TRAINING

INDUCTION TRAINING

New employees usually receive induction training to help them settle into their new job.

This will probably include:
- background details and the history of the business
- introduction to company/departmental policies and procedures
- introduction to colleagues and departmental managers
- tour of the building
- information about health and safety – for example, fire evacuation procedures
- tour of staff facilities – for example, canteen or staff room
- reinforcement of tasks and responsibilities associated with the job.

The main purpose of induction training is to ensure that the new employee settles quickly and comfortably into the organisation.

ON-THE-JOB TRAINING

'On-the-job' training involves the employees receiving their training at the place of work (using such techniques as work shadowing, apprenticeships and mentoring).

The main benefit of on-the-job-training is that it is less expensive than off-the-job training: employees are trained using equipment that they are familiar with and the training programme is tailored specifically to the needs of the organisation.

OFF-THE-JOB-TRAINING

'Off-the job' training involves the employees attending training courses away from their workplace (for example, at local colleges, conference centres and universities). This type of training is usually more expensive and the organisation has to pay temporary staff to cover the employee's duties while they are undertaking their training.

Training has a number of costs and benefits to both the employee and the organisation:

Benefits of training	Costs of training
Employees become more efficient at their job and so output increases.	The cost of training a large workforce can be expensive.
Motivation increases because employees are able to take on more demanding and challenging tasks.	Highly skilled and trained employees are in a better position to request pay increases.
Employee stress is reduced, and this can reduce absenteeism.	Output might be reduced while workers are taking part in training.
Staff are better prepared to embrace change.	Once trained, employees could seek higher-paid employment with another organisation.
The organisation gains a reputation as one that values and invests in its employees.	Temporary staff might have to be recruited to undertake the duties of those employees undertaking training.
Staff are more likely to be flexible and job rotation is therefore more of a possibility.	
Wastage and poor-quality output are reduced.	

TRAINING METHODS 1

DEMONSTRATION

This is sometimes referred to as 'sitting next to Nellie'. An experienced employee demonstrates a task and then the trainee undertakes the task. The more experienced colleague will be on hand to support the trainee. This method is best used when an employee is learning a new skill and when one-to-one training is required.

COACHING

The trainee is taken through a task step-by-step by a trainer who acts as a mentor or coach until the trainee has mastered the task. This method is used when it is likely that the trainee will require ongoing support because the coach will be on hand to offer help or advice when necessary.

JOB ROTATION

The trainee is assigned to different departments or sections of the business for a set period of time and is trained to undertake different jobs in each. This method is best used when there is a highly skilled or talented trainer in each department or section of the business to share their expertise with the trainee.

DISTANCE LEARNING

The trainee receives a pack of resources to work through at their own pace and usually undertakes assessment tasks at regular stages. Completed assessments can be sent to an external assessor to be assessed and these assessments can be accumulated to achieve an external formal qualification. This method is best used when the employee wishes to develop knowledge or skills in an area specific to them and at a pace that will not impact too much on their work–life balance.

ROLE PLAY

A trainee works with experienced colleagues and takes part in role-play exercises to help them develop the knowledge and skills required to cope with particular situations – for example, how to deal with a difficult or unsatisfied customer. This method is best used when an employee is likely to encounter a range of unpredictable situations as part of their job.

PRESENTATIONS

These are used to update or disseminate information from one employee – for example, a senior manager – to a large group of other employees or trainees.

VIRTUAL LEARNING FACILITIES

A **virtual learning environment** (**VLE**), or **learning platform**, is an e-learning education system based on the web where 'virtual' access to classes, class content, tests, homework, grades, assessments and other external resources are available. It also has a social space where students and teacher can interact through threaded discussions or chat.

Virtual learning can take place in 'real time', where teachers conduct live classes in virtual classrooms. Students can communicate through a microphone, chat rights, or by writing on the board. The teacher is able to present lessons through video, PowerPoint or chatting. Students are able to talk to each other and to the teacher. They can also collaborate with each other and answer or pose questions using the application tools to virtually raise their hand, send messages or answer questions on the screen that have been asked by the teacher or student presenter.

 THINGS TO DO AND THINK ABOUT

Consider the types of training listed here and on the next page before attempting the activity on p113.

TRAINING 2

TRAINING METHODS 2

Work-based qualifications

Many business organisations, such as Scottish Power and McDonald's, encourage employees to gain recognised qualifications to support their personal professional development. Scottish Power has its own 'open learning' unit, where employees can undertake short units of study in areas such as spreadsheets, word processing and databases. Employees are awarded an in-house certificate when they complete each course. These can be logged in their continuous professional development record. Work-based qualifications can ensure employees are well prepared for additional responsibilities or promotion.

APPRENTICESHIPS

Apprentices are taken on directly by organisations and they work alongside other employees. They are basically entry-level positions offered to someone who has limited to little qualifications. They are supported by their employer who provides them with a structured training programme to help train them in the relevant skills, abilities and qualifications. They may attend a day or two at college or university to learn any theoretical knowledge behind the practical skills.

TRAINING SCHEMES (CORPORATE)

Sometimes employees do not have the necessary skills or qualifications to fulfil the job role. Some organisations offer their employees the opportunity to participate in training schemes from English and Maths to apprenticeships and foundation degrees. Gaining a qualification through work can make a big difference to an employee's job, life and long-term career.

TRAINING SCHEMES (GRADUATE)

These are aimed at university graduates and may offer a period of on-the-job training over a two-year period (i.e. an internship or studying towards a personal qualification whilst working and being mentored by their employees such as in a law firm). The graduates can gain formal qualifications which are specific to their area of work. Similarly, people employed in accountancy, surveying and management have the opportunity to undertake study and become a registered member of their professional institute as well as gaining invaluable hands-on experience.

GOVERNMENT TRAINING SCHEMES

The government offers a range of training programmes for those employees who are between jobs. They sometimes also offer funding to certain employees to help finance the cost of training, particularly when they have been unemployed for a considerable length of time. The Human Resource Management department should ensure that a business is fully aware of all current government training initiatives and funding available.

STAFF DEVELOPMENT – CONTINUING PROFESSIONAL DEVELOPMENT (CPD)

Some organisations operate a programme of continuing professional development (CPD) to help employees achieve their full potential. Employees are one of the most important resources to an organisation, so investing in continuing professional development for the workforce will reap dividends in terms of employee skills, motivation and loyalty. A programme of continuing professional development offers an organisation four main benefits:

1   The organisation can offer all employees the opportunity to raise their performance to match that of the most experienced and talented employees.

2   The organisation can deliver high-quality goods or services.

3   The workforce will be highly knowledgeable and skilled and so should be more motivated.

4   The organisation will develop a wide pool of talented employees to help it achieve its current and future aims and objectives.

For some organisations it is company policy that all employees keep a formal record of their continuing professional development. They are required to evidence how they have updated their professional knowledge and skills over a one-year period. This is sometimes discussed or referred to during the staff appraisal process.

 **ACTIVITY:**

Read the case study below and then answer the questions that follow.

KFC: Have Fun Working With Your Mates!

At KFC QLD*, all employees receive extensive training, provided through using blended learning techniques (e-learning, on-the-job and formal classroom).

All Team Members receive comprehensive training.

All Shift Supervisors/Managers participate in our KFC Global Training curriculum (40 core competencies). The training is designed and facilitated by accredited professionals (internal and external) to ensure all Shift Supervisors/Managers gain the skills, knowledge and experience to operate our successful restaurants. Our KFC training is matched against National Qualifications Framework (NQF) and recognition of prior learning is available.

In addition, the company provides comprehensive training in the following areas:

- Leadership Development
- Coaching Skills
- Culture
- Interaction Management
- Fire Safety
- First Aid

- Food Safety
- Human Resources, Workplace Health & Safety
- Information Systems
- Financial & Operations Accounting
and much more...

Training continues throughout everyone's career with the Company to ensure employees are well qualified to seek promotion and fill vacancies within the organisation. So, for a career path that will meet your learning needs at every level, you are more than welcome to apply to join the KFC QLD organisation.

* KFC QLD restaurants in Queensland, Australia are owned and operated by Franchisee, Collins Restaurants Queensland   Pty   Ltd.

1   State the three main types of training used by KFC QLD.   (3 marks)

2   Outline the main advantages to both employees and KFC QLD of offering on going training to all staff.   (2 marks)

3   Explain why you think KFC QLD has linked their training courses to the National Qualification Framework.   (2 marks)

4   The case study suggests that KFC QLD seeks to fill vacancies internally. Outline two advantages and two disadvantages of internal recruitment.   (4 marks)

 **THINGS TO DO AND THINK ABOUT**

Specimen exam-style questions

Now that you are confident with this topic, try answering the following specimen exam-style questions in sentences.

1   Explain why the workforce is the most valuable resource to an organisation. (2 marks)

2   Describe some activities that may be undertaken by staff working in a Human Resource Management department.   (4 marks)

3   Describe reasons why staffing may change each year in a large organisation. (4 marks)

4   Describe two advantages and two disadvantages of **internal** recruitment.   (4 marks)

5   Describe any 3 types of testing that can be used in the selection process.   (3 marks)

6   Describe some of the activities that may be used to assess candidates at assessment centres.   (3 marks)

 **DON'T FORGET**

Most reputable organisations have an ongoing CPD programme in place

MOTIVATION

MOTIVATING STAFF

The Human Resources Department needs to understand what motivates the workforce, because a highly motivated workforce benefits business organisations through:

1   increased productivity
2   better quality output with less waste
3   reduced absenteeism
4   reduced labour turnover
5   improved time-keeping
6   fewer formal grievances.

A number of theories have been put forward to help businesses understand how employees are motivated at work. Two of these are outlined below.

MASLOW'S HIERARCHY OF NEEDS

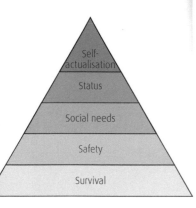

Abraham Maslow argued that most people want to work for more than simply money. He developed his hierarchy of needs theory based on his research about what motivates people to work. Maslow suggests that individuals have five levels of need and it is these that influence their behaviour.

- **Basic needs:** for food, drink, clothes and shelter.
- **Safety needs:** protection against danger, threat and hardship.
- **Social needs:** the need for belonging, acceptance, friendship and team membership.
- **Status or self-esteem needs:** reputation, recognition, achievement and status.
- **Self-actualisation:** the need to realise your own potential for continual self-development, and to be all you can be.

According to Maslow, the things at the top of the hierarchy are more important than those at the bottom. However, an individual will only strive to satisfy these higher level needs when the lower-level needs have been satisfied first. For example, a person who is hungry and cold will seek food and shelter first. Once they have been well fed and have secured accommodation, they will turn their attention to higher needs such as securing friendships and group/team membership.

HOW CAN A BUSINESS USE MASLOW'S HIERARCHY OF NEEDS TO MOTIVATE EMPLOYEES?

- **Basic needs:** a fair wage, a work canteen and staff room.
- **Safety needs:** job security, safe working conditions, pension schemes.
- **Social needs:** team work and perhaps providing social facilities like a gym or by organising nights out.
- **Self-esteem needs:** rewarding staff with status symbols like job titles, company cars, private offices, personal assistants and opportunities to gain professional qualifications.
- **Self-actualisation:** providing opportunities for employees to use their own initiative and assume leadership roles. They should also ensure that promotion structures are in place.

MCGREGOR'S THEORY X AND THEORY Y

Theory X assumes that workers	Theory Y assumes that workers
Are lazy and don't want to work. Can't be trusted. Have no initiative or ambition. Must be supervised all the time and forced to work. Work purely for cash.	Enjoy working. Want responsibility and opportunities to lead. Can be trusted to work on their own initiative. Will work hard for both financial and non-financial rewards.

Douglas McGregor describes two different assumptions that employers (managers) have about employees. He refers to these two assumptions as Theory X and Theory Y.

Theory X is about controlling and directing the workforce, whereas Theory Y is about trusting and empowering the workforce to do their job with little or no supervision.

contd

To some extent McGregor's theory appears to support the work of Maslow. Theory Y assumes that workers want to be involved in the decision-making process, develop professionally and work in an environment that is exciting and challenging where they can achieve their true potential. McGregor therefore argues that if employers (managers) adopt theory Y, employees will be naturally motivated, work harder and the organisations aims and objectives are more likely to be achieved.

HERTZBERG'S THEORY OF MOTIVATION

From his research, Hertzberg suggested that there were two sets of factors that organisations should consider when trying to motivate employees – hygiene factors and motivational factors.

HYGIENE FACTORS

Hygiene factors do not necessarily motivate employees. However, if these hygiene factors are not in place then this could cause **dissatisfaction** at work. Hygiene factors include company policy and administration, wages, salaries and other financial remuneration, quality of supervision, quality of inter-personal relations, working conditions and feelings of job security.

MOTIVATIONAL FACTORS

Motivational factors are based on an individual's need for personal growth, achievement and recognition. When motivational factors exist they can actively create job satisfaction. If they are effective, then they can motivate an individual to achieve above-average performance and effort. Motivational factors include status, opportunity for advancement, gaining recognition, responsibility, challenging/stimulating work and a sense of personal achievement and growth in a job.

FINANCIAL METHODS OF MOTIVATING EMPLOYEES

Time-rate payments	The employee receives a basic rate of pay per time period that they work (£6 per hour, £75 per day, £600 per week). As the pay is not related to output or productivity, the employee feels valued for the work they have achieved.
Piece-rate payments	The employee receives an amount of money per unit that they produce. Payment is therefore directly linked to the employee's productivity level. There is a possibility with this method that to boost their earnings, the employee will work faster and there will be a reduction in the quality of goods produced.
Commission	The employee receives a very small percentage – for example, 0.5% – of the value of the goods they manage to sell in a given period of time. This method is often used for sales personnel in life insurance, double-glazing and telesales.
Performance-related pay	This is a method of awarding an employee who has improved their performance or achieved a number of targets over a given time period – usually one year. It's common with managerial and professional workers such as bankers.
Profit sharing	Each employee receives a share of the profit earned by the business each year, with the aim of increasing employee effort, motivation and productivity. However, if the business makes low profits (or even a loss) then it will probably have a detrimental effect. Tesco uses profit sharing to motivate its employees.
Share ownership	The employee receives a part of each month's salary in the form of shares, usually at a discounted price. This provides employees with a lucrative savings plan because they can sell their shares after an agreed period of time. The aim is to motivate employees to work harder because if they do, the company will become more profitable, the share price will rise and the price of shares will therefore increase. Scottish Power and Bank of Scotland use 'share options' in this way.
Overtime payments	An employee can be offered these payments to work additional hours above those specified in their contract of employment. The payments are often at 'time and a half' or 'double time' – for example, £15.00 per hour instead of £7.50 per hour. The higher rate of pay aims to encourage workers to work longer hours and increase output.
Remuneration packages	Here, an employee is rewarded with fringe benefits or 'perks' over and above their formal salary. For example, some organisations offer employees private health schemes, pension schemes, subsidised meals, discounts on holidays and travel, cheap mortgages and loans, company cars, gym membership and discounts when buying the company's products.

THINGS TO DO AND THINK ABOUT

Some organisations such as Marks and Spencer, Bank of Scotland and Scottish Power offer very attractive remuneration packages to recruit, retain and motivate employees. Write a short report explaining why financial rewards on their own might not be sufficient to motivate all employees. Refer to the theories of motivation in your report.

MOTIVATION AND LEADERSHIP STYLES

RESERVED
FOR
EMPLOYEE
OF THE
MONTH

DON'T FORGET

Motivating some employees requires more than financial rewards.

NON-FINANCIAL METHODS OF MOTIVATING EMPLOYEES

Delegation	This occurs when a manager passes a degree of responsibility and authority for an area of their work down the hierarchy to a subordinate. The employee is motivated simply by the fact that their potential has been recognised.
Job enrichment	This involves giving a subordinate a degree of power over their own work – for example, the subordinate decides for themselves the best way to solve problems and how to tackle their assigned duties.
Job enlargement	This involves increasing the number of tasks associated with a job to challenge, motivate and multi-skill the employee.
Job rotation	This involves the employee performing a number of different tasks to make their job more varied and enjoyable. It also makes them more motivated. Marks and Spencer offer employees the opportunity to work in different departments within their stores for these reasons.
Quality circles	This is a group of workers who meet at regular intervals with their line manager to identify work-related problems, consider solutions to these problems and then recommend the one that they believe will be the most successful.
Teamworking	This involves grouping a number of employees together to complete a task. Usually, each member brings specialists skills or knowledge to the group. Because group members are dependent on each other to complete the task, individual members are motivated to contribute their part.
Worker participation	This is when workers are asked to participate in the decision-making process by contributing their ideas and suggestions.
Works councils	These councils consist of regular discussions between managers and representatives about how the business can improve the processes and procedures that relate to production of goods or services, training employees or quality control.
Worker directors	These are workforce representatives who participate in the meetings held by the board of directors. Worker directors are used in the USA and Japan but are not very common in the UK, because employers here often believe that they can slow down the decision-making process and 'leak' confidential information to employees.

LEADERSHIP STYLES

One of the fundamental roles of a manager or leader is to motivate subordinates through their own leadership. There are three main leadership styles: autocratic, democratic and laissez-faire. Each of these leadership styles has its own advantages and disadvantages.

AUTOCRATIC

Autocratic leaders lead with an 'iron fist' and will tell each employee what and how to do it. Feedback is not encouraged or used. Leaders that use this style distribute tasks the way they see fit without allowing others to make any suggestions. Employees can feel controlled and this could lead to a high rate of employee turnover.

This style of leadership limits creativity and independent thinking. It is not effective when employees want to work independently. It can, however, result in higher quality products and be very efficient when deadlines are tight.

DEMOCRATIC

Democratic leadership is consultative. The leader respects others' opinions and expects feedback. This style of leadership allows for new ideas or feedback to be suggested and considered and encourages independence and quality of thought. It is, however, less productive – a lot of time can be taken up with discussion.

contd

A democratic way of leading encourages workers to feel that they own part of the business, which will reduce employee turnover and increase employee satisfaction. It allows for greater creativity, motivation and engagement in a task and benefits both the worker and the leader. It's an effective style of leadership for meetings, because it encourages open discussion where suggestions can be made and problems can be aired.

LAISSEZ-FAIRE

Laissez-faire is a style of leadership in which a manager gives a task to an individual employee or group of employees and leaves them to decide the rest. There is no structure or strategy given, and as a result, employees often lose direction, creativity and drive. It is the least productive of the three styles.

However, it does improve the thinking skills of employees who are motivated to do the job, because they have to figure out how to complete the given task without any help. This style of leadership works best if done by professionals or experienced people, because they already know what to do and how to solve the problem.

VIDEO LINK

For more information on leadership styles watch the video at www.brightredbooks.net

ORGANISATIONAL FACTORS IMPACTING ON LEADERSHIP STYLES

Sometimes the type of leadership in the organisation may be affected by the following:

- The actual task to be performed – a more complicated task requires more direction (autocratic) whereas a task which requires innovative thinking or creativity would benefit from more employee participation (laissez-faire).
- The time available – less time to work on a project requires strict deadlines and less time for discussion, so a more autocratic style would be best.
- The skills and abilities of the workforce – highly skilled and experienced staff require less direction and supervision, so a democratic approach may work best.
- The personality of the leader – some leaders naturally lean more towards certain styles of leadership as a result of their character or temperament. Some people are too laid back to be autocratic.
- The corporate culture – a more chilled and open working environment encourages a laissez-faire approach.

ONLINE

For a great case study on this, head to www.brightredbooks.net

 THINGS TO DO AND THINK ABOUT

Specimen exam-style questions

Now that you are confident with this topic, try answering the following specimen exam-style questions in sentences.

1 Describe any two types of interview that can be used as part of the selection process. (2 marks)

2 Explain what is meant by induction training. (1 mark)

3 Describe some of the activities that are likely to be included in an induction training programme. (3 marks)

4 Describe the main costs and benefits to an organisation of providing ongoing training for employees. (8 marks)

5 Describe what is meant by a virtual learning environment. (2 marks)

6 Describe the significance of Maslow's and McGregor's theories of motivation to organisations looking for ways to motivate their employees. (6 marks)

7 Describe any four financial and any four non-financial methods of motivating employees. (8 marks)

8 Explain the difference between an autocratic and a democratic leadership style. (4 marks)

ONLINE TEST

Test yourself on motivation and leadership styles online at www.brightredbooks.net

APPRAISALS AND FLEXIBLE WORKING PRACTIC

STAFF APPRAISALS

The appraisal process allows the employee to reflect on how well they are performing:
- What areas of the job are going well?
- What areas of the job could be improved upon?
- What areas of the job are not going so well?
- What actions or support is required for performance to improve?

It is usually carried out at regular intervals (normally once per year) by the employee's line manager. The process can be as simple as an informal chat. Alternatively, it could require the completion of an appraisal form by both the employee and the line manager, which is then followed up with a formal interview/meeting.

PERFORMANCE AND DEVELOPMENT REVIEWS

In some organisations 'staff appraisal' is often called 'performance and development review'. The purposes of this review are generally to:
- assess performance over the year and identify areas of current performance that could be improved upon
- evaluate the impact of training that has been undertaken and to identify new training needs
- set performance targets that relate the employee's development targets to departmental objectives
- discuss and support career progression
- discuss the potential for promotion and/ or a pay review to motivate employees.

The performance and development review process should:
- clarify the role and expectations of the employee in their current role
- involve a discussion of actual performance during the review period and outline areas for future personal development
- ensure formal documentation is completed for use in deciding on matters such as employee rewards, promotion and future development requirements
- ensure that the member of staff is continuously made aware that their individual performance (related to expectations) is the purpose of the review
- not be an occasion for the member of staff to be confronted with how well he/she has performed or not performed or to discover that the 'goal posts' have moved without being told during the review period.

A performance and development review takes place between the employee and whoever he/she is responsible and accountable to – generally their direct line manager. Each manager has to give the appropriate time and attention to each member of staff as an 'individual' for the process to be of value.

Even when an organisation has a formal policy for giving systematic, job-related feedback on performance, many appraisal meetings between a manager and a subordinate result in frustrating and problematic experiences for both. Despite this, many organisations claim that participants say they obtain considerable benefits from the formal appraisal process.

ONLINE

Learn more about the types of staff appraisal schemes at www.brightredbooks.net

DON'T FORGET

An appraisal system is a two-way communication process between line manager and subordinate.

Advantages of appraisal	Disadvantages of appraisal
Staff who are performing well in their job and are perhaps suitable for promotion can be identified.	If the appraisal meeting is not positive the employee can become demotivated.
It's an opportunity for an employee to receive feedback on current performance from their line manager.	When a manager is responsible for many employees, the appraisal system can be time consuming and costly.
A positive appraisal meeting can increase motivation.	It might be the case that too many development needs are identified, which is stressful for the employee.
Development needs can be identified and addressed.	When development needs have been identified, the organisation should fulfil these – and this could be very costly.
Employee performance and future development needs can be linked to departmental or overall business objectives.	If an appraisal isn't conducted properly, some employees could perceive it to be threatening or feel that they are being 'checked up' on.

contd

ACTIVITY:

Working with a partner, conduct a simple appraisal meeting to evaluate how well you are performing in your role as a student. One of you should assume the role of appraiser and the other the role of appraisee. Some of the areas that should be discussed during the appraisal meeting are:

- What areas of your studies are going well?
- What areas of your studies could you improve upon?
- What areas of your studies are proving to be problematic?
- What action could the school or subject department take to help you overcome your difficulties?
- Are your current grades comparing well to your targeted or predicted grades?

Switch roles and then repeat the process again.

VIDEO LINK

Watch the clip at www.brightredbooks.net to see an appraisal interview.

TYPES OF APPRAISAL SCHEMES

There are a number of appraisal schemes in use:

- **One-to-one** – this appraisal involves the employee and their line manager having a face-to-face discussion usually on an annual basis. It is often a formal procedure with paperwork to be completed by both and can be linked to a review of pay/bonus.

- **360-degree or 360°** – most often, 360-degree feedback will include direct feedback from an employee's subordinates, peers (colleagues), and supervisor(s), as well as a self-evaluation. It can also include, in some cases, feedback from external sources, such as customers and suppliers or other interested stakeholders. This gives it a more rounded (i.e. 360°) evaluation as many people are contributing.

- **Peer-to-peer** – this is less formal as, rather than by a line manager, the review will be carried out by a colleague in a similar or identical position. This can be useful as employees may relax more and react better to constructive criticism given by a colleague than a manager.

- **Competency/behaviour appraisal** – a competency is an attribute, knowledge, skill, ability or other characteristic that contributes to successful job performance. Behavioural competencies are observable and measurable behaviours, knowledge, skills, abilities, and other characteristics that contribute to individual success in the organisation. This approach to appraisal seeks to identify and measure the competencies that are contributing to an employee's successful job performance.

- **Results based (against agreed targets)** – this approach to appraisal evaluates achievements against agreed, clearly stated targets (which were decided in advance between an employee and their line manager). This appraisal will draw on a range of evidence to determine if these targets were achieved and if not, what can be done to support the employee to achieve future targets.

ONLINE

Learn more about these flexible working practices at www.brightredbooks.net

DON'T FORGET

Flexible working practices can be used to retain highly valued employees.

THINGS TO DO AND THINK ABOUT

1 Describe two appraisal schemes that are commonly used to assess workplace performance. (4 marks)

2 Describe and explain the purpose of the following when recruiting new staff:
- Job description
- Person specification
- Reference (6 marks)

3 Describe a selection process that could be used to ensure that the best applicants are appointed to work in an organisation such as a restaurant. (4 marks)

4 Explain the role of testing in the selection of new staff. (4 marks)

5 Describe the main forms of training that an organisation could use. (4 marks)

6 Describe 'on-the-job' and 'off-the-job' training. (2 marks)

7 Discuss the value of an appraisal system. (3 marks)

8 Discuss methods that an organisation could use to ensure that its staff stay motivated. (4 marks)

DON'T FORGET

Flexible working practices offer employees a better work–life balance, which can ultimately benefit the organisation.

ONLINE TEST

Test yourself on this topic at www.brightredbooks.net

EMPLOYMENT LEGISLATION

AN OVERVIEW

The government has introduced a number of pieces of legislation primarily concerned with protecting the welfare and safety of employees. It is the responsibility of the Human Resources Management department to ensure that all employees (and managers) within the organisation are aware of employment legislation and how this legislation (or breach of it) can impact on the organisation.

Any breach of employment legislation can be very costly in terms of the impact on the organisation's reputation. The main pieces of employment legislation are outlined here.

THE HEALTH AND SAFETY AT WORK ACT 1974

This states the responsibilities of both the employee and the employer in ensuring health and safety in the workplace. The act states that both the employee and the employer have a responsibility to ensure health and safety. Employees must consider the health and safety of other people and not just themselves.

- **Employers' duties:** The employer must take every possible step to ensure that all machinery is properly maintained, all dangerous substances are stored properly, all staff are trained and made aware of potential dangers and that the working environment is safe and non-hazardous to the health of employees. All organisations are required therefore to carry out a risk assessment of the building, machinery and of each task that employees are expected to undertake. Employers should also appoint safety officers and encourage employees to join health and safety committees which will carry out regular inspections of the workplace to identify any potential dangers.

- **Employees' duties:** All employees are expected to behave in a reasonable manner at work and must not behave in such a way which could cause danger to themselves or other employees. They must cooperate with their employers (and immediate line manager) to ensure that all health and safety requirements are met. They must also take part in any health and safety training deemed necessary by the employer.

OFFICES, SHOPS AND RAILWAYS PREMISES ACT 1963

This outlines the minimum basic health and safety requirements that employers must meet. For example, it provides information on the requirements for toilet facilities, cleanliness and workplace temperature.

THE NATIONAL MINIMUM AND LIVING WAGE REGULATIONS (MOST RECENTLY AMENDED 2018)

This sets out the minimum hourly rate that must be paid to employees or apprentices. The rate payable depends on the age of the employee. You must be at least school leaving age to receive the national minimum wage and aged 25 to receive the national living wage.

The current (these rates are reviewed and change every April) national minimum and living wage rates are: 25 and over – £7.83, 21–24 year olds – £7.38 per hour; 18–20 year olds – £5.90 per hour; Under 18 – £4.20 per hour; Apprentices – £3.70 per hour.

Apprentices are entitled to this rate if they are under 19 or age 19 and in their first year of the apprenticeship. If 19 or over or in the second year or beyond of their apprenticeship, they are entitled to the minimum wage rate for their age.

EQUALITY ACT 2010

The Equality Act 2010 encompasses all of the following acts and regulations.

THE EQUAL PAY ACT 1970

This states that pay and working conditions must be equal for employees of the opposite sex who are performing the same job.

THE SEX DISCRIMINATION ACT 1975

This states that it is illegal to discriminate against an employee, or an applicant for a job, on the grounds of their sex or their marital status.

THE RACE RELATIONS ACT 1976

This states that it is illegal for an employer to discriminate against an employee, or an applicant for a job, on the grounds of their race, colour, religion or ethnic origin.

contd

THE DISABILITY DISCRIMINATION ACT 1995

This states that it is illegal for a business with 20 or more employees to discriminate against an employee, or an applicant for a job, on the grounds of their disability. Where necessary, organisations must make reasonable adjustments to the job or business premises to allow those with a disability to access the job and/or workplace.

EMPLOYMENT EQUALITY (SEXUAL ORIENTATION) REGULATIONS 2003

These regulations make it illegal for a business to discriminate against an employee, or an applicant for a job, on the grounds of their sexuality.

> ### ✚ DON'T FORGET
>
> Companies who do not adhere to employment legislation can face penalties and potential loss of reputation.

⚙ ACTIVITY:

Read the short case study below and answer the questions that follow.

Smart-Buy

An incident in which a forklift truck ran over a warehouse worker has landed discount supermarket giant Smart-Buy with more than £98 000 in penalties.

Employee Peter Francis suffered serious leg injuries at Smart-Buy's regional distribution centre in Barrow-in-Furness, Cumbria early in the morning of 26 November 2010.

He was stock checking goods on in-coming pallets when the forklift came through the curtains of a nearby doorway and ran him over.

When environmental health officers from Barrow-in-Furness Borough Council investigated the accident, they found Smart-Buy had failed to provide a safe system of work and its health and safety management system was substandard.

At Barrow-in-Furness Magistrates Court, Judge Harvey fined the retailer £70 000 plus £28 750 costs after it had admitted two breaches of health and safety legislation.

In April 2008, Smart-Buy was fined £40 000 following two separate incidents in which delivery drivers suffered serious injuries using a faulty loading lift at one of its stores. The following November, it was fined £55 000 after a 1-tonne safe fell on a deputy manager at a Birmingham outlet.

1 Name the piece of employment legislation that Smart-Buy has been found guilty of not adhering to sufficiently. (1 mark)

2 Describe any two responsibilities of employees and any 2 responsibilities of employers that are outlined in the legislation in your answer to question one. (4 marks)

3 Describe one likely effect on Smart-Buy's public reputation of high profile accidents like the ones mentioned in the case study. (1 mark)

4 Explain how poor attention to employee's well being might impact on their motivation? (2 marks)

5 Describe three steps you would advise Smart-Buy to take to ensure that they meet the requirements of the legislation named in question one. (1 mark)

💭 THINGS TO DO AND THINK ABOUT

1 Outline the benefits of the appraisal process for an employee. (4 marks)

2 Describe the four main types of appraisal schemes used by most organisations. (4 marks)

3 Describe the four flexible working practices that are potentially available to employees in large organisations. (8 marks)

4 Outline the main benefits of flexible working practices for both the employee and the employer. (8 marks)

5 State any two responsibilities of an employee and any two responsibilities of an employer outlined In the Health and Safety at Work Act 1974. (4 marks)

6 Name and describe any other two pieces of employment legislation. (4 marks)

> **ONLINE**
>
> Head to www.brightredbooks.net for activities, links and tests on employment legislation.

INDUSTRIAL RELATIONS 1

The terms 'labour relations', 'employee relations' and 'industrial relations' refer to the relationship between employers and employees. Employers have historically been in a much stronger position – which led to the growth of organised labour in the form of trade unions. Employers have realised the influence that trade unions can have on an organisation and have responded by establishing their own associations.

DON'T FORGET

Remember that a trade union will negotiate many other issues for its members other than pay rises (including length of the working week, working conditions and proposed redundancies).

ONLINE TEST

Test your knowledge of industrial relations online at www.brightredbooks.net

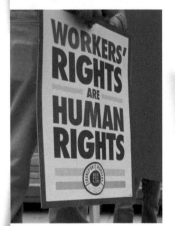

DON'T FORGET

Being a member of a trade union can bring the following benefits to members:
- improved working conditions
- protection against exploitation
- representation with employers
- financial and insurance services
- legal and technical advice
- training and education services
- improvements in pay.

EFFECTS OF POOR EMPLOYEE RELATIONS ON AN ORGANISATION

Poor industrial relations between owners/managers and the employees can have the following serious and negative effects on an organisation.

DEMOTIVATED WORKFORCE

This can lead to:
- decreased productivity
- increased staff turnover
- increased staff absenteeism
- poor quality output
- less cooperative staff
- resistance to the introduction of new policies or procedures.

INCREASED INDUSTRIAL ACTION

This can lead to:
- long-lasting loss of sales if the organisation cannot meet orders due to lost output
- reduced productivity, increase of unit production costs and decrease of profit margins decrease
- poor reputation and loss of customers and investors.

TRADE UNIONS: AN OVERVIEW

A trade union is a group of workers who join together to protect their interests and be more powerful when negotiating with their employers. Each employee who wishes to join a trade union must pay an annual fee. This contributes to the union's costs and expenses and supports workers who take part in industrial action.

Trade unions have four broad aims, which are to:
1 improve the pay of its members
2 improve the working conditions and the working practices of its members
3 support the training and the professional development of its members
4 ensure that their members' interests are considered by the employers when any decision is made which will affect the workforce

EXAMPLES OF HOW AIMS ARE ACHIEVED

Advises, represents and protects members:
- Advises members on procedures following industrial accidents, represents employees at industrial tribunals and gives general financial and legal advice.
- Ensures that members receive sick pay and other benefits to which they are entitled.
- Helps protect against redundancy, unfair dismissal, disciplinary action and discrimination.

Negotiates with employers:
- Improved pay and working conditions.
- Improved pension and retirement arrangements.
- Greater job satisfaction and better job security.

contd

Seeks to influence others:

- As a pressure group influencing employers and governments on legislation and other matters.
- Regarding improved social objectives, such as full employment and better social security.

TYPES OF INDUSTRIAL ACTION

Trade unions can take industrial action to try and influence employers. The main types of industrial action that can be taken are outlined below:

- **Boycott** – refusal to carry out a new duty or use a new piece of equipment.
- **Go slow** – employees deliberately work slower than normal.
- **Sit in** – employees refuse to work and simply sit in the workplace.
- **Strike** – a refusal to enter the workplace.
- **Overtime ban** – a refusal to work any extra time over the normal working hours.
- **Work to rule** – only activities written in the contract of employment will be carried out.

PAY BARGAINING

Many employers recognise the benefits that unions bring, and that they themselves gain from only having to negotiate with a single body representing a large group of employees. Some industries had union membership agreements requiring all employees to join a union but the 1988 Employment Act made it unlawful to dismiss an employee who refuses to join a union. (Employers are now also free to recruit workers who are not union members.) Trade unions are most closely associated with negotiating with the employers of a business on behalf of their members over the issue of pay. This is known as the 'pay-bargaining process' and involves three main stages as outlined below:

Stage 1
The employer outlines the wage increase on offer. The trade union submits their request on behalf of the employees for a pay increase, which they consider fair and necessary, with any conditions clearly outlined.

Stage 2
Both sides present their arguments at a 'pay-talk' discussion. A trade union will put in a 'pay claim', which will be based on one or more of the following points: 1 An increase in the cost of living (that is, inflation). 2 An increase in labour productivity rates (output). 3 To recruit and retain high quality employees. 4 To compensate workers for developing new skills or adapting to new working practices introduced by the employer. 5 To match the pay scales of rival businesses.

Stage 3
Negotiation process between the trade union and the employer where both sides will be required to compromise and be prepared to accept less than their original objectives.

WORKS COUNCILS

These are formal meetings of employer (management) and employees (employee representatives) to consider issues affecting the business and workplace. Works councils have the legal right to access information from management and have joint decision-making powers in many areas relating to employees.

CONSULTATIVE COMMITTEES

Consultation will take account of as well as listen to the views of employees and must therefore take place before any decisions or changes impacting on employees are made within the workplace. Making a pretence of consulting on issues that have already been decided is unproductive and may result in employees feeling mistrust about the process as it is already a 'done deal'.

Consultation does not mean that employees' views always have to be acted on, since there may be good practical or financial reasons for not doing so. However, whenever employees' views are rejected the reasons for doing so should be carefully explained. Equally, where the views and ideas of employees help to improve a decision due credit and recognition should be given.

THINGS TO DO AND THINK ABOUT

Choose one of the trade unions below and use the internet to investigate ways in which it serves its members. Present your findings as a short PowerPoint presentation.

- Educational Institute of Scotland
- Equity
- Fire Brigades Union
- Unsion

INDUSTRIAL RELATIONS 2

FORMAL DISPUTES AND GRIEVANCE PROCEDURES

These can be:

- collective – where issues are taken up on behalf of a group (or branch) of employees by their trade union representative. These are normally referred to as a 'dispute'.
- individual – these involve an individual employee only. These are normally referred to as a 'grievance'.

A dispute has a far greater impact on employee relations than a grievance because it is concerned with disagreements between a whole group of employees and their employer and usually arises due to matters directly affecting the group's terms and conditions of employment.

GRIEVANCES

Grievances are disputes between an individual employee and his/her employer or immediate line manager. To handle this kind of issue, organisations will establish a formal grievance procedure as outlined below. Such grievances are **initiated by employees**.

STAGES OF A TYPICAL GRIEVANCE PROCEDURE

> Employees raise grievances with immediate supervisor/line manager.

> If matter not settled, it is taken to the next level of management, and the employee may be accompanied by a friend or trade union representative.

> If the matter is still not resolved, it is taken to a senior management level, and the employee may take a representative as before.

> If the employee is still not satisfied he/she may appeal to the Managing Director.

Discipline procedures are also classed as individual disputes and are designed to provide fair treatment of 'misconduct' by employees. Discipline procedures are **initiated by management**.

ADVISORY CONCILIATON AND ARBITRATION SERVICE (ACAS)

The Advisory Conciliation and Arbitration Service was set up as an independent body by the government in 1975 to help settle industrial disputes and claims of unfair dismissal by employees. As the name suggests, ACAS offers three main services: advice, conciliation and arbitration.

ADVICE

ACAS representatives can be invited into a business by the two feuding parties (employers and trade unions) to offer their advice to both parties on the industrial unrest and the 'best' way to settle the unrest.

CONCILIATION

Conciliation is an attempt to get the two sides in an industrial dispute to resolve their differences. A conciliator listens to the arguments of both sides, and then tries to encourage the trade union and the employer to negotiate and compromise so that they can reach a solution that is acceptable to both parties.

ARBITRATION

Arbitration is the process of resolving an industrial dispute by using an independent person to decide the appropriate outcome. The arbitrator will look at the arguments put forward by both parties, and then he will arrive at a decision. The decision can be legally binding on both parties if this was agreed prior to the arbitrator's decision.

Pendulum arbitration is a type of arbitration in which the arbitrator will decide completely in favour of one party or the other, with no compromise or negotiation being allowed. It is likely, therefore, that both parties (the employers and the trade union) will make their demands more conservative and realistic than if the arbitrator was allowed to choose an outcome which was somewhere between the two.

EMPLOYERS' ASSOCIATIONS

Businesses in one sector of industry sometimes form an organisation to look after the interests of all businesses in that industry. For example, businesses in the engineering industry can opt to join the Engineering Employers' Association. This gives them the advantage of having a single strong voice with which to influence politicians and to deal with the engineering unions and media interest.

Employers' associations can influence government by campaigning for government grants, reductions in corporation tax and changes to employment law. Smaller businesses in particular benefit from membership of employers' associations because they can often access information and support that they wouldn't be able to finance on their own.

CONFEDERATION OF BRITISH INDUSTRY – CBI

This organisation attempts to represent the employers of all of the United Kingdom's industries. It is much stronger and more powerful than employers' associations as it's able to voice its opinion on any political matters that affect business in the UK. For example, it will have input into matters such as should the UK leave the EU or should the UK adopt the single European currency (Euro).

 DON'T FORGET

Industrial action can be costly for an organisation and can impact on its reputation.

 ONLINE

Visit the link at www.brightredbooks.net to find out more information on the work of ACAS.

✓ **ONLINE TEST**

Test your knowledge of this topic online at www.brightredbooks.net

 THINGS TO DO AND THINK ABOUT

Read the case study below and then answer the questions that follow.

Ardagh Glass

Workers at glass manufacturers Ardagh Glass in Yorkshire and Scotland will be balloted on industrial action, following a 'very inadequate' pay offer from the highly profitable firm.

Unite, the country's largest union, will be balloting its members on strike action and industrial action short of a strike. The ballot opens on Monday 8 July, closing on Monday 29 July.

Ardagh Glass employs about 1300 workers at sites in Barnsley, Doncaster and Knottingley in Yorkshire and at Irvine in Ayrshire. It made £65 million in pre-tax profit last year.

Unite's deputy regional secretary, Tas Sangha, said: 'Our dispute centres on the wage award for 2013. Our claim is for more than the current retail price index rate, which rose to 3.1 per cent in May.

'Our membership also made big sacrifices when the final salary pension scheme was closed and there have been changes to the sick pay scheme which were, again, detrimental to our members.

'Following months of negotiations, the company offered two per cent, way below the increase in the cost of living and this was rejected by 97 per cent of our membership in a consultative ballot.'

Unite's regional officer for the Ayrshire plant, Jim Winter, said: 'It is very disappointing that the management has refused to engage with the conciliation service ACAS and will not meet the trade union side without pre-conditions, which we don't think is conducive to meaningful negotiations.

'We are, therefore, going to a ballot for industrial action on this very inadequate offer, given that this company is highly profitable – profits that our members help generate.'

1 Explain, with the use of examples, what is meant by industrial action. (2 marks)

2 Describe one reason (from the passage) why the Unite union might feel justified in asking for a pay rise above the retail price index. (1 mark)

3 Outline the role of ACAS in settling industrial disputes. (6 marks)

4 Describe what is meant by 'a ballot for industrial action'. (2 marks)

TERMINATION OF CONTRACTS AND HR AND THE USE OF ICT

TERMINATION OF CONTRACTS

The final role of the HRM department is to make the termination of an employee's contract of employment as smooth and efficient as possible. There are a number of different ways in which an employee can have their contract of employment terminated.

REDUNDANCY

Sometimes it's necessary for a business to 'downsize' its workforce and make a proportion of them redundant – for example, during a recession, or a decline in the industry.

This process can be done in several ways:
- voluntary redundancy (where workers opt for a redundancy package)
- compulsory redundancy: 'last-in-first-out' (where the most recent appointments are the first to be made redundant)
- retention by merit (where the least effective employees are made redundant).

RETIREMENT

When an employee reaches the end of their working life, they want to retire and leave the organisation. Most employees will have paid into a works-based pension (during their working life) and so will be eligible for a lump-sum payout and a monthly private pension in addition to their state pension

TRANSFERS AND RESIGNATION

Some employees will leave an organisation to go and work for another organisation, often as a result of promotion.

ABSENTEEISM

Whether or not an employer can lawfully dismiss an employee for unauthorised absence depends on the reason for, and length of, the absence and the procedure that the employer follows. It will be difficult for an employer to argue successfully that its dismissal of an employee for one day's unauthorised absence that was taken for good reason was fair. However, if the unauthorised absence is prolonged, persistent and/or not for a genuine reason, dismissal is more likely to be fair, provided that employer follows a fair procedure.

DOWNSIZING

Downsizing occurs when an organisation permanently reduces its workforce. Corporate downsizing is often the result of poor economic conditions and/or the company's need to cut jobs in order to lower costs or maintain profitability. Down sizing can cause anxiety among a workforce and so it should be done in a sensitive manner following official and legal procedures stated in employment law.

DISMISSAL

When an employee breaks their contract of employment, their services are no longer required by the business and they are dismissed. Dismissal can take place for a number of reasons, including sexual harassment, racial harassment, bad timekeeping, sleeping on the job and compromising the integrity of the business.

However, if an employee feels that they have been unfairly dismissed they can take their case to an industrial tribunal. This is a small court that deals with claims of unfair dismissal and discrimination from employees against their (former) employers. If the employee is successful in claiming that they have been unfairly dismissed, then they are eligible for re-instatement in their previous job, as well as a financial compensation (to cover loss of earnings, and financial hardship and suffering).

HUMAN RESOURCES AND THE USE OF ICT

Like all other functional departments in the organisation, the HRM department will make use of the most up-to-date information communications technology to improve the efficiency of the work that they do. The Human Resource Management department may make use of the following:

- **Databases** – these applications could be used to store employee personal data. Having employee's records stored electronically means data can be retrieved, amended, printed and shared easily.
- **Presentation Software PowerPoint** – this can be used to deliver information to large numbers of staff at any one time. The presentations can include images, videos, sounds/music files. Presentations can be shared easily via e-mail or company intranet.
- **E-diary** – these allow meetings and appointments to be created and shared. Reminders can be set, and appointments cannot be double booked. These are useful for HRM departments when scheduling appointment slots for interviews.
- **Video Conferencing** – this allows for presentations, meetings or interviews to be held with a number of people who may be in different locations.

Computerising the work of a department comes with both costs and benefits.

COSTS

- hardware and software
- installation
- staff training
- loss of working time while training takes place and the cost of employing specialist training staff
- loss of efficiency until staff are familiar with the system
- errors/glitches in the system, causing loss of working time
- possible data loss or corruption and breaching data protection legislation
- possible commercial espionage and information theft through computer hacking
- health and safety implications and possible costs of equipment to prevent eye-strain and backache

BENEFITS

- increased speed of information handling and decision-making
- flexibility of integrated systems
- increased production and administrative efficiency
- enhanced reputation with investors, customers and competitors
- competitive edge – until newer technology is adopted by rivals
- reduction in staffing costs
- facilitates home working

 THINGS TO DO AND THINK ABOUT

Specimen exam-style questions

Now that you are confident with this topic, try answering the following specimen exam style questions in sentences.

1 Describe two forms of industrial action and one effect each action could have on an organisation. (4 marks)

2 Describe the steps that employees could take if they feel they have been unfairly treated in the workplace. (4 marks)

3 Describe three forms of legislation that would affect the running of an organisation. (6 marks)

4 Describe the purpose of:
- The Health and Safety at Work Act 1974
- Equalities Act 2010 (3 marks)

5 Describe the role of each of the following in supporting employees and employers when disputes occur in the workplace:
- Trade Unions
- ACAS (4 marks)

 ONLINE TEST

Test your knowledge of this topic online at www.brightredbooks.net

SOURCES OF FINANCE 1

THE ROLE AND IMPORTANCE OF FINANCIAL MANAGEMENT

The efficient management of finance is key to the success or failure of a business organisation. The finance department has to:

- ensure that there are **adequate funds** available to enable the organisation to achieve its objectives
- ensure **costs are monitored and controlled**
- ensure there is **adequate cash flow** (to cover payments going out)
- maximise and maintain **profit levels**
- generate appropriate **financial information** for managers and decision-makers.

The work of the finance department includes:

- calculation and payment of wages and salaries
- ensuring financial records are kept up to date
- preparation of budgets
- paying trade payables and credit control
- gathering information for the preparation of annual accounts
- analysing accounting information using ratio analysis.

SOURCES OF FINANCE: AN OVERVIEW

A business can access many different sources of finance. The most important source of finance for most businesses is **internal**, in the form of retained profits (retained earnings) – that is, profits that have been ploughed back into the business to generate more profits in the future.

Advantages	Disadvantages
Retained profits do not cost anything as the business is not paying interest on borrowing. Using retained profits is also cheaper than issuing new shares or debentures as it avoids administrative costs.	Re-investing profits may mean less funds available to pay dividends to shareholders.

But a business also needs **external** sources of finance, which can be short term, medium term or long term.

SHORT-TERM SOURCES OF FINANCE

BANK OVERDRAFT

A bank overdraft is a method of short-term borrowing that enables a firm to continue trading over a short period when its need for cash exceeds the money it has available.

An overdraft is an agreement with the bank that the business can draw from its current account up to a certain amount more than it has in the account – the 'overdraft limit'. Interest is charged only on the amount overdrawn, and any cash paid into the account reduces the amount of the overdraft. Many firms have a permanent overdraft facility to tide them over difficult times such as the end of the month, when staff must be paid before income from sales (sales revenue) has been received.

Advantages	Disadvantages
A bank overdraft is simple to arrange. Interest is calculated on a daily rate on the amount overdrawn.	Can be expensive if used for a long time due to interest charges. If the overdraft limit is exceeded the facility may be withdrawn.

DEBT FACTORING

Debt factoring involves the firm selling its debts to a 'factor' for less than its face value. The factor collects the full amount owing from the debtor (trade receivable) and the factor's profit is the difference between the two. This can enable firms to avoid cash flow problems by recouping debts that might otherwise not be repaid by their customers.

Advantages	Disadvantages
The factor chases up the unpaid debt, saving the company time and money.	Factors tend to be interested in only large outstanding debts as they can earn more profit. The business does not receive the full amount of the outstanding debt.

TRADE CREDIT TERMS

Negotiating a longer period between receiving goods from suppliers and having to pay for them (or a shorter period between sending goods to customers and receiving payment from them) can provide a firm with more cash to use in the short term.

Advantages	Disadvantages
When a business can negotiate longer payment terms with suppliers, this can improve their cash flow position.	Discounts for prompt payment are lost. If payment is made outwith the credit period, suppliers could be reluctant to sell the business more goods on credit.

 THINGS TO DO AND THINK ABOUT

Use the internet and visit the websites of the following banks:

- Clydesdale Bank
- Barclays Bank
- Bank of Scotland

In your workbook, note down the features and advantages for a private limited company of arranging a bank overdraft (as a short-term source of finance) with each of the banks above.

 ONLINE

Learn more about debt factoring by following the link at www.brightredbooks.net

 DON'T FORGET

If a firm is not profitable, extensive use of short-term sources of finance will ultimately lead to greater losses.

 ONLINE TEST

Want to test yourself on sources of finance? Head to www.brightredbooks.net

SOURCES OF FINANCE 2

MEDIUM-TERM SOURCES OF FINANCE

BANK LOANS

Bank loans are the most common way to get medium-term funds (usually about 2–4 years). They are often used to purchase machinery or other assets, and will need to be repaid in full by the end of the agreed payment period. Banks normally charge a higher rate of interest on loans than they do on overdrafts, because they regard them as being more risky. Businesses pay back the loan in agreed instalments during the period of the loan.

Advantages	Disadvantages
Repayment is usually made in fixed instalments over a set period, and this makes budgetary control easier.	Newly formed or smaller businesses are usually charged higher rates of interest.

HIRE PURCHASE

Hire purchase is often used to obtain equipment or vehicles. The cost of the item purchased, plus interest, is paid in equal instalments over a set period of time. The item is owned by the hire purchase company until the last instalment is paid.

Advantages	Disadvantages
The cost of purchase is spread over a period of time, making it possible to purchase fairly expensive assets.	High rates of interest can make this an expensive way of financing the purchase of assets.

LEASING

Leasing is another term for renting. A business can rent assets such as equipment or motor vehicles, rather than having to raise the finance to buy these outright.

Advantages	Disadvantages
Leasing means that the equipment can be changed on a regular basis and will therefore be up to date.	Leasing over a long period can be expensive. The equipment is not owned by the business and is therefore not an asset to them.

GOVERNMENT GRANT

A grant is a sum of money given to an organisation that doesn't need to be paid back. Unfortunately, grants are usually only given to new businesses starting up, or to businesses that will create jobs in a deprived area of the economy.

Advantages	Disadvantages
A grant doesn't need to be repaid. It is usually given to the business in one lump sum.	It is usually only given once; it might not involve a large amount of cash; it could be tied to a specific project that the business must undertake.

LONG-TERM SOURCES OF FINANCE

MORTGAGES

This is a long-term method of borrowing used, for example, to buy premises (property). Interest is added to the loan at the beginning, and the whole amount is usually repaid in equal monthly instalments over a period of (usually 25) years. The rate of interest charged will depend on the length of the mortgage and the collateral (security) offered. The longer the loan and the higher the collateral, the lower the interest rate will be. Mortgages are often used by small private limited companies (which cannot issue shares or debentures) to raise large amounts of money.

Advantages	Disadvantages
Repayment is over a long period of time – for example, 25 years. Fixed interest rates can be arranged so that the organisation knows what its monthly payments will be for the foreseeable future.	Mortgages are usually secured against a property – failure to meet monthly repayments will result in the property being repossessed. Usually a 10 per cent deposit on the value of the property is required up front. When interest rates are not fixed, monthly repayments can vary greatly depending on current interest rates.

contd

DEBENTURES

Public limited companies can borrow money by selling debentures, which are long-term 'IOUs'. Debenture holders receive interest annually and the firm must repay the loan at the end of the specified period of time – for example, 15 years.

Advantages	Disadvantages
Large amounts of capital (equity) can be raised. The company only has to pay interest each month/year.	If the business fails to make interest payments or repay the debenture at the end of the repayment term, the debenture holder will be able to seize assets from the business. Debenture interest must be paid, even if the business makes a loss.

CROWDFUNDING

Crowdfunding usually takes place via social media or crowdfunding platforms online. It is a method of raising finance through the collective effort of friends, family, customers and individual investors. This approach to raising finance taps into the collective efforts of a large pool of individuals. With crowdfunding, interested investors can opt to invest anything from a few hundred pounds to many thousands of pounds.

Advantages	Disadvantages
Social media and online crowdfunding platforms mean you have access to thousands of accredited investors to share your fundraising campaign with. Huge amounts of finance can be raised.	You may end up with many investors in the business and so control could be lost. If you don't reach your funding target, any finance that has been pledged will usually be returned to your investors and you will receive nothing.

'SALE AND LEASEBACK'

Here, the business sells assets such as machinery to a finance company and then leases (rents) them back from the company.

Advantages	Disadvantages
Selling the asset generates large amounts of capital (equity) for the business. The business is no longer responsible for repairs and maintenance.	The businesses assets are reduced, which could make it difficult to secure future finance. Paying 'rent' over a long period of time can be more expensive than actually purchasing.

SHARE CAPITAL (EQUITY)

Just as a sole trader or partners can add more of their own money to their business, a company can issue more shares (preference (preferred) or ordinary (equity)) – as long as its **issued** capital (equity) (the value of shares actually sold to shareholders) is less than or equal to its **authorised** capital (equity) (the maximum value of shares the firm could issue according to its Memorandum of Association).

Advantages	Disadvantages
Large amounts of capital (equity) can be raised. Shareholders benefit from limited liability. Finance raised does not have to be paid back in the same way as a loan or debenture.	The administration costs involved in issuing shares can be expensive and usually have to be paid 'up front'. The selling price of shares is subject to demand and the selling price can rise or fall. Public limited companies are only authorised to issue a certain amount of shares.

VENTURE CAPITAL (EQUITY)

Venture capitalists – often referred to as 'business angels' – provide loans to those businesses that a bank or other lender consider to be too risky. In return for lending the money, they usually acquire a share in the business.

Advantages	Disadvantages
Those businesses with a risky credit rating can secure finance from a reputable source. Large amounts of finance can be raised.	Not suitable for short-term financial requirements. Part-ownership of the business could be requested to secure the finance.

THINGS TO DO AND THINK ABOUT

Think about the following key factors that a business will have to consider when sourcing finance:

1 **How much** finance is required?
2 What will the cost of the finance be – that is, how much **interest** will be charged?
3 If the finance has to be repaid, **how long** will the repayment period be?
4 What sources of finance will be most **suitable** to meet the financial needs of the organisation or its planned project?
5 Potential lenders views of the organisation including possible **risk factors**.

CASH BUDGETS

BUDGETARY CONTROL

A budget is a statement of future expectations. It covers a specified time period such as a month, a quarter or a year. It is normally expressed in financial terms but other types of measurement can be used – for example, an overtime budget is expressed in labour hours.

WHY ARE CASH BUDGETS IMPORTANT TO MANAGEMENT?

Plan	Budgets allow management to plan ahead and set aims, targets and strategies on how to achieve them. By identifying where cash is being spent and where it is being earned, management can plan to finance, for example, short-term cash flow problems or long-term expansion.
Organise	A business needs to organise its resources so that they are in the right place, at the right time with the right quantities. Cash budgets give management the information to be able do this effectively.
Command	Each departmental head will have a budget for routine requirements. They must manage their budgets effectively and understand their limits when making one-off requests for additional finance for specific jobs, projects or capital expenditure.
Coordinate	Budgets ensure that everyone in the organisation is working towards the same aims and objectives and that the work of one department fits in with the work of other departments. Budgets from each department will allow management to keep a clear overview of the operation as a whole, with surpluses of cash in one department being used to offset shortfalls of cash in another.
Control	These budgets allow managers to measure, evaluate and compare actual results with planned expenditure and income, giving them a degree of control over the organisation's finance.
Delegate	Management can delegate responsibility for holding, recording and spending departmental budgets or project budgets to the departmental manager or project leader.
Motivate	Delegating budgets in this way leads to increased motivation, because staff feel trusted and empowered.

CASH BUDGETS STATEMENTS OF CASH FLOW

A cash budget is prepared on a regular basis. It is a forecast of receipts and payments of cash. The information contained in a cash budget represents **estimated figures** of the cash position of an organisation over a given period of time, and is used to highlight potential **shortages or surpluses** of cash resources that could occur. It therefore gives management time to put the necessary financial arrangements in place to address these.

Negative cash balances will alert the business to arrange **overdraft facilities** from the bank in plenty of time. Expected surpluses of cash allow the business to arrange **short-term investments** of money.

Expected surpluses can also be used to invest in the purchase of, for example, new equipment or machinery.

Cash budgets are normally set out as shown in this example:

Example: Predicted Cash Budget for Ms Sandra Grant who runs a florist business

Time period	Month 1 April £ (000)	Month 2 May £ (000)	Month 3 June £ (000)
Opening balance (1)	100	105	115
Add income (2)			
Cash sales (Sales revenue)	20	40	30
Receipts for credit sales	35	30	20
Total income	55	70	50
Total funds for the period (3)	155	175	165
Less expenses (4)			
Purchases	14	18	20
Payments of Credit Purchases	2	3	4
Petrol	4	5	8
Administration	5	7	5
Wages	20	22	23
Rent	5	5	5
Total expenses (5)	50	60	65
Closing balance (6)	105	115	100

contd

NOTES ON THE CASH BUDGET

1 Opening balance
This is the money that the business has at the start of the time period.

2 Add income
Both sales revenue and receipts from trade receivables are recorded. Any other cash income can be recorded in this section.

3 Total funds for the period
This is the total amount of cash available to the organisation each month during the budgeted time period.

4 Less expenses
All individual expenses involving the movements of cash are identified, including payments made for credit purchases.

5 Total expenses
This is the estimated total amount that will be spent during the month.

6 Closing balance
This is the total income for the period, minus total expenses for the period. The closing balance for one month becomes the opening balance for the next month.

 **DON'T FORGET**

It is unlikely that you will be asked to prepare a cash budget in your final exam.

 ONLINE

Head to www.brightredbooks.net for more information and activities to enhance your skills in cash budgeting.

Cash budgets can identify where and why there are cash flow problems:

Causes of cash flow problems	Addressing cash flow problems
Tying up too much cash in inventory – often referred to as over stocking.	Invest in an advertising campaign and offer discounts to encourage sales revenue to reduce inventory levels.
Offering too much credit to customers and allowing credit customers too long to pay.	Sell assets that are no longer required by the business to generate income/cash.
Taking on large loans with high rates of interest.	Public limited companies could issue additional shares.
Low levels of sales, which means low sales revenue.	Find cheaper suppliers to reduce outlay on purchases.
Owners taking too much money (drawings) out of the business or companies declaring dividends that are too high.	Reduce drawings or, in the case of companies, reduce dividends.
Purchasing expensive non-current assets that could be leased instead.	Ask trade payables for longer to pay and negotiate for both trade and cash discounts.
Increasing business expenses.	Tight control of business expenses.

CASH BUDGETS AND SPREADSHEETS

Most finance departments use computer software – spreadsheets – to prepare cash budgets more quickly and efficiently. Once formulae have been entered into the spreadsheet, the business can 'experiment' with different figures for income and business expenses to identify their impact on cash flow.

 THINGS TO DO AND THINK ABOUT

Specimen exam-style questions

Now that you are confident with this topic, try answering the following specimen exam-style questions in sentences.

1 Outline some of the routine tasks undertaken by the finance department. **(4 marks)**

2 Explain the difference between **internal** and **external** sources of finance. **(2 marks)**

3 Briefly describe three sources of long-term finance available to a public limited company. **(6 marks)**

4 Outline two reasons why a business should prepare a cash budget. **(2 marks)**

5 Describe some of the reasons why a business can encounter cash flow problems. **(4 marks)**

 DON'T FORGET

Managers can use spreadsheets to identify the impact of income and expenditure on cash flow. This helps with decision making.

 ONLINE TEST

Head to www.brightredbooks.net and test yourself on this topic.

FINANCIAL STATEMENTS 1

Public limited companies are required by law to prepare and publish a set of annual accounts and Scottish private limited companies are required to provide Companies House in Edinburgh with their annual accounts. Financial statements consist of an **Income Statement** and a **Statement of Financial Position**.

These financial statements are useful to stakeholders because they provide a guide to the profitability, liquidity and efficiency of a business.

DON'T FORGET

The following stakeholders – banks, shareholders, lenders, HMRC and investors – have a special interest in the accounts of a business.

INCOME STATEMENT

This is a historical review of the revenue (income) and expenditure of a business for the previous financial year. The account can be divided into two distinct sections:

THE TRADING SECTION

This compares the value of sales to the customer with the value of the sales at cost price (that is, the purchase price paid by the business for the goods from their suppliers). The main activity of any organisation involved in trading is the purchase of goods and the subsequent 'selling on' of those goods to the customer at a higher price. The difference between the **Sales Revenue** and the **Cost of Sales (purchases)** is the **Gross Profit**.

Items that appear in the Trading Section include:
- **Sales Revenue**
- **Purchases** (goods purchased from a supplier, such as cash and carry)
- **Returns inwards** (sales returns – that is, goods returned by customers)
- **Returns outwards** (purchase returns – that is, goods returned to the cash and carry)
- **Carriage inwards** (delivery charges – the cost of bringing inventory into the shop/business)
- **Inventory at the start** (of the trading period)
- **Inventory at the end** (of the trading period)

In fact, the Trading Section of the Income Statement details **any items** that relate to the **sales or the cost involved in making those sales.**

Example:

Lesley McCallum has provided you with the following information relating to Buzzy Bee, a public limited company that makes and sells honey-based products. From the information provided, prepare an **Income Statement for year ended 31 December 20...**

	£
Sales (Sales Revenue)	104 285
Purchases	45 628
Returns Inwards (sales returns)	531
Returns Outwards (purchase returns)	135
Inventory at Start	5432
Inventory at End	6102
Carriage Inwards	365

Buzzy Bee Plc
Income Statement for year ended 31 December 20...

	£	£	£
Sales Revenue			104 285
Less returns inwards			531
			103 754
Less Cost of Sales			
Inventory at start		5432	
Add: Purchases	45 628		
Carriage inwards	365		
	45 993		
Less returns outwards	135		
		45 858	
		51 290	
Less inventory at end		6102	
		45 188	
			45 188
GROSS PROFIT			58 566

contd

THE PROFIT AND LOSS SECTION

This section of the Income Statement calculates the **final profit or loss** that an organisation has made over a financial time period. It starts with the gross profit figure calculated in the Trading Section less any business expenses. Any additional income raised by the organisation (not directly linked to trading) is then added to calculate Profit for the Year.

Items that will appear in the Profit and Loss Section include:
- discounts received
- commission received
- rent received
- profit on the disposal (sale) of assets
- business expenses such as:
  - wages
  - carriage outwards
  - rent
  - rates
  - insurance
  - advertising
  - bad debts allowance
  - telephone
  - stationery
  - any other general expenses.

Example:

Buzzy Bee plc
Income Statement for year ended 31 December 20...

	£	£	£
Sales Revenue (1)			
Sales Revenue			104 285
Less returns inwards			531
			103 754
Less Cost of Sales (2)			
Inventory at start		5432	
Add: Purchases	45 628		
Add carriage inwards	365		
	45 993		
Less returns outwards	135		
		45 858	
		51 290	
Less inventory at end		6102	
		45 188	
			45 188
Profit and Loss Section starts here:			
GROSS PROFIT (3)			58 566
Less expenses: (4)			
Wages	26 390		
Carriage Outwards	560		
Rent	4400		
Rates	1400		
Insurance	600		
Advertising	2000		
General Expenses	1354		
Telephone	460	37 164	
		21 402	
Add Gains (5)			
Discount Received		200	
Profit for the year (6)		21 602	

NOTES ON THE INCOME STATEMENT

1	Sales revenue	The revenue that the business receives from selling goods and/or services to its customers.
2	Cost of sales	The cost of purchasing goods from a supplier or cash and carry.
3	Gross profit/loss	The difference between sales revenue and the cost of sales. This money is earned directly from the trading activities of the business – that is, buying low and selling high.
4	Gains	This is any other revenue that the business receives – but not directly from buying and selling.
5	Expenses	All the necessary expenses incurred by the organisation to carry out its day-to-day activities – for example, electricity, advertising and telephone.
6	Profit for the year	The money that the organisation has left once all expenses have been deducted from sales revenue. This is the reward for running a successful business.

THINGS TO DO AND THINK ABOUT

Preparing simple Income Statements

From the following information prepare the Trading Section of the Income Statement for Jamie Wilson for the year ended 31 December 20...

	£
Sales Revenue	27 500
Purchases	15 350
Sales Returns	250
Purchase Returns	50
Inventory at 1 January 20	1750
Inventory at 31 December 20	1950
Carriage In	100

(a) Suggest two ways in which Jamie could increase his gross profit.

(b) Explain the difference between sales returns and purchases returns.

DON'T FORGET

Gross profit is improved when a business can buy inventory at a low price and sell at a higher price.

DON'T FORGET

Net profit (profit for the year) can be improved if business expenses are tightly controlled.

FINANCIAL STATEMENTS 2

THE STATEMENT OF FINANCIAL POSITION

This is a statement that shows the **assets** of an organisation (what it owns) and its **liabilities** (what it owes to others) at a particular point in time. Although it is generally drawn up at the end of an accounting period, a Statement of Financial Position can be drawn up at any time.

In particular the Statement of Financial Position shows:
- **the value of the organisation's assets** – for example, property, vehicles, machinery, equipment, inventory, trade receivables, cash and cash equivalents
- **the liabilities of the company** – for example, equity, trade payables and bank loans
- **the equity of the business** – for example, (in the case of a sole trader) the equity invested or (in the case of a company) the total value of the shares owned by the shareholders.

Example:

A typical Statement of Financial Position for a limited company would look like this:

Buzzy Bee Honey Company Ltd – Statement of Financial Position as at 31 August 2...

	£	£	£
Non-current Assets (1)			
Premises (Property)			130000
Machinery			30000
Vehicles			19000
			179000
Current Assets (2)			
Inventory	27000		
Trade Receivables	13000		
Cash and cash equivalents	7000	47000	
Less Current Liabilities (3)			
Trade Payables	8000		
Dividends owing (Other Payables)	2000		
Tax owing to Inland Revenue (Other Payables)	2000	12000	
NET CURRENT ASSETS (4)			35000
(Working Equity)			
NET ASSETS (5)			**214000**
(Equity employed)			
Financed by:			
Issued share Equity (6)			105000
Reserves from Income Statement (7)			29000
Shareholders' Interest (8)			**134000**
(Shareholders' Funds)			
Add Non-current Liabilities (9)		80000	
			214000

Both sides of the Statement Financial Positi should agree

NOTES ON THE STATEMENT OF FINANCIAL POSITION

1	Non-current assets	Items of value owned by the organisation (such as property, equipment, furniture and vehicles) that will generate income. Without these assets the organisation would not be able to operate. These assets will probably be in the organisation for some years.
2	Current assets	Items owned by the organisation that will be used up, sold or converted into cash within 12 months. They include inventory, trade receivables, cash and cash equivalents.
3	Current liabilities	Debts owed to outside organisations that must be repaid in the short term – usually in less than 12 months. They include trade payables, bank overdraft (cash and cash equivalents), dividends due to shareholders and taxation owed to the government.

contd

4	Net Current Assets	Total current assets minus total current liabilities. The value of the current assets should always be greater than the value of current liabilities or the business will encounter cash flow problems and be forced to sell their non-current assets to pay short-term debts. Without non-current assets the business would probably be unable to continue to operate.
5	Net assets	Non-current assets + net current assets. This shows the net value of the business once short-term debts have been repaid.
6	Issued Share Equity	Money invested in the organisation by the owners or shareholders. In return for their investment they will receive a dividend payment (share of the profit) in proportion to the amount of shares they hold.
7	Reserves from Income Statement	Profits retained by the organisation after the payment of dividends to the shareholders. Organisations will use these profit reserves to finance expansion at some later date – it is like keeping money back for a 'rainy day'.
8	Shareholders' funds	The total of all issued share equity (ordinary and preference shares), all reserves and any retained profits.
9	Non-current Liabilities	Debentures (long-term loans) or mortgages where the debt repayment will be over a number of years.

NOTES ON THE STATEMENT OF FINANCIAL POSITION FOR THE SOLE TRADER

1	Equity at start	The value of the owner's investment at the start of the accounting period + any retained profits (retained earnings) accrued in previous trading periods.
2	Profit	The value of profit for the year taken from the Income Statement.
3	Drawings	The value of resources that are withdrawn from the organisation by the owner(s) for their private use. These can be taken in the form of cash, goods or services.
4	Equity at end	The value of the owner's capital (equity) at the end of this financial period.

 **ACTIVITY:**

1 State two advantages of using spreadsheets in the preparation of a cash budget.

2 Decribe how a cash budget can enable managers to fulfil a number of management functions.

3 State what is meant by the term annual accounts.

4 Describe the difference between a business's gross profit and profit for the year.

5 List four typical expenses that a business is likely to encounter.

6 Describe the main reasons why a business prepares a Statement of Financial Position.

7 Using examples, explain the difference between non-current assets and current assets.

8 Using examples, explain the difference between current liabilities and non-current liabilities.

 THINGS TO DO AND THINK ABOUT

Research task (Annual Accounts)

Use the internet and search for the financial statements of one of the following organisations – Tesco, Marks and Spencer, Sainsburys or Morrison's. Find one piece of information that would be of interest to different stakeholders with a vested interest in the financial statements of these organisations.

Present your findings in a business report in the form of a PowerPoint presentation.

 DON'T FORGET

Don't worry – you probably won't be asked to prepare a Statement of Financial Position!

 **ONLINE**

Head to www.brightredbooks.net for some more activities.

 **ONLINE TEST**

Test yourself on financial statements online at www.brightredbooks.net

RATIO ANALYSIS 1

THE INTERPRETATION OF FINANCIAL STATEMENTS

All public (plc) and private (ltd) companies are required to provide financial statements (Income Statements and Statement of Financial Position) at the end of each accounting period.

Her Majesty's Revenue and Customs (HMRC) uses the information to determine the **corporation tax** (tax on profits) payable by the organisation.

Sole traders, partnerships and private companies **are not legally required** to make their financial statements public, although many are forced to provide these when attempting to borrow from banks or other financial institutions.

Public limited companies, which obtain money by issuing shares, **are legally obliged** to publish their financial statements.

As you can see from the table below, many people – including rival companies, investors, lenders and trade union representatives – use the information contained in published accounts to make informed decisions.

Trade unions and employees	Government/Inland Revenue	Owners or shareholders
Banks, financial institutions and other lenders	**USERS OF FINANCIAL INFORMATION**	Trade payables
Managers	Investors	Members of the public

WHAT DO THESE STAKEHOLDERS WANT TO KNOW?

- **Managers** – are mainly interested in how to improve profitability and to identify where costs can be reduced. Increased profits are sometimes linked to bonuses for managers!
- **Owners** – are mainly interested in profitability and the return that they receive on the money invested in the business. They will also compare this return to the return possible with alternative investment opportunities.
- **Trade Payables** – are mainly interested in the business's liquidity position and their ability to pay for goods that they have purchased on credit.
- **Trade unions** – are mainly interested in profitability as this will provide a guide to realistic wage rises that employees should be seeking.
- **Members of the public** – are mainly interested in the profitability of an organisation and any potential growth. If a business is experiencing financial difficulty and is under threat of closure, it could cause unemployment in the local area in which it operates.
- **Banks and other lenders** – are mainly interested in the profitability and liquidity of a business. Loans will only be offered to those organisations which are able to meet agreed repayment terms and conditions.
- **HMRC** – this government department is interested in the profits earned by a business because this will allow them to determine the tax that should be paid by the business.
- **Investors** – will be interested in profitability and the potential return on any investment made in the organisation.

Careful study of financial statements can provide an enormous amount of information about the performance of a business organisation. For example, it is possible to examine the Trading Section of an Income Statement and discover more than just the gross profit figure. By interpreting the data available and making comparisons with figures for previous years, or with similar organisations, or by analysing the relationship between different figures, it is possible to find the real indicators of the future success and financial security of a business organisation.

The types of questions that can be answered by interpretation of the financial statements include:

contd

INTERPRETATION OF INCOME STATEMENTS

- Was this year's trading result good or bad, **compared** with last year or with a **rival company**?
- Has the **gross profit improved** this year, compared with last year?
- Are we making **efficient** use of our inventory? Is it proving popular with customers?
- Does our profit for the year figure **compare favourably** with those of other organisations in the same industry?
- Are business expenses being tightly controlled?

INTERPRETATION OF STATEMENTS OF FINANCIAL POSITION

- Do we have enough working equity to avoid cash flow problems?
- Are we making enough use of available trade credit?
- Is our level of trade receivables comparable with that of our industry competitors?
- Are non-current assets being used effectively to generate profits for the business?
- Are there sufficient current assets to meet current liabilities?

PURPOSES OF INTERPRETATION

To offer long-term security, most if not all business organisations will be interested in the following:

- **Profitability** – is the organisation earning more than it is paying out?
- **Liquidity** – does the organisation have enough money to pay its bills?
- **Efficiency** – is the organisation making the best use of its resources?

Managers obtain information about each of the above from careful interpretation of the financial statements using a variety of different **accounting ratios** – a process commonly referred to as ratio analysis. The ratios to be used are selected according to the theme being investigated.

USES OF RATIO ANALYSIS

Ratio analysis is used to:

- compare the current year's performance with that of previous years
- compare the performance of the organisation with those of similar organisations
- interpret information to identify why differences occur and how best to improve performance in the future
- analyse the information for forecasting/budgeting
- assist in the management decision-making process.

LIMITATIONS OF RATIO ANALYSIS

Ratio analysis has the following limitations:

- Information contained in financial statements is **historical** – it happened in the past – so there is not much you can do about it.
- **Like must be compared with like** – any comparisons made must be with businesses of similar size and in the same type of industry.
- Findings might not take **external factors** such as a recession or the effects of inflation into account.
- Factors such as the skill of the workforce, location of the business and skills and experience of the management team are not normally taken into account when calculating ratios.

 ONLINE

Head to www.brightredbooks.net for further activities on this topic.

 **DON'T FORGET**

Ratio analysis can be used to examine the **profitability, efficiency** and **liquidity** of a business.

 THINGS TO DO AND THINK ABOUT

As indicated above, different ratios are selected according to the theme to be investigated. The ratios described over the next few pages fall under the headings of **Profitability, Efficiency** and **Liquidity**.

 ONLINE TEST

Test yourself on this topic at www.brightredbooks.net

RATIO ANALYSIS 2

PROFITABILITY RATIOS

GROSS PROFIT RATIO

Purpose:	To measure the percentage of profit earned on the trading activities of the organisation or, in simple terms, to measure how many pence of gross profit is earned out of every £ of sales.
Used by:	Managers/directors to compare one year's trading with trading in previous years or with other similar businesses.
Limitations:	No realistic comment can be made unless trends are over different time periods, or comparisons are made with other, similar organisations.
Improvements:	To improve the gross profit margin the organisation can either purchase cheaper supplies, or increase the selling price to the consumer.
Formula:	$\dfrac{\text{Gross profit}}{\text{Sales (turnover)}} \times \dfrac{100}{1}$

PROFIT MARK-UP

Purpose:	To measure how much has been added to the cost of goods purchased (from suppliers) as profit.
Used by:	Managers/directors of a business to compare year on year and with other similar companies.
Limitations:	No realistic comment can be made unless trends are over different time periods, or comparisons are made with other, similar business organisations.
Improvements:	To improve the profit mark-up the organisation can either negotiate discounts with current suppliers, find cheaper suppliers, or increase the selling price to the consumer.
Formula:	$\dfrac{\text{Gross profit}}{\text{Cost of sales}} \times \dfrac{100}{1}$

PROFIT FOR THE YEAR RATIO

Purpose:	To measure the **overall profit** of the firm after all expenses have been taken into account or, in simple terms, to measure how many pence of profit for the year is earned out of every £ of sales.
Used by:	Stakeholders such as managers/directors/current investors and HMRC, who all have a vested interest in the net profit (profit for the year) of the business. (Comparisons will be made year on year and with other similar companies.)
Limitations:	No realistic comment can be made unless trends are over different time periods, or comparisons are made with other, similar business organisations.
Improvements:	To improve the net profit (profit for the year) margin the organisation must reduce expenses or increase gross profit.
Formula:	$\dfrac{\text{Profit for the year}}{\text{Net Sales Revenue}} \times \dfrac{100}{1}$

RETURN ON EQUITY EMPLOYED

Purpose:	To measure the percentage return on the equity invested in the business – perhaps the owner of a business could earn more by simply investing their money in a bank or elsewhere. Similarly, shareholders want to know how much return they are making annually on the shares they have purchased in the business.
Used by:	Managers who want to know how well the equity is being used to generate profits and by current investors (shareholders) who want to know the rate of return being given on the equity they have invested. Potential investors will want to know if the return from one company is better/worse than from other companies. (Comparisons will be made year on year and with other similar companies.)
Limitations:	This ratio uses **historic costs** of the business's assets. If asset values are inaccurate then the equity employed figure will also be inaccurate.
Improvements:	An increase in profit for the year, with everything else remaining equal, will improve the ratio.
Formula:	$\dfrac{\text{Profit for the year (before tax)}}{\text{Opening equity*}} \times \dfrac{100}{1}$ (*share equity in the case of a company)

ONLINE

Head to www.brightredbooks.net for further activities on this topic.

LIQUIDITY RATIOS

CURRENT RATIO

Purpose:	To measure whether the business has sufficient current assets to cover payment of current liabilities. Has the firm enough 'working equity' to meet all short-term debts? The ratio compares assets that will become liquid in less than 12 months with liabilities that are due in the same time period.
Used by:	Managers/directors/banks and other lenders to make comparisons year on year and between companies. These stakeholders want to know that the business is liquid and can meet all short-term debts.
Limitations:	There is no ideal ratio or benchmark, though it is commonly accepted that this ratio should be 2:1 (twice as many current assets as there are current liabilities).
Improvements:	A business might try to increase its current assets or find ways to decrease its current liabilities. If the current ratio is too high it could mean that funds are better employed in the business to generate more income rather than sitting in cash or in a bank or tied up in inventory.
Formula:	$\dfrac{\text{Current assets}}{\text{Current liabilities}}$ Answer is always shown as ?:1

ACID TEST RATIO (SOMETIMES CALLED QUICK RATIO)

Purpose:	To measure if the company has sufficient liquid assets to cover current liabilities, in a crisis situation. Inventory is removed from current assets as it cannot be guaranteed that the business will be able to sell it quickly enough to generate cash to pay debts.
Used by:	Managers/directors/banks and other lenders.
Limitations:	If a business has a slow inventory turnover, the acid test ratio should, ideally, be 2:1. With a fast inventory turnover, the ratio can be less than 2:1 without causing alarm.
Improvements:	This ratio can be improved by the use of an efficient inventory control system.
Formula:	$\dfrac{\text{Current assets} - \text{inventory}}{\text{Current liabilities}}$ Answer is always shown as ?:1

DON'T FORGET

There are six main accounting ratios which should be used to analyse accounting information.

ONLINE TEST

Test yourself on ratio analysis at www.brightredbooks.net

 THINGS TO DO AND THINK ABOUT

Specimen exam-style questions

Now that you are confident with this topic, try answering the following specimen exam-style questions in sentences.

1 Explain the role of the finance department in an organisation. (4 marks)

2 Describe the financial statements that are produced by an organisation. (3 marks)

3 Describe the type of information found in published accounts that stakeholders might find useful. (5 marks)

4 Describe the financial information that potential stakeholders could use to decide whether or not to invest in a company. (4 marks)

5 State two different sources of long-term finance that are available to an organisation such as a plc. Give an advantage for each source identified. (4 marks)

6 A cash budget is an accounting statement that an organisation would prepare before purchasing a new non-current asset. Describe its contents and how it would be used. (6 marks)

7 State four sources of cash flow problems and suggest a solution for each source. (4 marks)

8 Explain why managers use cash budgets. (4 marks)

9 Describe reasons for the cash flow problems that can affect an organisation. (5 marks)

10 Firms use ratios to analyse their annual accounts. Describe reasons for using ratios to analyse performance. (2 marks)

11 Describe ratios that could be used to ensure that appropriate levels of profitability and liquidity are maintained. (5 marks)

12 Explain the limitations of using accounting ratios. (3 marks)

13 Describe any three accounting ratios and justify their use. (A different justification must be used each time.) (6 marks)

14 Explain the reasons why managers use accounting ratios. (4 marks)

INDEX